Flight of the Dragonfly

FLIGHT OF THE DRAGONFLY

A MOTHER'S HARROWING JOURNEY TO BRING HER DAUGHTERS HOME

MELISSA HAWACH

HarperCollins*PublishersLtd*

Published by HarperCollins Publishers Ltd.

First Canadian edition

HarperCollins Publishers Ltd
2 Bloor Street East, 20th Floor
Toronto, Ontario, Canada
M4W 1A8

www.harpercollins.ca

Library and Archives Canada Cataloguing in Publication

Hawach, Melissa
Flight of the dragonfly : a mother's harrowing journey to bring her daughters home / Melissa Hawach.

ISBN 978-1-55468-087-0

1. Hawach, Melissa. 2. Parental kidnapping—Canada. 3. Parental kidnapping—Lebanon. 4. Mother and child. 5. Mothers of kidnapped children—Canada—Biography. I. Title.

HV6604.C32H39 2008 362.82'97092 C2008-900863-4

RRD 9 8 7 6 5 4 3 2

Printed and bound in the United States

To my dearest angels, Hannah and Cedar

Author's Note

This book—about an intensely emotional time in my life—is as accurate as I could make it. Dialogue has necessarily been reconstructed from memory. Names have been changed only where I feared harm might come to the person described, and such changes have been flagged for the reader. *Flight of the Dragonfly* is my true story.

PREFACE

As I write this letter late in the summer of 2007, Hannah, you are six and Cedar, you are on the verge of turning four (as you remind me constantly). On a beautiful sunny day in southern Alberta my family is here to help us out in the yard. I watch you all from the window of the kitchen and I laugh, Cedar, at the outfit you have put on: pink moon boots, yellow cotton shorts, a hooded bunny jumper, and every piece of play jewellery you can find. You, Hannah, on the other hand, have dutifully and sensibly put on play jeans and donned rubber gloves to look the part of yard-duty supervisor.

I can hear you, Hannah, organizing. Telling everyone what needs to be done or eagerly volunteering to assist the adults in their tasks. Your grandfather (he will always be Bumpy to you) and your uncle Brendan are outside building a dog run and you are laying out wood and setting out nails according to size. You, Cedar, on the other hand, are dancing in front of the picture window, singing one of your endless songs about rainbows, "balentimes" (valentines) and best friends. This counts among the many moments this summer that I have caught my breath at how lucky I am that you are here with me, how far we have come, and how the present moment contrasts so sharply with the nightmare that was the summer of 2006.

Some day you will both read *Flight of the Dragonfly*, and I thought it important to write this letter to explain to you both my intentions and my hopes for the book. I owe this to you since this is not just my story but yours as well, and one that involves people who are important and meaningful in your lives. I hope you can understand that I have done my best to tell the tale with as much respect to your involvement as I possibly could without sugar-coating the truth of what happened.

The story, in a nutshell: In the summer of 2006, you went to Australia on what was supposed to be a three-week vacation to visit your Lebanese cousins and uncles and aunts, and your *dodo* (grandfather) and *data* (grandmother). You were halfway around the world when I realized an awful truth: You had been taken by your father into a Middle Eastern country just freshly launched into an ugly war with Israel. Losing you both—and you were gone from my life almost totally for six months—was the worst loss I have ever endured, and I pray I will never have to face its like again.

I believe that this book, painful as it will be for you to read in places, may help other "left-behind parents" and children facing a similar crisis. For many reasons, some practical, I decided to write the book when the wounds for all concerned were, and still are, raw and tender.

Like most parents, I want you to learn from my mistakes and to make better choices than I did. Much of what kept me moving forward during those dark days was my way of leading by example—even in your absence. I needed to show you both that it is not acceptable to be manipulated and bullied by the people in your life. But at the same time I never lost sight of what was best for you. "At what cost to my children?" was the question I asked myself repeatedly before every major decision on my marathon journey to find you and get you back. I hope you both feel that I abided by that all-important guideline.

Perhaps when you have children of your own you will comprehend the intense pain and desperation I felt while you were gone. My driving force was also my greatest fear: that you would both think I had abandoned you, that I no longer wanted you. You, Hannah, did not believe your father when he told you and Cedar that Mommy had left you both. You challenged him, I know, over and over again. But the longer we were apart, the greater the risk was that you would succumb to that horrible lie, and I could not bear the thought of you two angels carrying that in your little hearts. As the three of us lay in the same bed at night a few days after I finally had you back with me, the fear of losing you still gnawed at me.

God was listening to my anguish that night, as He had many nights before, and this brought me much peace. That night, I realized that my greatest fear had been laid to rest. You now knew the truth and would never ever again even consider the thought that I had abandoned you. Especially you, Hannie. I knew at that moment—no matter what happened in the days ahead—that you would tell your younger sister how far I had travelled, how much all of us here at home had done, how much you two were loved and valued and missed.

You both should know and remember this important fact: You were born out of love, and your father and I married with the very best of intentions. What happened between the two of us was our fault, not yours, and I will be sorry for our drama touching your lives until my last day on this earth.

I am hopeful that by the time you read this, Hannah and Cedar, you will be in regular and healthy contact with your father. However, more critical to me now is that you both have the opportunity to grow up feeling secure and safe with every opportunity to become beautiful, kind and gifted—qualities I already see in you as children. If, through this book, I can help educate other parents and possibly spare some pain and anguish, then this has been a worthwhile endeavour.

During the tortuous and tangled ordeal of tracking you both down, the dragonfly became my symbol of hope. For "the team" at home in Calgary—Bumpy and Nanna, your uncles and aunts, our many friends, the dozens of people who helped us here and across the ocean and who go on helping us—the dragonfly was our totem, our good luck charm.

Only days after we learned you had been taken, two large black dragonflies entered our old house on Copperfield Gardens. Many people in Saskatchewan and Alberta were talking about the extraordinary numbers of dragonflies seen that summer. I have always loved dragonflies: When I was a tree-planter as a young woman in British Columbia, these mosquito hunters were my best friends. Later, when I was in Australia studying to become a helicopter pilot, I was reminded often how close those flying machines come to matching the flight of the dragonfly.

For some time, Hannah and Cedar, you and I had been collecting dragonfly paraphernalia, like the small piece of stained glass that still hangs from the rear-view mirror in my mini-van. My brother Adam, who does not normally make such utterances, voiced his belief that dragonflies in the house were a sign. "The girls' spirits," he said, "are with us and they're somehow aware that we're looking for them." Adam caught the dragonflies and set them free. There was no thought of killing them. Everyone knows you do not kill a dragonfly.

Cedar, you were too young, but Hannie, I know you remember that house in Calgary with the little porch at the front where you two would play and ride your tricycles. Inside that house was where the search for the two of you began. From that most unlikely command post, we cast a net as wide as the world, and it seemed like every second day someone would come to the house with a dragonfly story. Sightings of swarms, landings on shoulders, chance encounters, so many that it struck some of us as strange. But we took heart when an old Cree medicine woman told one of us that the dragonfly ranked among the most powerful symbols on the totem. The literal English translation of the Plains Cree word for dragonfly is "by two," and it apparently refers to the creature being powerful both in the water and in the air.

The dragonfly can rest its wings. Its part in the journey is now over and our own new journey, my precious ones, has begun.

Forever with all my love,
Momma

1

King-hit

Three a.m., July 19, 2006. A call in the small hours of the night rarely brings welcome news. But this one, to my house in western Canada from my brother-in-law in eastern Australia, was stunning, even nauseating.

In Australian slang, there is a phrase to describe a blow delivered without warning. The Aussies use it often in their sports pages, as both noun and verb. Key to the phrase is the element of surprise and the devastating result. There was no denying: I had been *king-hit*.

Joe Hawach—the husband from whom I had separated ten months beforehand—had taken our daughters, five-year-old Hannah and two-year-old Cedar, on a three-week vacation to see his Lebanese-Australian relatives in Sydney. I had approved this arrangement, but most reluctantly, for it seemed a long time for my young daughters to be apart from me. On the other hand, I did want them to have a relationship with Joe's family and all their Australian cousins, whom the girls adored. I put in the girls' luggage various pins and stickers and pencils—all emblazoned with red maple leafs—that Hannah and Cedar could hand out as souvenirs.

I was, and am, a stay-at-home mom with a mother's keen sense of detail and preparedness. I had taken steps to ensure that Hannah and Cedar would not be bored or become difficult for their father on the long trip to Australia via Vancouver and Hawaii. As Joe and the girls walked onto the plane in Calgary on July 1, he was carrying the travel kit I had prepared for him: my portable DVD player and new movies, batteries, decongestant for the girls' ears if the flight caused them pain, Tylenol, Band-aids, snacks, extra clothes. I was sure I had thought of everything. Clearly, I had not.

On our other trips to Australia, I always gave Hannah and Cedar a wash-up and rubdown with baby cream upon arrival in Hawaii so they would feel more comfortable and refreshed for the last leg of the journey. I even scrounged some American cash because I knew that when they stopped in Hawaii it would be in the middle of the night and only concession stands would be open. Making things easier for the girls had always been my task, not Joe's, and I had done everything I could to make the marathon trip smooth sailing. I wanted the girls to be well occupied and less inclined to ask their father the inevitable question: "Are we there yet?"

But for all my elaborate precautions against every contingency, my instincts told me that something was not right about this trip. I will never again ignore such instincts. For one thing, at the airport there was a problem with one of their tickets. It was taking a very long time to sort out and Joe asked me to take the girls to an airport coffee shop while he dealt with it. My suspicions were aroused, and I remembered something that Hannah had mentioned to me earlier that month: Her father had apparently told them that he was going to take them to Italy to eat pasta. I immediately called Joe on the phone at the time and asked him: Did he have travel plans beyond Australia? He just laughed at me for believing Hannah's story.

We snacked at the restaurant, but the ticket hassle seemed no closer to being resolved. I made my way back to the counter with the girls to see what was going on, but after twenty minutes the girls' impatience with the process overwhelmed my suspicions, and I took them to a mock plane on display in the terminal to ride and play in. I parked my suspicions, dismissed them as nosiness.

Joe was taking with him an enormous amount of luggage, but this, too, I rationalized. I myself had bought gifts for Joe's family, including large items from the golf store where I worked part-time—a tour bag for his youngest brother, Jean-Paul, and a new driver for Pierre. Joe had also packed purchases for his siblings, who had drawn up wish-lists of jeans and other items. Earlier, as he had loaded the girls' luggage into the van, he'd had to rearrange everything. "It's all this stuff I bought for my family," he'd said. That had sounded right. They often did that. No worries, as the Aussies say. What should have raised an eyebrow is that Joe himself was the one who brought up the subject of all the luggage. He was a man who never offered excuses, and now he was offering one.

I would suffer enormous guilt during my ordeal for ignoring my gut instincts. I should have been more focused on what was best for the girls, even if it meant questioning Joe or causing dissension. I was so busy trying to keep the peace and take the high road—for the sake of the girls.

The vacation was originally to have been four weeks, but I insisted that I would come to Sydney after two weeks to see the girls. Joe was extremely understanding, and lowered the time away to three weeks. He did not want me coming to Sydney, and only later would I understand why.

Joe and the girls departed Calgary, and through phone and a video link, I maintained daily contact with them. The video link was mostly for the sake of Cedar, who was then too shy to speak on a telephone. I had even sent ahead letters to their paternal grandparents so the girls would have mail from home to open every day. The girls and I had planted pumpkin and watermelon patches in the backyard of our house on Copperfield Gardens, and I sent photos so Hannah and Cedar could see how our garden was coming along. I sent photos, as well, of the house itself along with a smiling mother-and-daughters shot taken the day they left. I worried that Cedar, especially, might feel abandoned and, on the advice of a psychologist, had taken all these precautions to maintain the bond between my daughters and me. I wanted them to know I was there.

But two weeks into the holiday, on July 15, Joe stopped taking my calls. All communication ceased. I left messages asking that he telephone, sent him e-mails asking that he call, but heard nothing back. Three more days passed.

When I called the Hawach family number in Sydney on July 19, just past midnight, Joe's youngest brother, Jean-Paul, answered. He hung up when he realized it was me. At first, I thought that maybe there had been an accident and Jean-Paul did not want to be the one to tell me. In a panic, I called back repeatedly but each time got the answering machine until it was full. Eventually, someone there unplugged the phone.

Now I began to pace the house, racking my brain for someone to call. I had an idea of calling friends in Sydney, people I had worked with in the past, imploring them to call the family business, a string of restaurants called Positano's, and ask for Joe. Maybe, I thought, a local call would get past this mysterious and frightening stonewalling. I thought of Nathan, someone who once worked for me in a Sydney restaurant, a man who knew Joe and the Hawach family. I got on the computer, searched his number on the Internet, and up it came. Nathan was home, thankfully, when I called.

"No worries, Mel," he said, and he promised he would call back when and if he got through. Nathan was trying to calm me, reassure me, but he had to have been rattled by how frantic and desperate I sounded. Listening to me must have been like hearing the sounds of someone drowning an ocean away.

I felt a little better knowing that someone there, a friend, was helping. I was lying on the couch next to the phone, and I must have drifted off to sleep. Finally, Pierre Hawach—a twenty-eight-year-old lawyer and one of Joe's younger brothers—called me in the middle of the night on July 19.

"Oh my God, Pierre," I said, "what's going on?"

He stammered a bit and paused, then began again. "I'm really sorry. I hate to be the one to tell you this," he said, "but . . ."

I started screaming, "No, nooo!"

Again, I thought he was going to describe a car accident or some misfortune that had landed one or both girls in hospital. My first thought: I'm twenty-four hours away from being next to them. It was, I imagined, my worst fear.

"No, don't worry. They're fine," he said. "Everyone's fine."

"Then what's going on?" I asked him. "What's really going on?"

"I don't know how to tell you this," he replied, "but Joe's taken the children overseas and I don't think he's coming back."

Now I collapsed on the floor. I was screaming and wailing, could not catch my breath or breathe. I ran out the back door and was kneeling on the grass, retching with the phone still in one hand. I was making strange yowling sounds like an animal just caught in the steel jaws of a trap. I could not for the life of me process this information.

My daughters have been kidnapped by their father.

"Nooo," I kept saying, over and over again. I must have said that word a hundred times. "No! Why didn't you call me? Why did this happen? I don't understand."

"We tried to talk him out of it," Pierre replied, sounding angry. "What did you want me to do? What was I supposed to do? I am not sure what has been going on over there for the past ten months, but you obviously have a different picture of events than we do here."

I have no words to convey my disbelief, my shock, and above all, my confusion. Why was Pierre angry with me for being so upset? Why did Joe do this? How could a father do such a thing to his own daughters? The ten-month separation with Joe had been so amicable. This couldn't be happening. Was I crazy? Was he?

I started to pace and rock and could not stop moving. Maybe, I thought, all this motion will help clear my mind. I was like a boxer in a ring, ducking this way and that. Dazed by a punch I never saw coming, trying to shake off the cobwebs and fearful of more blows to come.

I was so distraught on the telephone that Pierre said he would hang up and call again shortly, which he did. We spoke only long enough for Pierre to say he would speak with his father, Louie, and that we would talk again after that. By now, all my dashing both inside and outside the house, my crying and my yelling had awoken two friends staying with me that night—Patrick and Rayanne. They kept trying to take the phone from me and when I ran out to the backyard and fell to my knees, they desperately tried to get me back inside. They had no idea what had induced my hysteria. Their only thought was that unless they got me inside and calmed me down, a neighbour would call the police to complain about the noise. I didn't care about that. This phone call had struck me senseless.

My daughters have been kidnapped by their father.

Through tears, I tried to make my friends understand what I myself could not. Rayanne was a childhood friend visiting to help me cope with what I thought was a three-week separation from my daughters. Another old friend, Stephanie, had been with us earlier, and we had all passed a pleasant evening together. Patrick was Patrick Lalande, a colleague from the golf course where I worked part-time. A friendship had formed in the spring and blossomed into something more, but it was all very new and tentative, and his being there that night had less to do with our budding romance and more to do with practicalities: My house was closer to the golf course than his was, and he had spent a late evening working—with the prospect of an early morning shift. His morning, though, would look nothing like the one he had planned.

Still reeling, still in our pyjamas (which would pass on the street as clothing), both of us distraught and no doubt unkempt, Rayanne and I drove to the place nearby that Joe had been renting—one floor of a house on Midland Crescent. We knocked on the door but failed to rouse the landlady, a woman named Pearl who was also Joe's bookkeeper. We looked in the garage window, trying to see his car, but it was too dark inside.

There was a moment that night when Rayanne and I felt a little like characters in a Nancy Drew novel. I was on her shoulders, peering into the landlady's garage for a sign of Joe's car, and she wobbled under my weight. But whatever humour that moment possessed is felt only in hindsight. We both fought nausea the whole time, and Rayanne—a mother herself—suffered a physical collapse when she got back home. For my part, I felt like I had been kicked in the stomach.

Now Rayanne and I drove to Joe's office. All signs to the contrary, we were looking for evidence that he was, after all, coming back to his adopted country and his business, a paper company called Amcan.

Amcan rented warehouse space and an office area at National Fast Freight Inc.—a massive warehousing operation close to our house in south Calgary. The warehouse is about the size of an airport hangar, with dozens and dozens of huge bay doors at the back where semitrailers load and unload their cargo. Amcan was just a drop in Fast Freight's bucket. At the back, we found the security guard for the parking compound who, on hearing our story, kindly let us in. We repeated the tale to one of the nightshift workers at the main dispatch office. He, too, was shocked and sympathetic, and he escorted us upstairs to the Amcan office.

I walked in, and I just kept saying, "Everything is gone. Everything is gone." The computers, the books, the office furniture. I opened the drawers of a remaining desk, hoping to find something. Still in disbelief, I walked out to the adjoining warehouse area, where our footfalls echoed in the emptiness. I had been in this same warehouse eight weeks before and had seen the big papercutter and pallet after pallet of paper, hundreds of them, each stack two metres high and arranged according to the paper's thickness. I kept thinking, "I must be in the wrong place," but then dismissed the thought. This was all quite real.

The man in the dispatch office said that Joe had sold all his stock some six weeks earlier. All that remained in the office were a pile of scrap paper in a box and, in it, on top, art by Hannah and Cedar—a drawing of the family. A family now very much in tatters. Was Joe leaving me a message? Was this a mean gesture? At the time I thought not, though later I wondered.

Rayanne and I returned to the bed-and-breakfast place on Midland Crescent that Joe had been renting for several months; it was where he'd had the girls as part of our shared custody arrangement (one that saw the girls living mostly with me and one we had achieved amicably without lawyers). By now, Pearl was up and about. She was astonished that Joe had taken the girls—but not by his departure.

The space Joe had been renting was as bare and echoey as his office. In the bedroom closet, amid dozens of forlorn-looking coat hangers, were two golf shirts the girls had given him for Christmas, but everything else was gone. I did retrieve one keepsake that Joe had left behind: Two 8 by 10 black-and-white photos, one of each of the girls, framed in green, which they had given to him on Father's Day a month before. Hannah's photo I had taken in the backyard, Cedar's at the Calgary zoo.

The landlady told us that Joe's car was gone. That it wasn't his car anyway, just one he had rented from a friend after selling his own, and that he had given the borrowed car back. Joe had apparently told Pearl he was leaving "for good" and had talked about taking the girls to visit relatives in Lebanon. It seemed Joe Hawach had been planning this spectacular move for a long time—close to a year, I learned later. I had been royally duped, and the evidence of that fact would mount in the coming days.

* * *

Back at the house on Copperfield, the three of us—Patrick, Rayanne and I—huddled and shared what information we had. Patrick had found a web site for Canada's Department of Foreign Affairs in Ottawa and the name of Jean-Marc Lesage, head of the Canadian government's Our Missing Children program. Patrick had left an urgent message.

I needed someone to tell me what to do, but the thought of waiting for the phone to ring seemed unbearable. So Rayanne and I hit the road once more, this time heading north.

En route to the airport (it seemed a slim hope, but I thought maybe someone there could help us), I called the Golf Depot, where I had been working one day a week while Joe had the girls. I was supposed to work that day and made the difficult call to my boss to tell him I would not be coming in for my shift and that I was unsure of when I would be back. He was shocked but offered any support that I needed.

Within minutes of my hanging up, his partner, Cher, called me back and offered advice. Her words were important to me, for this woman was no stranger to heartache. Her daughter had been murdered in Mexico by a drug lord a few years earlier. She had experienced deception on a grand scale and knew how important a thick skin is to staying the course. Cher told me that it was okay to cry and be sad but it was now time for me to get mad and be tougher and smarter than Joe and those helping him, that my daughters were counting on me.

As Rayanne and I sped around Calgary, I continued to make calls on my cell phone. Mind and body were both racing: My mind casting back over my conversation with Pierre, replaying what he had said, looking for clues. My body, coursing on adrenaline, trying to get done all that needed to be done.

I called Asia Pacific, one of the major paper companies Joe dealt with. He had said he was seriously considering merging with this firm and had gone—or so he told me—to the firm's annual meeting in Toronto the previous month. I called the man in charge and left a message: "Please call. It's an emergency." He did call back right away, and I learned that he and Joe had spoken several months before, when Joe indicated he was exiting the paper business and needed to liquidate his stock. But there had been no discussion of a merger or partnership.

"I'm very sorry," the man told me. "I hope you find your children. If I hear anything, I'll let you know."

When Rayanne and I arrived at the airport, we went to the Air Canada desk and spoke to the representative there. The rep called the Airport

Authority Police on duty to speak with us. Rayanne and I waited impatiently on some chairs until they came. We were not surprised, but there was little they could offer us or do for us. The little information they gave us told me only that parental kidnapping is a very common occurrence and that we were up against all kinds of red tape.

Meanwhile, back at Copperfield, Patrick had received a call back from Jean-Marc Lesage. He had briefed Patrick on what we needed to do: report to the police, and get a very good lawyer since I needed to get custody of the girls in order for the police to take meaningful action. Patrick called the police, who told him they would send someone over. He then began looking through the phonebook for a lawyer. He was having difficulty knowing who to pick when he hit upon an idea: He called a lawyer who was a member of the golf club for advice and was in turn given the name of Richard Bennett, a Calgary lawyer with decades of experience in criminal and immigration law. The golf club contact praised Richard's intelligence but also his "great heart and great passion"—traits we would need, Patrick was cautioned, because of the explosive situation we were facing.

By now, Rayanne and I had arrived home from the airport. As we waited for the police to arrive, I became more and more antsy. I called the Calgary Police Service again and was told that the attending officers were tied up with a major traffic accident but that they were trying to send the Victim Assistance Unit. I waited. Four excruciating hours passed.

Two male constables in uniform—both sturdy men in their mid-thirties—arrived at my door at about 11 a.m. This marked the first time in my life that police officers had come into any place I called home. The constables apologized for the long delay. I suppose, in hindsight, I should have invited them into the house, offered them coffee at the kitchen table. But I was too frantic for that. They stood just inside the front door, and one took notes while I paced back and forth and told them what I knew. (I could not sit. In fact, I did not sit for weeks. I would eat standing. Only sleep, when it came, would stop all motion.)

"Are you sure your husband is gone?" the officers wanted to know. I told them about the phone call from Pierre Hawach.

Joe's taken the children overseas and I don't think he's coming back. . . .

"Did your husband have permission to take your daughters on vacation?"

"Yes," I replied, and showed them a letter of permission I had written for Joe to take with him. I also told the officers that the vacation time had been spelled out in a separation agreement. I ran down to the basement to get it, but the document, kept in a brown envelope, had mysteriously disappeared. The simple three-page agreement set out the financial terms of our separation and the fact that we were to share custody of the girls. (We downloaded the template from a web site that made it clear: The document was only legal if it was notarized and filed in court—which we did not do.)

"And when is he supposed to return?"

"July twenty-first," I told the policemen. These officers must have heard many stories like mine, but I was impressed by how sympathetic and sensitive they were. They were not so much consoling as respectful. July 21 would have to pass, they said, before Hannah and Cedar could be declared "missing" and charges could be laid against Joe. Charges? Did I have a sense at this point that an actual crime had been committed? I knew only that what Joe had done was wrong, but the word *crime* had yet to enter the narrative.

(I am no lawyer, but I do understand that "kidnapping" and "abduction" mean something quite specific under criminal law. And while Joe would eventually be charged with parental child abduction, I do want to emphasize that when I use the words *kidnapping* and *abduction* in these pages, I mean them in the most ordinary way. My babies had been taken, a moral outrage had been committed, plain and simple. It will be for the courts to decide on any charges and whether the legal definition of those words applies in the case of Hannah and Cedar.)

The word *loopholes*, though, terrified me when one of the officers used it. I had signed a letter that specifically gave Joe permission to travel with the girls *only* from Canada to Australia via Hawaii and back to Canada again. The girls were scheduled to return on the 21st of July, the permission letter stipulated, "unless due to unforeseen circumstances or illness that date needed to be amended." I could not believe that an unscheduled trip "overseas" could possibly fall into that category. But could it? In those first hours of crisis, I was unfamiliar with the legalities of my new circumstances, and it deepened my panic not to know what my rights were.

The officers also informed me that they had checked Joe's name on their computer system before arriving. They told me he was under investigation for a recent theft of paper from the warehouse that was the base of operations for Amcan, his paper company. For me, this information reinforced my deepening suspicion that Joe had taken the girls with no intention of returning to Canada.

The officers suggested that after July 21 I go to family court with a lawyer to try to get custody orders in place. They also urged me to type up a full statement of events from when I first met Joe until that present day.

At about 11:45 a.m., the officers left. I was extremely exhausted from lack of sleep, but day one of this ordeal had only begun.

Cher's words were still ringing in my ears. I told myself that I would not be dismayed, I would not become a statistic, I would never give up.

* * *

Now absolutely certain that Joe was gone, I started making the calls I was dreading—to my family. My father has a heart condition, and I hated to add to his stress, but I desperately needed the support of my mother, my father, and my three brothers. I called Mom first and broke the news to her, and she, in turn, called my father—then in Detroit on business. My youngest brother, Brendan, lives in Calgary, but my other brothers, Doug and Adam Engdahl—like my parents, Jim and Judy Engdahl—live in Saskatchewan. They all dropped everything and made plans to drive west to my house on Copperfield eight hours away.

"Don't worry," my father told me on the phone. "Hannah and Cedar are coming home. Don't think for a minute they're not. Our priorities in life have just changed, that's all. We'll figure it out. Don't panic."

It was good to hear that. In fact, I *had* to hear it—or sleep would not come. Every night for the next six months, I would ask Patrick to say those words to me. "They're coming home, Mel," he would say. "They *are* coming home."

* * *

I was no longer wrestling with a twenty-one day absence from Hannah and Cedar. Pierre's statement that the girls were "overseas," the landlady's mention of Lebanon, the fact that Joe had an uncle living in that country: I could not yet be sure, but all signs were pointing to the girls and Joe being in Lebanon.

On the other hand, this made absolutely no sense. Joe had never shown an interest in teaching the girls Arabic, did not speak at all highly of Lebanon and said that people there always wanted something from you if you were from the West. His mother, Gladys, not Joe, taught me some Arabic, along with Lebanese cooking so I could teach the girls.

And yet, if the girls were indeed in Lebanon at that moment, then they were in an extraordinarily dangerous place. Hezbollah militants based in Lebanon had struck at targets in Israel with grenade and rocket attacks and, on the morning of July 12, kidnapped two Israeli soldiers. Now the Israel Defense Forces, like enraged bees whose nest has been jostled, were following the militants home, and the casualties, both military and civilian, were mounting. In "the July War," as they would call it in Lebanon, the red earth ran red with blood, most of it innocent. Whole neighbourhoods, twelve-storey apartment buildings, were reduced to rubble, razed to the ground by artillery and air strikes. Families who lived where the militants either lived or sought refuge were crushed or burned to death. Bridges and roads were bombed out, along with water lines and power lines. As the shelling continued and the fires continued to burn in the torrid Mediterranean heat through July into August and on into early September, when a ceasefire finally took hold, taps and toilets ran dry and the power was lost. Thirst and the threat of disease loomed almost as large as the bombs that rained down day and night.

Israeli planes also dropped propaganda leaflets all over southern Lebanon, laying the blame for the carnage on Hassan Nasrallah, the leader of the Lebanese nationalist party, Hezbollah. "Hassan is playing with fire," one leaflet read in Arabic script, "and that is why Lebanon is burning." Worst hit was the south and its border towns and villages, but bombs landed in northern Lebanon as well. There was no safe place. Somewhere in this savaged land were Hannah and Cedar.

How, I asked myself, could Joe risk the lives of the daughters he loved? Such a move went against everything that I thought I knew about him as a father. I expected harsh treatment towards me, but not towards the girls. I worried about his mental stability, which only fuelled my hypervigilance. I had to push from my mind the thought that my estranged husband was mentally unbalanced and therefore capable of hurting our daughters.

* * *

Patrick spoke to Richard Bennett that same afternoon of July 19 and set up a meeting. Good lawyers do not come cheap, and while Richard would in coming months not bother to clock all his hours—and he would give me his home and cell numbers to be used at any hour, without charge—the first matter of business was his $5,000 retainer fee. Patrick's roommate, a good and loyal friend, came to Richard's office with a loan in that amount. Day one not even half over, and the first whopping bill had already come in.

On the way home from Richard's office I called Pierre again (he had not called me back as promised), and he told me that he would get his father to call me and explain things further. Within about twenty minutes Louie called me back from Sydney.

"Not to worry, sweetie," he told me. "The girls are in a safe place. I've done you a favour: I've sent Gladys with them. We need to work this out. Joe is not coming back to Canada. So you'll have to come here." He made it sound so simple, as if the most natural thing in the world was for a father to run off with his children, giving the mother no choice but to follow.

Louie said he would get Pierre to call me back to explain things, so clearly I was being passed around like a hot potato from father to son. I was so hungry for information to help me figure out what was really going on. Pierre called back and by this time I was sitting in my van in the back alley parking spot behind the house on Copperfield. I was still so emotional, but because I wanted to keep Pierre on the line for as long as I could, I made every effort to be steady and rational. I was begging him to help me and to find out more of what I needed to do. What did Joe want? What did he hope to accomplish by taking Hannah and Cedar to the Middle East?

"I spoke to both of the children on the telephone this morning," Pierre told me. "They are in good spirits and think they are on a holiday." I insisted on knowing where they were.

"Are they in Lebanon?" I asked him.

Pierre paused. In hindsight, a meaningful pause, but I did not want to risk having him hang up by pressing for specifics.

"Are they in the Middle East?" I asked.

"Yes," he said, promising to call back, though he never did. We never spoke again.

My biggest and overwhelming concern was for my daughters' lives and getting them out of wherever they were in the Middle East. The girls believed they were on holiday, and I now clung to that thought. It sounded like such a happy and carefree thing, and it helped erase that other image—the girls confused and lonely and terrified by the sights and sounds of war—that would have driven me crazy. What if, I thought, the girls had been abducted by a stranger? The unknown and the unthinkable would have unravelled me even more. What Pierre told me was a gift. It allowed me as a mother to be more rational, or relatively so. For all that, in those first twenty-four hours immediately following Pierre's call, I was spinning.

Later that night I tried to call Pierre again and he did not answer. I kept trying to get him on the phone. No answer. Finally, I e-mailed him and told him that my parents were on their way to Calgary and that once they got here, I would not be able to stop this whole thing from snowballing. I was trying to make it urgent that he help me without issuing a threat. I basically said that if he was not helping me he was against me and that if he got caught up in all of this—however innocent his involvement may have been—I would protect no one but my daughters. My message, like my phone call, was never answered.

I walked into my backyard through the back gate and lay down on the three-seater outdoor swing that the girls and I had sat on so many times. For the first time in nearly thirty-six hours, I slept.

* * *

Those first few days and weeks that followed Pierre Hawach's phone call became a blur of meetings and phone calls and new obligations—and not much in the way of sleep. My life had been truly turned upside down, and emotions and tensions continued to run high. Nothing was happening fast enough for me, and I was clinging to the hope that all this activity meant that things were actually falling into place. Still, there was no denying one fact: A formidable team had formed to address my hideous loss.

It was like that line from the Bible that delineates Christ's genealogy: "Abraham begat Isaac; and Isaac begat Jacob; and Jacob begat Judas and his brethren . . ."

The Calgary police officers had suggested I seek a court order to achieve sole custody of the girls. On day one, with Patrick's help, I had acquired the services of two terrific lawyers—Richard Bennett and his colleague, Kelly Stewart, a family lawyer. Two days later, on July 21, we went to court to seek sole custody of Hannah and Cedar. The two lawyers also set in motion the terms of the Hague Convention, an international treaty signed by both Canada and Australia, and specifically designed to help left-behind parents. The treaty stipulates that a child abducted by a parent *must* be returned to that child's country of origin for a custody hearing. Had Joe set foot back in Australia, the girls would very likely have been taken from him, put into the care of Australian social services, and Joe and I would have presented our respective cases, first at a preliminary hearing in Sydney, then at a Hague hearing in Calgary.

The process is not quick. Preliminary hearings alone can take up to two months. There are many games that the abducting parent can play to slow proceedings—including accusing the other parent of being abusive or negligent. In such a circumstance, the country the children are in (Australia, for me) would have to ensure that the allegations were untrue before sending the children home. For this reason, I was advised to start collecting reference letters from Hannah's and Cedar's teachers, doctors and other close contacts so that when and if any allegations flew, I could deal with them. The bottom line was that getting the Hague Convention working for us offered a chance to get the girls back on home ground.

Richard, in turn, suggested we hire the services of Bison Security Group, a local team of private investigators (most of them former police and RCMP officers) who work closely with the Calgary police. On day two, Bison came on board in the form of two investigators, Darryl Stark and Lovell Bowen. The latter advised me to get in touch with the Missing Children Society of Canada. I had not known this non-profit organization existed, but it would prove invaluable (it was the MCSC that had urged me to collect reference letters). Calgary police detectives John Hebert and Theresa Garagan were assigned to my case, and they would likewise offer enormous help.

Within fourteen days, arrest warrants were issued against Joe on two counts of parental child abduction, and extradition orders were sworn against him. These documents were also filed with the Canadian Police Information Centre, who then filed the information with the RCMP, who then informed the International Criminal Police Organization (Interpol). The latter outfit appeared to be distressingly slow to act, several months in fact, but eventually Joe's passport was assigned a red flag, and the girls' passports yellow flags (to indicate they are minors). These cautions meant that for Joe, to cross any border was to risk detention.

All those working on my behalf—lawyers, police detectives, private detectives, experts on child abduction—had a wealth of experience, and they were all telling me the same thing just days into my nightmare: We're moving forward quickly and expeditiously, much quicker than normal. Joe had not just taken the kids into the Middle East. He had taken them into a country under attack, and he was already entangled by serious criminal charges back in Canada. Those two facts gave what might have been just one more parental kidnapping a lot of weight.

We would gather at Richard's office, often several times a week during these early hectic days. When I was not in these meetings, or researching on my own, I was working on my police statement—an eighteen-page, single-spaced document that took nearly two days to produce. I would dictate and Krista and Shauna (the partners, respectively, of my brothers Brendan and Adam) took turns keying in my story. This proved to be a long and difficult, very emotional and, above all, embarrassing process. "Melissa Hawach's Statement," as it would be labelled, detailed several disturbing—and to this point, largely undisclosed—incidents from my married life. I made Krista and Shauna promise not to talk to my brothers about the specifics of some of the abuse described in those pages.

In light of the kidnapping, certain incidents from the recent past now leapt out at me. In the statement, for example, I described a meeting that took place days before Joe and I separated. My mother and father had just learned of the abuse in my marriage, and they had gone to discuss it with Joe and his mother, Gladys—who had flown from Sydney to Calgary to support her son during this emotional time. At one point during that meeting, Joe lost his temper. He was, I was later told, literally beating his chest as he screamed, "You can't take my girls away from me!" What was so disturbing—my mother was frightened by this outburst, my father just stunned—was that it seemed to come out of nowhere. My parents had simply told Joe that they thought it best that I be apart from him for the time being.

Melissa Hawach's Statement ends, "I never doubted his hatred for me. But I never in a million years thought that he would deny the girls the right to grow up with a mother who loves them." Proof of that hatred was his taking the girls from me.

* * *

On July 19, that interminable first day, I sent Joe an e-mail message. Under "subject," I had written "please," and the text read: "Please find it somewhere in your conscience to call me. I need to hear the girls' voices. However much you must obviously hate me, it will be detrimental to the girls' well-being and mental state. If you love them, do not cut me out. I am begging you."

Several days later, he did call. It was heart-stopping, realizing that it was him on the line, and that Hannah and Cedar were likely there with him in the same room. When the initial shock of the call subsided a little, I focused on staying steady and calm. Yelling and arguing, I knew, would accomplish nothing. Still, my body shook all through this call, which only lasted a few minutes.

Joe did let me talk to Hannah, and that was hard—for different reasons. It was so good to hear her voice, to know that she was well and, for the moment, safe.

"I love you," I told her. "Are you being a good girl?"

"Yes," Hannah replied, "but Cedar is being naughty. We're playing cards with our cousins."

Joe, I knew, had his hand on the telephone. He had warned me: He didn't want a long chat. For my part, as wrenching as it was, I wanted this conversation to be normal for Hannah. But the line was not the best. There were pauses, as if the words were taking their time to travel all those miles between us, and if we spoke at the same time, the voices would cancel each other out.

Finally, I said to Hannah, "I miss you. I hope you're having fun."

Then my mother got on the line and she, too, had a brief and teary talk with her granddaughter. Mom and I both felt that we had been, for several precious minutes, thrown a lifeline. Then it disappeared.

* * *

Joe had called once. Might he call again? In those first few days and weeks, the tension in the house on Copperfield Gardens could be overwhelming. Every time the phone rang we jumped in case it was Joe Hawach with a new demand. He was so cold. Our talks felt like a kidnapping negotiation—though, of course, without a ransom demand. His demands were of a different sort, and I would learn about them very soon. I would hear his voice and immediately feel rushes of panic and anger and loss: The girls were there with him, but on only two occasions and only briefly did he ever let me speak to Hannah. Cedar still shied away from the phone. And Joe would never, of course, say precisely where he was. During these conversations, a hush would fall over the whole house, and everyone there would be forced to watch and listen and endure all that I was enduring. I had to park my fury and all my emotion; I had to focus. What we needed was information.

The calls would be recorded on a speakerphone, and later replayed. Everything Joe said, everything I said, was later dissected and endlessly analyzed. Had he offered any new information that might prove useful to our side? Had I said the right thing, or the wrong thing? What should I do differently the next time he called?

At 11 a.m. on July 25, day six, Joe called again. And again my body shook under the strain of these surreal circumstances. He told me that if I wanted to see the girls again I would have to sign "a parenting plan." The binding document would be filed in the courts but not actually considered by the courts, it could not be changed, nor could the girls leave Australia until they were sixteen years old.

Kelly Stewart, my family lawyer, very much doubted whether any court in Australia would have approved such a plan, which explained Joe's insistence that no judge actually examine the document. When courts make decisions about children, she explained, they always use a "best interests" test. Was Joe's plan in the best interests of Hannah and

Cedar? Clearly not. Courts tend to favour joint custody so that both parents have a say in major decisions (concerning a child's health, religion, education and residence)—and Joe, by taking his daughters into a battle zone, had shown he needed help with his decision-making. Kelly also pointed out that courts like flexibility in agreements about children so that agreements can change as circumstances change. The plan Joe had in mind was etched in stone, non-negotiable and to be signed privately. It looked to us as if the "best interests" being served by this plan were those of Joseph Hawach.

Through e-mails that followed from Joe, and through later discussions between Richard Bennett and Louie Hawach, I learned a little more about the preconditions to this "parenting plan." I was to sell my house on Copperfield Gardens, put $50,000 in an Australian trust account (to be my source of income) and go live in Australia—or never see Hannah and Cedar again. (I'm presuming the $50,000 figure represents the sum of what Joe had paid me from the sale of our matrimonial home plus what he had paid me in child support.) No discussion of these terms. No debate. It felt like blackmail, pure and simple.

During these early days, as part of the cat-and-mouse game between my side and Joe's side, I sometimes played along to a certain extent. In a telephone conversation with Louie Hawach (after first consulting with Richard and Kelly), I did allow Louie to believe that I was preparing to sell my house, create the trust account and come to Australia. I did not want to shut down any options, and I would plead with Louie (and later Joe's uncle, Sid Hawach, a lawyer) to fax us the parenting plan. It never came.

Privately, though, I was appalled and disgusted. Louie, his family, certain people I had considered friends in Australia: Did they think they had the right to know where my daughters were while I did not? How many of them were communicating with Joe while pretending not to? As for Joe's draconian plan, I found it one-sided and completely unacceptable.

E-mails, four in total, were exchanged between Joe and me in these first days. Me in what felt like a command post in southern Alberta, Joe somewhere in Lebanon, where a real war raged.

Within two weeks of the abduction (and with the help of Krista's stepfather), we posted photos on the Internet of the girls and of Joe and

Gladys. "Have you seen these missing children?" the web site asked, with details of the kidnapping and an e-mail address. The photo—me with my sunglasses perched on my head and smiling, Hannah on my right and Cedar on my left, both laughing with their eyes closed and hamming it up for the photographer—was taken the day they left. We sent the photo to friends, urging them to send it to their friends, on and on. Around the world went those images of Hannah and Cedar.

First, though—on July 26, day seven—we posted a "fake" web site aimed only at Joe and meant to dupe him into revealing his general location. I had sent him an e-mail that read "I can't believe it has come to this. May God help you." I then mentioned the web site and its name. This one, with a tag slightly different from the one that would follow, was called bring-hannah-and-cedar-home.com. We used an invisible web tracker (StatCounter.com) that allowed us to monitor and track any visitors to the web page in real time. Within hours of the poster first going up, we got a hit from somewhere in Lebanon. I remember my father shouting in the living room at Copperfield Gardens, "We got him! We got him!" Well, not exactly.

That same day Joe called me on the phone. He was furious. "Keep that web site up," he told me, "and you can't talk to the girls." He gave me one day to take it down, and we did.

Also on that day, Detective John Hebert of the Calgary police e-mailed Joe, offering him a chance to tell his side of the story. "This can be undone," John wrote him, holding out an olive branch. No reply.

On July 29, Joe called my cell phone again, this time at 12:49 p.m. (Connor Tapp, who works for the Missing Children Society of Canada, later traced it to a phone booth in Tripoli, Lebanon). The quality of the line was good, with no pauses.

I was at that moment shopping at the Millarville farmer's market in southwest Calgary. My mother and Krista had gone to the market to purchase food and fresh vegetables, and they had taken me with them. Only later did this occur to me: My family had made it a point never to leave me alone. They were obviously concerned about my mental state. I may have seemed tough and focused, but just below the surface was a blubbering wreck.

I had another reason for being at the market that day. In what may have been the one form of denial I was allowing myself, I was always buying items for the girls—and the market vendors offered hand-sewn clothes and handicrafts, as well as fresh produce. If I saw something that Hannah or Cedar might like, I would purchase it and set it aside. This was one more way of telling myself that sooner or later they would be home. My mother did the same.

Now Hannah was on the line, sounding in good spirits, talking about a big celebration they were going to, how they had bought fireworks. It was a hot sunny day in southern Alberta, and I sat on a stoop and cried while I talked and told my daughter repeatedly: "I love you, Hannah. I miss you." It must have been strange for others to behold, a very private scene unfolding in a very public place.

Joe came on the line. I begged him to call me soon so I could speak to Hannah again, but he offered no promise of that and hung up the phone. The call, my cell phone clock told me, had lasted precisely four minutes and thirty-five seconds. This marked my last telephone communication with Hannah. Almost five months would pass before I heard her voice again. I went on sending e-mails and text messages to Joe, but all communication from him once more abruptly ceased.

* * *

In the days and weeks that followed, Joe Hawach's strategy became clearer: He had rung up $25,000 on our American Express card, and he went on using the card a while longer until I was finally able to cancel it. (Though it was a Catch 22 decision: Should I let him go on using the card so we could track his whereabouts? Or should I cancel the card and try to minimize my mounting debt?) By then, the list of purchases had hit $36,000. He had also taken out half a dozen other credit cards and spent the limit on each one. I found out about these debts only after I got the mail from Amcan re-routed to my home address.

With Joe gone and in hiding, I was responsible for all these charges, along with a rash of his business debts that poured in as the days went by. Financially crippled, he thought, I would be forced to sign the binding arrangement he had in mind: the girls living in Australia (and not allowed to leave until each had reached the age of sixteen), and their mother allowed to see them but with full custody granted to their father.

Four days before he left Canada, Joe and I had actually talked about Lebanon. Ever since the Israelis pulled out of Lebanon in 2000, the Israeli-Lebanon border had been tense. Hezbollah and the Israeli army had for years taken potshots at each other, but these were just skirmishes, little brush fires that flared and then were doused. This was different.

The war had just begun, and I wondered aloud if Joe's relations there were safe. He said that his sister, Suzie, and her husband were thinking about going to live there, that it was safer than you might think—especially in the north. I told him that choosing between living in a country where bombs rain down and one where they don't is a no-brainer. Besides, Suzie had just given birth, she loved Australia, and even contemplating moving to Lebanon made no sense to me. Later, as I replayed this and other conversations looking for clues and insights, I wondered if Joe was actually preparing me for the thought of Hannah and Cedar in his ancestral—and war-torn—home.

Having the girls grow up in Lebanon was not an option for me. But neither was signing Joe's custody deal. "Like making a deal with the devil," my Australian family lawyer, Mark Whelan, would later tell me. I still could not believe that my husband was capable of doing all that he had done. And I could not believe that my husband's family—whom I adored and who had taken sides against me—would acquiesce to this lunatic strategy of using children as pawns in a custody battle. One betrayal was stacked upon another.

And so began my nightmare, a mother's worst.

2

Mel the Tomboy

I was born Melissa Mae Engdahl in 1974, in the northern Ontario town of Thunder Bay. The family name was actually Isaacson—the name of my great-grandfather, who had come to Saskatchewan from Sweden in the 1930s. Family lore has it that someone in the distant past felt that Isaacson was too hard for non-Swedes to spell, and that Engdahl—the name of a valley in Sweden—was an easier moniker.

It says Melissa on my birth certificate, but almost everyone in my circle of family and friends calls me Mel. I am the eldest of the family, with three younger brothers—Adam, Doug and Brendan. My father, Jim Engdahl, fifty-six as I write this, grew up poor, dirt poor, in Kelvington, a town of a thousand people in central Saskatchewan. He tells stories of sleeping in a bed of straw, of sharing a 400-square-foot shack with six siblings and his parents, of not having running water or electricity until he was in the early grades of primary school. The Engdahl farm was too small to support such a brood, and there was never enough money to buy farm machinery or more land. Young Jim Engdahl and his siblings would be hired to pick rocks in the fields of neighbours for 50 cents an hour. I remember as kids being driven across the prairie in our old 1987 Chev, a blue wood-panelled station wagon, to visit relatives and we would pass dilapidated, falling-down outbuildings. "Is that where you lived?" we would ask my father. We never really knew whether my father's stories were historically accurate or whether they were meant to drive home a point: You kids have no idea how good you've got it. Both were true. He was giving us a sobering history lesson.

Mom, Judy Engdahl, had also come from a poor family. Her father worked at three jobs so his wife could stay home and look after my mom and her four brothers. My mother was extremely organized—as she had to be with four children and her husband often gone on business trips. She was a cleanliness fanatic who ran a tight ship at home. Driving a car, she would put her hands precisely at 10 o'clock and 2 o'clock, never once got a speeding ticket, never had an accident. Her driving record was as clean as her house.

Once, when she was driving one of the boys to hockey practice (with three other kids in tow), she was being extra cautious—a winter storm had just hit and road conditions were awful. A police officer pulled her over and asked for her licence and registration, and then asked her if she had been drinking. My mother—who has never been a drinker, even socially, a very proper woman with impeccable manners driving a car full of children—found the question preposterous.

"No!" she replied curtly. "Have *you*?"

I started laughing (my mother was actually sassing a cop), then Mom immediately turned contrite as she realized she was talking to someone in authority. Nothing came of her outburst but it was a very funny moment.

My friend, Andy, has known me since Grade 5, and he says he learned sarcasm from hanging around the tightly knit Engdahl household. There was a lot of laughter in that house, a lot of fun. Andy and I would get into trouble—mild trouble, nothing serious—for laughing in class or getting caught drawing cartoons of our friends to alleviate boredom. There was never any romantic attachment between Andy and me. He was like a brother to me, and I like a sister to him. But where I was blonde and fair, Andy—of Syrian blood—was dark and olive-skinned.

My father's grim past notwithstanding, he has done pretty well in business: first in banking and then, later, handling finances for a mining company. Along the way we moved around a lot, from Thunder Bay to various towns in Saskatchewan: Prince Albert, St. Louis, Yorkton, Moose Jaw. In a twelve-year span in my youth, I lived in eleven different houses. We finally ended up in Saskatoon—a city of 220,000 souls on the bald, flat prairie in the middle of Canada—where I spent most of primary school and all of high school.

I remember my childhood as happy. My best friend from those days, Rayanne, says I was "the planner." She recalls that when we were both in Grade 2, young Melissa concocted a scheme to sell bananas and wash cars at a sidewalk kiosk to raise money for track suits. Adidas track suits coloured purple and yellow and white. I was from the start outdoorsy, athletic, entrepreneurial.

Someone once asked me—in the wake of Hannah and Cedar's abduction—if I ever experienced anything like that as a child. Was I ever lost or separated? I never was, but I do remember going through a phase when I was about ten worrying about death and the repercussions of death: never being able to put my arms around my mother, father and brothers again. No more touching, no more hugs. That fear kept me awake at night for a long time. I would go into my brothers' rooms in the middle of the night and rouse them, ask them to play with me or talk to me so I would be spared such thoughts.

The only other childhood trauma I remember was meningitis, which I contracted in the summer of 1985 when I was eleven years old. The inflammation of my brain—which very nearly killed me—went undiagnosed for four months, leading to crushing migraine headaches and total paralysis from the hips down. Before they had a diagnosis, doctors had to perform a number of spinal taps on me using a *very* large needle. Only my mother had the stomach to be present and hold my hand through that ordeal. My father, whose spirit is willing but whose stomach is weak, had to pass. He still says that one of the happiest days in his life was seeing me walk, with support, as my body finally rallied from that devastating blow. I was in hospital and confined all that time, but I absolutely refused to use a bedpan and expose my body to strangers. Far too embarrassing for a Catholic girl like me. No matter how long it took, I was going to drag myself to the bathroom. And I did.

When I see Hannah in the morning—not fully awake, cranky and stubborn and on the verge of exploding—I see myself. I was sometimes like that as a child, and I'm still like that to a certain extent. I do not always greet the dawn with a handshake and a smile.

I was a typical tomboy and played all kinds of sports, often competing at elite levels on teams my father coached. Baseball was, and remains, my favourite sport. I still play it, still love diving for balls in centre field. I played competitive baseball in Canada and later in Australia when I lived there. I still play fast-pitch.

After being tested as a child in Grade 4, I was enrolled in an advanced academic program called Extended Learning Opportunities, or ELO. I always felt like I did not quite belong in those classes, since most of my fellow pupils—many of them gifted—seemed so much smarter than me. We would study whatever struck our fancy: inventions, potholes, the stock market, palaeontology—sometimes at the University of Saskatchewan (which offered the opportunity to examine dinosaur bones). It must have been funny to see all these little eleven-year-olds with their backpacks cruising around the campus.

I continued in ELO at Bishop Mahoney High School, with advanced classes in algebra, biology and, my specialty, English (I wrote a thirty-five page "novel" in Grade 10). But math had always been a struggle for me, and I was not surprised when my Grade 10 algebra teacher politely asked me to return to the mainstream program.

In high school, I did no drugs, no booze. I had a small group of friends connected with my various interests—sports, drama, student council, my boyfriend's pals. I dated the same boy from Grade 10 until my first year in university. I was the school valedictorian the year I graduated, but the choice between my friend Andy (also president of the student council) and me was so close that the principal called us both to the office to announce the decision.

That year I also earned a reputation as a troublemaker of sorts. I had been playing on the school basketball team for four years, and it bothered me that "the team room," as it was called (it was really a locker room), was available only to male athletes. I did some research on the number of athletes, male and female, playing on school teams. I got a letter from the Catholic school board to show that cheerleaders, too, were athletes and part of the sports program. (I have to say that while I was somewhat allergic to the concept of cheerleaders, I did have friends on the squad.) All this to make the case with some of my own teachers, the football coach and the principal that the team room should be shared. Eventually, the room was shared and later a new team room was built for the girls.

Underneath my yearbook photo in my graduation year was this

caption: "I want to be the first female prime minister." A lot of students write something similar in their yearbooks, and I am now embarrassed to rank among them.

I had ambition, and no shortage of flaws. Around my friends, I can put on a cocky manner for their amusement. But those around me and close to me must also bear my endless questions. If there is something I do not understand, I will insist on more and more detail, and those on the receiving end of this barrage may think I doubt them. So I try to choose my words and my tone carefully, but I invariably put my foot in it.

The girls on my ball team know that I always tell it like it is, and they see my rowdy and blunt side. I often forget that feelings can be hurt. Mostly I just try to be funny—at my own expense and that of others—but always in good fun. It would break my heart to know I had hurt someone.

You might think by all this that I am the sort to swim against the current. That is only partly true. In religion class, I wanted to know why women cannot become priests and argued the point with my teachers. At the same time, I do not like being in conflict with family members or the law. Catholic guilt is a powerful thing. A psychologist I saw in Australia (just after I got married) observed the contradiction in me: an independent and strong woman who tended to get involved with men on whom she became dependent.

In my youth I was seen as spirited, independent, adventurous, spontaneous, impulsive. The mini-van, the soccer mom, the *hausfrau* who sprays her kitchen counters with antibacterial cleanser every afternoon: Those days were off in the future. One summer after high school, Rayanne and I shouldered our backpacks and went off tree-planting in northern British Columbia when most of my friends at home were waitressing and pumping gas.

I did most of a degree in psychology at university, until I was hit by the travel bug. I had met an Aussie while tree-planting and I soon found myself living in Australia. This was the early 1990s, and I was working as a tour guide on the weekends in Sydney—leading skiing tours for a company called Alpine World to the Snowy Mountains of Australia and, once a year, the Rocky Mountains back home. During the week, I worked as the daytime manager at a Swiss restaurant in Sutherland, a southern suburb of Sydney.

And I was living with Brad—the most serious romance of my life to that point. Along with two friends of Brad's, we shared a bungalow on Murrawal Road near Stanwell Park (a gorgeous national park) with cliffs behind and the Pacific Ocean in front. I remember the beauty of the place, how relaxed it made me feel. Brad and I shared many interests: hang-gliding, bungee jumping, surfing, travel, the outdoor life. From our balcony, I could smell saltwater, watch the sun rise over the beach below and feel that forest breathe.

Hoping to catch on full-time with the touring company, I dropped the restaurant job and took a course at a travel college. With my studies occupying me most mornings, I got a job working the noon to 3 p.m. shift at an Italian restaurant on York Street in downtown Sydney, just a block from the college. The restaurant was Positano's, run by Joe Hawach.

The Hawach family—a tight and warm clan headed by the family patriarch, Louie Hawach—operated a string of restaurants, all called Positano's. Louie and Gladys had emigrated from Lebanon and ran a fruit shop in Sydney until Joe, just twenty-two, launched the first Positano's—in the central business district (or CBD) of Sydney. The downtown restaurant served a business luncheon clientele and had a fabulous wine list. The Positano's in the south Sydney suburb of Cronulla (a restaurant we later renamed Cheeky Monkey) had a loyal clientele, and great care was taken with the service. Finally, there was the Positano's in Parramatta—a western Sydney suburb—that catered mostly to tourists.

These were Italian restaurants (specializing in wood-fire pizza with the music of Dean Martin and Frank Sinatra often playing in the background), and I suppose the Hawaches could have passed for Italian. Everyone in the family had worked at some point in the restaurants and spoke Lebanese most of the time. Lebanese culture was a powerful force in their lives.

The Hawaches were part of the Lebanese diaspora—300,000 in Australia claim Lebanese heritage, along with a like number in Canada. In the United States, the number is three million and in Brazil, a staggering nine million.

I worked at Positano's for nearly a year—for Joe, but never with him—and when I graduated from the travel college, I got a job as an agent with a sister company of Alpine World and told Joe Hawach that I was leaving. He tried to convince me to stay but I had other goals in mind.

I wanted to fly helicopters. The helicopter passion derived from my time as a student working in logging camps in British Columbia and Alberta. I always liked to push myself, and I also wanted to be sure of my motivation to become a pilot (I often examine my motives, thoughts and behaviours—probably too much). A helicopter pilot's licence is more difficult and more expensive to get than an airplane pilot's licence, and I wanted to know: Was I really in love with flying? This wasn't about making my mark as a woman. This was a test of my passion.

For the next year, I worked as a travel agent while studying for my helicopter licence by correspondence. Then came a call, in 1998, from Joseph Hawach. He was opening two more restaurants (the second and third Positano's) and needed someone he could trust while he was not around. No one in the Hawach family was available. Would I be interested?

Joe did trust me. When I first worked for him, he would put extra cash in my pay packet. Looking back on it, I can see he was testing my honesty. When I told Joe I had been overpaid, he would insist I keep it—"for all your hard work."

Joe had already researched how much it would cost for me to fly two hours a week at the aerodrome, and he made me an offer that included enough to cover that flying time. The trade-off was that I would work some eighty hours a week at all three Positano's restaurants, with one day off. For me, it was a dream come true. I was also terribly flattered. Joe was not pursuing me romantically, I'm as sure of that now as I was then. We worked at separate places. What Joe needed was a trustworthy employee cum supervisor, and he has a way of weighing your currency—of doing or saying something that will compel you in the direction he wants you to go.

Brad, meanwhile, took my old job as an international tour guide. We were both working absurdly long hours, he was away on weekends (including my one day off) and I was fully entrenched with my helicopter flying and work. Brad was pursuing another path. An electrician by trade, he spent every spare moment surfing, hang-gliding or involved with Alpine's many social events. We began to drift apart over the next six months.

Brad is such a talented and dynamic individual, a kind man and a free spirit and maybe one of the gutsiest and bravest people I have ever met. We shared many adventures around the world and a few of them got us into tight spots, but he always rose above the difficulties, kept me calm and worked things out.

One time we were hiking off the trail in Stanwell Park and we got lost. Brad decided we should climb an escarpment to get our bearings. I got to a point where I could neither climb (too steep and nothing to grab onto) nor descend (the rock was crumbling and giving way beneath my hiking boots). I was losing equilibrium. Brad calmed me, talked me through it, and we managed to get up onto a lip.

Another time we were surfing the waters off Stanwell Park. That coast is known for its riptides, and this day, Halloween, there was a big nor'easter swell and wind, and I got caught in it. I ditched my surfboard and tried to swim out of it but got nowhere. From shore, Brad saw me struggling and swam out ahead of the lifeguards, but he couldn't get me in either. By now the swell was four feet high. By timing the waves, we got onto a tiny island of rocks without dashing our bodies. The lifeguards had by this point spotted us, and though they could have rescued us with ropes, there was talk at the time of cutting back on lifeguard services and someone decided that a more dramatic rescue would make the news and generate public interest. So we were winched up into a helicopter and our photos—me wrapped in a blanket on shore—made the front page of a small local newspaper. For me the real story was Brad's bravery. He was a fearless guy.

When Brad told me he wanted to fly helicopters, too, I knew we could not compete with each other. He was a true flier and adventurer, and I could never stand in the way of that ambition, nor would I want to. Brad was Brad: When the wind was wrong for flying, it meant the wind was blowing offshore—great for surfing. Everyone loved Brad. I do not regret that we broke up because I think it was the right thing, but it hurt a great deal and I was a long time grieving that relationship.

I was also feeling the urge to settle down. I had lived for a time in a van with my dog, but I was tired of that seat-of-the-pants lifestyle. It seemed to me then I had started many things in my life but never finished them, and that, too, left me dissatisfied.

I took an apartment on the beach at Cronulla, in south Sydney, close to the Positano's where I was working most of the time. Joe and his best friend were equal partners in the restaurant, but when the friend split with his long-time fiancée, the Cronulla restaurant visibly suffered. Though I felt bad for the co-owner, a sweet man but absolutely distraught over the fracture in his personal life, I felt duty-bound to inform Joe. He and the friend deliberated over how to unravel the partnership. At first, this other man was supposed to buy Joe out, but in the end the reverse happened. The parting of ways was bitter and acrimonious, with Joe changing locks at the restaurant and hiring security guards in what is best described as overkill. I, meanwhile, began to work more hours at the other Positano's locations.

I worked with Joe Hawach and Joe's brother Pierre, and we made a wonderful team. We laughed a lot.

There was never, I thought, any physical attraction between Joe and me. But one day at the restaurant, not long after Brad and I had gone our separate ways, Joe came up behind me and put an apron around me, and there it was. The attraction took me by surprise, but the real surprises were yet to come.

Later, Joe would tell me that a fortune-teller in Los Angeles once predicted that he would marry a fair-haired woman from North America. Did he make it up? I don't know. But what I did know—for he told me—was that he had no desire to marry a traditional Lebanese woman. It seems he wanted me.

3

Swept Away

The actual premarital courtship lasted all of four months, but I had spent the entire year before that working for Joe Hawach—and not spending much time thinking about him. In the open kitchen of the restaurant, everyone who cared to look was afforded a view of Joe's "plumber's butt" as he dug in the fridges below the pizza-making shelves. I remember remarking in my own mind on his total disregard for what people saw and thinking at that moment, "I wonder what sort of woman he's going to end up with." It seemed like he cared about nothing (save money and business), yet he drove a Porsche Boxster and he was very fussy about his suits. He was an enigma to me, an oddball, yet I knew he was smart and capable.

Joe was just a few months younger than me, and he was imposing in many ways. At the tender age of twenty-two, he had begun running his own restaurant. That impressed me. At six-foot, one inch and 260 pounds, he was once a gifted athlete who had played professional rugby until a knee injury cut short his career. He was charming, he was handy, and he loved the finer things in life—elegant food, music, architecture. And I loved his corkscrew, curly black hair. He was, in a word, *exotic.* I think he, on the other hand, was impressed by my work ethic, how reliable I was, how I could just take charge of a restaurant and not come undone by the chaos that restaurants are prey to.

I remember once having a cappuccino on a break when I first started to work at the Positano's in Parramatta. There was this elderly man (or so he seemed to me) on his hands and knees scrubbing a cupboard. It did not seem right that I should be lounging while he was toiling away down there. So I just put my coffee down, grabbed a brush and joined him. This was, of course, Louie Hawach. From that point, he and I enjoyed a warm connection. He was always so sweet and good to me: He would bring me flowers from the fruit market.

I loved the Hawach family, all of them. They were all hard workers who admired other hard workers, and I was one. "You work like a horse," Joe's mother, Gladys, used to tell me.

Louie had very little education. He spoke English with a heavy accent—four parts Lebanese, one part Australian. He was little and loud and explosive, with the temper of a petulant child. He was always threatening to break the legs of people who crossed him. But he was such a tiny man (who never hurt anyone) that the effect was more comic than fearsome.

Warm and caring and, like many men, hard pressed to express his feelings, Louie always had tears in his eyes at family functions and was forever lecturing Joe about how family mattered most and how concerns over money paled beside a rift or argument in the family. On the other hand, Louie had that fear that many immigrants never quite shake: No amount of money would ever make him feel comfortable or set. He could win the lottery and he would go on working and saving, working and saving. He did not know how to rest or pause, how to put his feet up and relax. He arrived in Australia quite poor with no English and he often said that his dream was to buy each of his six children their own house.

Louie and his eldest son, Joe, were alike in many ways. Louie brooked no challenge from his wife or daughters, and Joe would take no sass from his sisters. The Hawach family was a clan, and Louie and Joe stood on the highest rungs of its ladder.

Joe is quiet and closed, where I am more of an extrovert. We were exact opposites (and maybe it's true about opposites attracting). I liked how he took care of those he cherished, his fierce loyalty, his fine taste. I liked the fact that he had travelled widely in the United States, so interest in travel was something we shared. I would give him popular books on psychology: *The Bridge Across Forever, The Road Less Traveled.* We would go to musicals, good restaurants (we were both foodies). And given what happened later in our marriage, it is shocking to admit: He made me feel good about myself. He made me feel valued.

I started "seeing" Joe in June 1999 and I was liking him more and more. I admired how he could appear to be calm even when he was actually quite upset. I liked how he handled people who worked for him and how he always saw the bigger picture. An employee would make a mistake or do something wrong, and Joe would not succumb to the emotions of the moment. He was controlled, and maybe I admired that. I was still suffering from the breakup with Brad, and even took time off work in July of that year to take a two-week holiday in the Whitsunday Islands, in Queensland, with my mother. I was having a hard time controlling my emotions, and there was Joe, with a pretty good grip on his. Maybe I saw this as strength and was drawn to it.

One night that year, after dinner and over cigars and Scotch in the restaurant when the patrons had all gone and we had the place to ourselves, I proposed to Joseph Hawach. That's right, *I* proposed to *him*.

I knew he was waiting for me to recover from my previous relationship, and that if one of us was going to pop the question, it would have to be me. I did not get down on bended knee, but looking back on it, I have to admit: I was infatuated and I had had it with adventure. Joe stood for family, stability, the prospect of children.

We got married in Our Lady of Lebanon Church late in 1999. Only after we were married did I learn from my new husband's mother that Joe had twice tried to call off the wedding. His mother—a devout Maronite Catholic who makes pilgrimages to holy places in Lebanon—had to convince him that I was a good choice, a good Roman Catholic, a good soul. (The two branches of Catholicism have much in common and I felt quite at home at the Maronite church in Sydney.) In hindsight, what matters most about this is that the groom kept a rather vital piece of information from his bride. He had profound doubts about his choice, and I never knew till the deal was done.

Looking back on it, I should have heard the ringing of alarm bells. They were not faint.

Were we both too young? Lacking in judgement? Was the match of cultures a mismatch? Or would waiting even another year to marry

Joseph Hawach have failed to reveal the dark side of him? In any case, we would later both make the same claim: "You're not the person I married." I thought he was more progressive, less tied to conservative Lebanese culture. In fact, I thought he opposed that culture and I believed him when he said he would never marry a Lebanese woman. Maybe he himself failed to realize the depth of his ties. He thought I was more traditional, more pliable perhaps. There were serious expectations on both sides, and they were quickly dashed.

Andy, my lifelong friend, thinks the world of me and has said as much on many occasions. As loyal friends do, he lauds my qualities and he forgives my flaws. "But you know," he observed not long ago, "I can't remember a time when you were not with a boyfriend or a man in your life." He could not fathom why such a strong and independent woman seemed so ill at ease flying solo, even if only briefly.

Andy, though, was not always around. There were indeed times when I was not in a relationship—first-year university, third-year the same. I was not a young woman who "dated." I had relationships.

Before I was married, I would get up at 4:30 a.m. twice a week and drive to the Albion Park Aerodrome in Sydney. In part, that's why I was working seventy and eighty hours a week at Positano's: to fund those pricey flying lessons. I used to fly a Bell 47 helicopter for an hour or two in the still air of the morning. Used as a trainer and with a long history of both commercial and military use (the *M*A*S*H* television series—that black comedy about the Korean War—used them), the Bell 47 is some 32 feet long with a 280-horsepower engine. Flying one gives you a feeling like no other: You're on top of the world. How many times when I was in hiding later on did I wish for one of those choppers to magically appear so I could fly us all out?

Trying to get out of a country severely rocked by war and beset by security issues, its borders on all sides looking like armed camps, soldiers with machine guns at every barbed-wire checkpoint and tanks on every corner, huge areas of cities and towns reduced to rubble, the skeletons of burnt-out cars strewn along every highway—if I had had a crystal ball, that's what I would have seen. Just months into my marriage, though the crystal ball was fuzzy on the details, one thing was crystal clear: The picture was far from idyllic.

4

The Unravelling

In my marriage to Joseph Hawach, my wearing pants (not dresses) was an issue. Not shaving my legs was an issue. My playing baseball was an issue. My taking university courses was an issue.

When I married Joe, I had known him for two years. I knew his family and I had experienced firsthand their generosity and goodness. I used to go to the market in the very early morning with Louie Hawach to buy produce for the restaurant, and sometimes when I worked late at the Parramatta restaurant, I would sleep on the Hawach family couch.

Born in 1975, Joe is the eldest of six siblings, and I liked them all. I liked Joe's mother, Gladys, who has a great sense of humour. It seemed to me, though, that the family was consumed with the business and finances, and I tried to introduce activities that would get them interacting in ways that I was used to with my own family. At Christmas, I bought board games for us and, over the holidays one year, I organized a funny skit about the restaurant. I dressed up as Joe—with a huge curly Afro, a big cigar, a wad of cash and a black marker line to accentuate my plumber's butt. Joe's younger brother Jean-Paul played Louie and kicked nearly everyone out of the restaurant. All the family watching this parody, including Joe and Louie and Gladys, were killing themselves laughing. The skit remains a good memory.

The Maronite Catholic priests from Our Lady of Lebanon Church would come to the Hawach's main house on Prospect Street in Parramatta for lunch, and Gladys always wanted me there for the comic element. After the meal, I would hand the clerics plastic gloves and point them to the stack of dishes in the kitchen waiting to be washed. My irreverent clowning seemed to offer a much-needed counter to the quiet and reserve and all-business sensibility that sometimes consumed the Hawach clan.

I would go to church with Joe's brother, Pierre. I liked the other Hawach brothers—Eddie (who could do anything in a restaurant, from cook to serve to manage) and the youngest brother, Jean-Paul (a professional rugby player)—his sisters, Suzie and Janet, and cousin Fred. After Joe and I were married, they all worked hard at various times at the family's restaurant in downtown Sydney.

English was the language of service in the restaurant; Lebanese was the language the Hawach family would resort to when emotions ran high. I liked the spirit and fun of the place, the Lebanese neighbourhood in Rosehill, how everyone lived around the corner. Family, community, roots: These matter to me. In the Lebanese culture, children are cherished and adored, as no doubt my own children would be cherished and adored. I was many thousands of miles from home, stepping deeper and deeper into a culture within a culture (the Lebanese within the Australian), yet feeling very much at home. I felt secure with the Hawach family.

And I *loved* Lebanese food, as would my daughters. *Baba ghanoush* (eggplant purée), *labneh* (yogurt cheese), *hummus* (chickpeas), *za'atar* (a spice mix of thyme, sesame seed, salt and ground sumac and baked on bread).

Perhaps, had Joe and I lived together for some time before taking the plunge, some of the cultural differences between us would have been revealed. But that really was not an option. Cohabitation would have shown great disrespect to his family, and I did not want that.

Joe and I got married on November 14, 1999. I was not keen on picking out bridesmaid dresses and table centrepieces: I had no interest in such matters, but mostly I was appalled by the idea of spending ridiculous amounts of money on one day. In the Lebanese culture (and in many others), though, a lavish wedding is a status symbol. I prefer things simple but I knew that it meant a lot to Joe's mother as he was the eldest son. I also knew that his two sisters (who were bridesmaids) had their own ideas about what they liked and what they would be comfortable in, so I just let them pick what they wanted to wear.

We walked to Our Lady of Lebanon Church and held the reception at the house. Joe and my brothers had peeled the shrimp, part of a fantastic potluck buffet with lots of seafood dishes. I did my own makeup and we had a friend come and do my hair. The Hawach family no doubt thought I was a little too low key about the big day but I just did not think that bigger meant better. Both Joe and I later bragged that we kept the entire wedding (including the honeymoon and the rings) under $10,000.

My brothers and my parents, of course, came to the wedding. My mother had already met Joe during an earlier visit; he had taken her out to dinner and, at first, she liked him. My family was somewhat overwhelmed by Lebanese culture—the music, the loudness. All of them had the same thought: the book and movie *Not Without My Daughter*, about the disastrous union of an Iranian man and an American woman. My folks were uncomfortable with my choice of husband, but that discomfort was never expressed.

We had our honeymoon in Paris, and my new husband was very romantic and seemed very much in love with me. And I loved him. But even then, just days into our marriage and our life together, he expressed disappointment. He thought there would be more sex, and he was not shy about voicing his complaint. "Are you frigid?" he would ask. "Are you a lesbian?"

Trust and intimacy are connected. You share, you open up, and that leads to closeness. You most certainly have to trust that your partner won't hurt you, and Joe had a way, early on, of destroying that trust. Being with him presented a totally different dynamic from what I was used to. I had grown up with three brothers and we were always cutting each other up, mocking the other, roasting the other. The Hawaches did not do that. Maybe he was hurt by things I said in jest, and he would hold on to the resentment. We didn't understand each other from the earliest days of our marriage.

The honeymoon was not relaxing at all. We wanted to see too much of Europe in just three weeks. Still, I have good memories of our touring. I remember fondly the tapas bars in Spain—we loved Spain and went out every night. I remember a three-star restaurant where the sommelier (wine steward) was this huge man with a cup at his belt, the bill arriving in an ornate silver box, Joe forced to wear a borrowed jacket with a fat golden crest because he had left all his suits at this awful hotel in Paris . . . We travelled so hard, so far and so fast that the motor in our rented car burned out. A metaphor for a marriage that would do the same.

Years later, Joe would tell me the honeymoon was a terrible disappointment. Was it really? Were we on different honeymoons? How could I have remembered a much better time? Was this part of Joe's crazy-making (a form of emotional abuse in which one partner tries to make the other feel crazy for not remembering things)? Or was this revisionist history? Did he really mean it when he told me that he was so disappointed that he prayed the plane taking us home would crash?

While in Paris—sitting with my husband at a McDonald's restaurant, in fact—I came up with a name for the new Thai-food restaurant that Joe was going to start up in Sydney. We would call the restaurant Cheeky Monkey. The name sounds light-hearted, and, for a time, the excitement of launching the new place took our minds off our own rocky beginning.

Things got better. Joe was kind and gentle again. He could be so charming, almost charismatic, but it seemed the two sides of him—the light and the dark—were always warring. He believed that what gave him an edge in business was his confidence and cocksure manner. The corollary, though, is that the second he entertained the possibility that his thinking or his behaviour were not the best, doubt entered the picture, and he could not have that. Joseph Hawach is not an introspective man.

Neither does he have much of a sense of humour. But I do remember lying with him in bed one morning when we were still living with his parents and laughing hard at his father's antics. We could hear Louie cursing in the bathroom after he stepped in water in his sock feet.

Louie would do outrageous things to customers—like toss them out for complaining about the price of a fruit salad. He was a little man with a huge heart who showed his love for his family the only way he knew how: by working in the restaurant around the clock. The comic side of Louie was something both Joe and I could laugh at together.

But then Joe would erupt. He was a controller and a scorekeeper: It was all about winning. I would write long letters to him, explaining what I was feeling, expressing the hope that we could work through our problems. I would leave the letters on the kitchen table, but he would pointedly ignore them. He would get upset if I wore pants five days in a row (he kept count); if I did not shave my legs (not something I ever worried about), he would call me a lesbian. I had coached a rep girls' basketball team in Sutherland and had been athletic all my life. Suddenly I was supposed to be a glam girl? I was shocked that Joe could be so cruel—and make such absurd demands.

In these rows, both Louie and Gladys would take my side, but that did not make things any easier for me. I learned that Joe had suffered in the past from depression, something I had never seen in the time I had known him. There was much I did not know.

My roller-coaster ride had just begun and, as the years passed, the peaks rose higher and the valleys got lower, the whole ride ever wilder. One day early in 2000, just one month into my marriage, I was working with Joe at the restaurant downtown when I turned four people away because the only table left was too small to accommodate them. Actually, they themselves made the decision since they weren't interested in waiting for a bigger table to free up. Joe started yelling at me, something he had never done, and he asked to speak with me in the back alley. I remember making a joke to the chef as I walked outside—"Uh-oh, I'm in trouble." I was trying to introduce some levity into the situation, but my gut told me that I was, indeed, in trouble. I had no idea how much.

"You fucking moron!" he screamed. "Are you retarded?" I was shocked, gob-smacked. No one had ever spoken to me like that in my life. Normally, if someone yells at me, I yell back. But I cannot remember whether I did or not. All the customers and staff could hear my husband through the open window, strafing me with his words.

A pattern began to unfold between Joe and me. I would do something that would make him angry and he would "punish" me. He would take off his wedding band and tell me it was staying off until I started acting "properly" (that is, doing exactly what he said, with no sass). He would take away my credit card and lock the till. This was the measure of his control, and my capitulation, in those days.

The news of my pregnancy seemed to soften Joe. For a while.

We were living on Eastcote Road in North Epping, a nice older section of north Sydney. The spot was gorgeous (with a view of the heavily forested Lane Cove National Park below) though our stately brick house perched on a cliff needed work: Black mould was ubiquitous inside, and termites had been feasting on the back wooden deck. Joe loved architecture and though we polished the floors and made the place look nice, the real solution was to knock the whole thing down and start over. In this heritage-conscious neighbourhood, though, change came slowly, and Joe spent a year wrangling with neighbours and the local council over the plans he had in mind.

A horticulturist had previously owned the property, so it was landscaped but badly overgrown. A perfect habitat, it turns out, for deadly funnel web spiders. Backpacking friends from Saskatoon travelling through Sydney would stay with us and we would hire them to hack away at the brush. They would come in every day with their tally of spiders killed: Eight or nine was a typical number.

Funnel web spiders, the males especially, have a reputation for aggressively rearing up and attacking. They rank among the most venomous spiders in the world, and their bite can be life-threatening to the young, the aged or the infirm. I am not afraid of spiders, and I had had the experience in Australia of entering a car, flipping the rear-view mirror and having a huntsman or wolf spider land in my lap. (Though some huntsman spiders look like tarantulas and their leg-span can be almost twelve inches wide, they are mostly benign.) But as a pregnant woman, I now wanted an expanse of lawn on the property—not hiding places for attack insects.

Two months into the pregnancy and five months into our marriage, I got the first taste of just how cruel my new husband could be. I was working a night shift with him. I was learning some of the ropes in the kitchen while Joe served. I cooked a pizza, but the oven was too hot and, as a result, the pizza did not cook properly inside. We made it right. But the evening just kept going off the rails.

Later, a couple came in, regular customers who knew me by name, and they waved to me. There was only one other customer in the restaurant—a man who ordered a salmon, medium-rare, which I cooked. Turns out it was not rare enough, and Joe came back into the kitchen and started yelling at me. I am emotional by nature, but now I was pregnant with hormones raging. And, with the open kitchen, everyone could hear our exchange.

"Get out there!" Joe said. "You serve, and I'll cook!"

I was bawling, I was embarrassed, and I refused to wait on tables in that state, and oh, did that make him mad. At the end of the night, I cleaned up the kitchen and I walked out into the back alley. I was not going to wait for a ride with him; I was going to take the train home. I got halfway down the alley when I heard Joe come up behind me. He grabbed me by my hair and sweater (something I had bought on our honeymoon in Paris, a green turtleneck now twisting in his hands) and he dragged me so forcefully I was choked and short of breath. He forced me back to the restaurant and shoved me against the shelves. I was both angry and scared.

Now he blocked the doorway, and I just said quietly, "Get out of my way." He would not move, and I just kept staring at him and repeating, "Get out of my way."

Finally, he did, but as I passed he kicked me in the lower back and into the hood of his car parked in the alley. I got up and walked to the train station, and went home to our place in North Epping, where I called Gladys. I was weeping but I would not tell her why on the phone.

Gladys arrived with Suzie, her youngest daughter, who was then about fifteen. But I was at this point still protective of Joe. Suzie, I thought, did not need to know about this side of her eldest brother. Later, in private, I did tell Joe's mother what had happened. She kept saying, "Oh my God, oh my God."

Then Louie entered the picture and at one point he asked me, "What did you do for him to do this?"

"If I was your daughter," I said to Louie, "and some other man had done this, would it matter what I had done?" He said nothing.

On our own, I asked Gladys the obvious question: Had Louie ever done this to her? She was adamant that he never had. The only drama that I ever witnessed between them was occasioned by Louie's obsession with work. He would come home religiously every Sunday for the Hawach family lunch but he never took his wife on a vacation, and our attempts at tricking him into doing so would involve the whole family—first to act as co-conspirators to get him to leave the restaurant, and then to act as nurses to assuage Gladys's anguish when the trick subsequently failed, as it usually did. (Though we did succeed one time in getting him to take Gladys to Adelaide on a trip.) I loved Louie and I loved Gladys, and I told them so, but

I was quite open with them. "I don't want," I told them, "your kind of marriage—where my kids have to trick my husband into taking a holiday with me, and I don't want to get hospitalized with some mysterious ailment so my husband will sit with me for a day."

Later, Louie and Gladys and Joe and I all met at our house to discuss the whole tawdry business. Most of their discussion was in Lebanese, which really angered me. Joe's defence, apparently, was that I had tricked him. I was not the wife he thought I would be.

Fair to say, neither was he the husband I thought *he* would be.

* * *

Eventually we sold the house in North Epping, a forty-minute drive from Positano's downtown. We rented a place just a five-minute drive from the Cheeky Monkey restaurant that I was then managing—a two-bedroom apartment on the top floor of a three-storey building at the quiet end of the beach in Cronulla. There was a park nearby and a playground. We were starting to think and plan like the soon-to-be parents that we were.

There occurred a handful of other incidents of abuse—both physical and psychological. Times when my husband would make no eye contact or say anything to me for weeks at a time. We argued in a café once, when I was six months pregnant with Hannah. My brother Adam was visiting then and helping me manage the Cheeky Monkey restaurant while I was home trying to cope with a pregnancy-related illness.

Joe and I had a fight about Adam, who was a total natural at managing the restaurant, a born salesman, a people person and a very hard worker. No matter. My husband was forever attacking my family and I was forever defending. Joe stormed out and drove off, leaving me in the café. With no money in my pocket, I had to walk the 10 kilometres home along the highway. I kept thinking that Joe would cool off, reconsider, come back and give me a lift, but he never did. The walk home took me two hours.

I did tell a Jesuit priest I knew in Sydney about these events. An elderly Irish priest whom Joe very much respected, he had a degree in psychology and counselled me after the breakup with Brad and prior to my marriage. Joe and I were seeing him one time, and Joe started to justify what he had done by talking about how angry I had made him.

The priest just cut him off. "No. Lay a hand on her again," he told Joe, "and I'll call the police myself."

Still, for all that, I held out hope that things would change. All my studying of human psychology had pointed me to my belief in human potential and the possibility for change. I really wanted the marriage to work. To me it was simple: I did not believe in divorce, and if I had disappointed my husband I would fix it, somehow. I would see a therapist, and I did. (This psychologist warned that the cultural differences between my husband and me were insurmountable and he advised me to quit the marriage. But I thought then, and still believe, that the therapist was culturally biased, so I stopped seeing him.)

Maybe, I thought, the birth of our first child and fatherhood would transform my husband.

5

Hello, Hannah Anne

My daughter was born in the first month of the year 2001. We chose her names, Hannah Anne, to honour Joe's maternal grandmother, whose name is Hannah (and because we liked the name), and my own maternal grandmother, Anne. My mother came to live with us in Sydney for a month before the birth and two months after, to help ease this voluble infant into the world.

Joe clearly loved his new daughter and was devoted to her, but there was a limit. He would occasionally get up in the night to change Hannah's nappies but would resent spending too much time with her. His job was the business. Mine was house and home. As the German expression says, for me it was all *Kinder, Küche, Kirche* (children, kitchen, church).

That entire year passed without any major dramas between my husband and me, other than minor arguments. We moved into a house owned by his parents so we could live rent-free for a year because Joe had a new dream now: moving to Canada for a fresh start in both business and marriage. We began to talk about new ventures in Canada—maybe a furniture shop or another restaurant. Through a friend in Milperra in southwest Sydney, Joe got interested in the paper business and the possibility of opening a plant in Canada. The more he researched (and he was good at that), the more the wheels began to turn. Joe has only a high school education but his business sense, his savvy, his gift for analysis: All that is bred in the bone.

Early in 2002, he sent me off on a little three-day holiday cum research mission—a trade fair in Bangkok. It was nerve-racking (militants had just blown up an Aussie bar in Indonesia and while I was in Thailand a mall in Manila was likewise targeted), but this was my first holiday in a long time and it brought back fond memories of all the travelling I had done in the past.

Before leaving on this trip, I wrote Hannah a letter—should something happen and, God forbid, I did not return. It was a letter telling her how much I loved her and what a beautiful baby she was. I gave it to Joe and asked him to keep it for her "just in case." He became emotional about it and I even saw a tear in his eye as he said, "Make sure you come back!"

I did come back—with paper samples, Thai silks, import/export manuals, and a long list of paper mills in Southeast Asia. Joe was looking over all this stuff and I could see the wheels turning, his mind clicking. Pretty soon there was paper tacked up on the walls, like a scene out of *A Beautiful Mind* (the movie about a troubled math genius with a penchant for plastering walls with newspaper and magazine articles as he looked for patterns in news stories). One possibility was to create a paper company in Australia, but Joe soon discovered that expatriate Southeast Asians had the Australian market cornered.

North America, on the other hand, was largely the domain of one company whose virtual monopoly others had tried, and failed, to break. Joe saw a real opportunity. So he hooked up with my brother Doug. Joe would be the front man, Doug the sales force. Together, they would create a company called Amcan, importing paper from Southeast Asia and selling it to commercial printers in Calgary.

Joe then scouted the city and bought a beautiful new house on Mountain Park Drive in the southeast corner of Calgary, in a subdivision known as Mountain Park. My friend Andy's father, a real estate agent, helped Joe make the purchase (and later remarked privately on Joe's arrogance).

Andy and his wife, Simone, had Joe as a house guest for several weeks before Joe took possession of the house. They, too, were left shaking their heads at my choice of husband. "He was hard to talk to," Andy told me later. "He was not much of a conversationalist. He liked to watch

The Sopranos on television, and that was about the only time he said anything. Simone and I just could not connect with him." To be fair, Andy hastened to add that his affection for me may have clouded his judgement, so that no husband could possibly be good enough for me. Both Andy and Simone also observed that Joe could be absolutely charming—when he wanted to be.

I moved in to the Mountain Park house with Hannah in February 2003. Joe, by this time, had returned to Australia but he joined us in Calgary once he had sold the restaurant in Cronulla. We were delighted by our new digs. There was a park across the street, with swings and slides, a man-made lake close by and a little mall around the corner with a pre-school centre where Hannah would go for two hours, twice a week. Everything seemed so clean and fresh and new.

By now, I was three months pregnant with my second daughter, Cedar Lourdes, who would be born in Alberta in September 2003. We chose those names simply because we liked the sound of them. We had brainstormed on a name, an Arabic name, so maybe it was Joe who tossed out the name Cedar—also the symbol of Lebanon, the evergreen tree prominent on that country's flag and coat of arms. Lourdes, of course, is a major Roman Catholic shrine in southwest France where the Blessed Virgin Mary is said to have appeared to a young French girl in 1858. Before we left Sydney, Joe's relatives—a lovely couple who live in Lourdes and who brought with them water from the shrine—paid us a visit. Gladys would rub the water on my belly before Cedar was born and even urged me to drink it. I declined.

Hannah had been difficult as an infant, colicky and inclined to fight sleep (she did not sleep through the night until she was almost four years old and she often slept in my arms in a chair). Rarely did she fall asleep without being in my arms. All I did was carry her and rock her—it's why she and I still have such a deep bond.

Breastfeeding her, though, was a nightmare, an absolute nightmare. I persevered for eight months before finally—with the help of lactation specialists—succeeding in feeding Hannah pain-free. At one point, I wore a whiffle ball, a perforated tennis ball cut in half, to let the air get to my poor sore breasts and to cure the mastitis. I was determined to breastfeed Hannah, and I did.

I remember one time going out with my family to a restaurant in Sydney and excusing myself every twenty minutes to go to the washroom to use a breast pump. My milk production had dropped, so this was the appropriate regimen. But I also had with me a bottle of formula—just in case. Later, I dumped what I thought was the formula down the drain, but I erred. What I had pitched was the breast milk, the product of three hours' labour. That night, I literally cried over spilt milk. Hannah was a challenge (we later learned that she had a gastrointestinal problem, called reflux, which causes gas pain and which eventually resolved itself).

The breastfeeding experience with Hannah taught me a great deal about myself and my perseverance. In the debate among mothers about breast versus formula, I am of the school of thought that the mom should do what makes her happy—because her baby will, in turn, be happy. I simply refused to give in and offer Hannah formula. In the end, the lactation specialists told me how proud they were of me and that they had never seen a case as bad as mine. I felt that if I did not succeed with my first child, how could I possibly breastfeed any future children? With Cedar, I had no problems and was mellow and mature enough to use formula if I felt my nipples getting near the sore point they had reached with Hannah.

Cedar, as a baby, was happy and easy and bright. Where Hannah hardly slept, Cedar just drifted off so easily I would sometimes have to wake her up. The two girls are completely different personalities. Hannah is kind and thoughtful, and takes very seriously her role as the older sister. She is always thinking about how someone might feel. If there is a pupil at school who is shy and quiet and not being treated kindly, Hannah is the first one to defend that child.

But Hannah also has the fire of a gifted athlete. She loves, just loves, sports. She has her own golf clubs and we would also go to the batting cage together to work on our baseball swings soon after we arrived in Alberta. She is so focused and intense, and I love that about her.

I remember one time she was running a mini-marathon at her kindergarten sports day. The teacher led the race—for three-quarters of the distance—and the rule for the children was that they were not allowed to pass her. Such young runners have no concept of distance (or of conserving energy) and they would otherwise just bolt (and collapse long before the end of the race).

I was waiting at the finish line, and all I could see as the runners rounded the corner was Hannah in the lead. There were some fifty runners all told, boys and girls, and she was a year younger than most of them. The look on her face, the determination, was what made me so proud. Her cheeks were beet-red and her arms were pumping like pistons. No smile, no looking around, she was just focused on the finish line. There was a car parked on the road, and it forced her to pause ever so briefly and go around it. A boy took the advantage and beat her by a foot, but that was one of my proudest moments.

Hannah is also an organizer, and she has to have order and structure in her life. Tell her a friend is coming over and she right away starts to plan the day, right down to the smallest detail.

Hannah needs to be played with; Cedar can play by herself for hours at a time. Cedar is now the clown, now the princess, now the ham, and she knows how to captivate an audience. Maybe she is aware of how cute she is, for she knows how to endear herself to people with snuggles and cuddles. She is very good-natured, but when she puts her mind to something she is a force of nature (which is either admirable or a royal pain, depending on the circumstances and your point of view). Cedar is also particular about her name: She is not Cedar Lourdes Hawach, just Cedar—like Cher or Madonna.

The four of us, then, settled into our imposing stucco house on Mountain Park and made it our own. We painted it a slate grey and I planted a beautiful tulip garden at the front. Joe was very particular about the front lawn, which he always kept trim and free of weeds, and we worked together on the back yard. We installed a circular pool, made a flagstone patio with fairy lights for barbecuing, rebuilt the deck.

Just one month before Cedar's birth, there was another incident with Joe. What precipitated this was an argument, typical of ones we had, with him maligning, and me defending, my family. When the whole thing began to escalate, I went to the phone: I'd had enough. I was going to call the police. He ripped the phone in the kitchen out of the wall, then the other two upstairs. At one point, I tried to run outside but he grabbed my hair and pulled me back into the kitchen. Then, as I ran to the front door, he blocked my path. He would not let me out of the house (I wanted to call neighbours), so I simply retreated to the bedroom and there I stayed. I thought better, then, of calling the police. My behaviour bore all the hallmarks of classic battered wife syndrome.

Joe later came up to the bedroom and said he was sorry and he convinced me not to do anything (like call the police). For the longest time, I told no one of the abuse. My family, I worried, would never forgive him, nor would my friends. It would have meant the end of hope, and there was always hope, wasn't there? I could make him happy, couldn't I?

But that day marked a turning point. Looking back on it, I can see that from that moment on, I began to dig in my heels. For all kinds of reasons, Joe would never again lay a hand on me in anger. I fought hard for the marriage—because of the children, because I was embarrassed about it failing, because the pain of divorce is so intense. But I had a right to be safe, and I began to realize how pathetic I was (rushing home between ball games to clean the house from top to bottom, vacuum and do laundry in hopes of pleasing my husband and to eliminate any possibility of complaint). I was a desperate housewife—desperate to make my husband like me.

Joe Hawach was a doting and devoted father. After work, he would make a point of spending time with Hannah and Cedar. A vigorous father-daughters wrestle would always come first. In the car, Joe and the girls would play music and sing songs. And he was very patient with them, more patient than I was.

Our parenting styles were not at all the same. He was looser with them, less inclined to impose discipline. When Hannah had problems going to sleep, I would try reward charts, which Joe thought silly. The Lebanese culture prizes and adores children, and he was in that mould. He thought Hannah and Cedar were amazing. There was no doubting the bond between Joe and his daughters.

And there were times when he could be so sweet and thoughtful—to me. Several years into our marriage, we took a trip to Las Vegas, the first trip since our honeymoon. The occasion was something called "The Big Smoke"—a convention that gathers the makers of fine cigars. Joe loved his cigars, and I, too, would, on rare occasions, join him—though I couldn't bring myself to finish one. Joe had booked both the convention and accommodation online (it was not a cheap package), and he was disappointed and upset when we got to our hotel room and found it gross, with mould on the ceiling. Joe took a cab out to the airport, rented a car, and eventually he found other accommodation.

He really wanted the weekend to be special, and it was. I remember it fondly. Six thousand people packed into the ballroom of the Mandalay Bay Hotel and Casino, most of them puffing on all the free samples—Arturo Fuentes and other exquisite cigars, before trying the Glenfiddich Scotch and Hennessey cognac, smoked salmon and every fine food imaginable. We had a wonderful time.

My oldest friends, though, such as Stephanie and Rayanne, could not fathom my choice of husband. "I never felt you were a match," Rayanne would say later. "I felt the house was divided into his and her duties." Stephanie remarked on how quiet and uninterested Joe was in getting to know her and my other friends. He could be unspeakably rude, even puerile: If a conversation was boring him, he would pointedly stare at the ceiling. Relations of mine from Saskatchewan would visit the house and Joe would retreat to a downstairs television, refusing even to say hello. And yet if a man were to visit the house, a man who might prove a useful business contact, Joe turned on the charm.

Both Stephanie and Rayanne observed a change in me. The dynamo they knew from high school days, the free-spirited adventurer who had dashed off to plant trees, travel the world and fly helicopters: She had been muted. "Joe was able," says Stephanie, "to crush a little of your spirit, to take away your confidence and control you—by not speaking to you for weeks at a time." Joe was conveying a message to me: "I know how to hurt you, so don't hurt me."

Meanwhile, other challenges to the reeling marriage presented themselves. They say family and business make poor bedfellows. It may be true. My father, who has spent a career putting together venture capital deals, was wary of involving family and business.

When Doug joined Amcan, Dad tried to get the partnership in writing. Joe listens to no one. Though born in Australia, he is virtually a child of the Middle East marketplace: He would haggle, cut deals, operate under the table if he could. Doug, on the other hand, plays by the book. The two sides fought a lot, and I was continually forced to act as mediator, often defending my husband even when the complaints sounded eerily familiar. Doug and Celeste (then his girlfriend, now his wife) lived with us for a year—rent-free for six months and salary-free for three months, and Doug and Joe would later clash over who owed what to whom.

* * *

Doug initially met Joe at our wedding, and his first impression was of a shy man. It puzzled my brother—who was used to the cut and thrust and sheer boisterousness of a large, loud family—that a man from an even larger family could be so withdrawn. Later, Doug would change his vocabulary and use the word *antisocial* to describe my husband.

Doug and my brother Adam had worked together creating and operating two pro shops at arenas in Saskatoon—selling hockey equipment, sharpening skates, cleaning hockey gear. The collaboration had worked well, so Doug clearly did not share my father's antipathy towards mixing business and family. Besides, as far as Doug was concerned, Joe never was family. He was a business partner, the money man, and Doug would later thank his lucky stars that Joe resisted putting in writing their partnership, a tortured one almost from the beginning.

"He was fairly lazy," Doug would say later. "And, for whatever reason, he loved to dupe people. For him, it was a competition." If pulling the wool over people's eyes was an Olympic sport, my brother complained, Joe operated at the world-class level. Doug would call the office frantic about filling an order: A magazine, say, needed a huge supply of paper, pronto. Joe would beg off, saying he was in a meeting, but Doug would later check the credit card logs and find that Joe, at the moment Doug called, was playing a round of golf.

"He was very generous," Doug would tell me, "but then I saw why. That meant you *owed* him something. He loved that power because he was power-hungry. He was also clever, but he thought he was smarter than he actually was."

Maybe this story illustrates the point. It's funny to recall it. Joe once backed an Amcan truck into a van in a parking lot. The other driver was in the now dented van, paint from the truck matched that of the van, and Joe had the audacity to claim he didn't do it and he made a big scene. The driver was livid. An Amcan employee happened to be in the truck with Joe, and I later asked him what had happened.

"Did he hit the van?" I asked him.

"Well," he replied, "I felt a bump, I saw the dent. Joe's my boss, but . . ."

Joe had this sense of entitlement, as if a prince's blood flowed in his veins. I remember his sister Suzie back in Australia complaining about "the boys on their pedestal" and their male privileges. Gladys expected the girls to cook and clean, but the boys never did.

The exceptions, though, were Louie and Joe. Louie would do the dishes when Gladys was not well, and Joe would likewise occasionally do them for me. If Joe had just been a big jerk all the time, it would have been easier to walk away. But because he was often very charming and gracious, I was inclined to think that there was something wrong with *me*, not with him. Chauvinistic and patriarchal Joe may have been, but it wasn't that simple. That alone doesn't explain him.

After he left Amcan, Doug would say he did not want to think about the company and his former partner—they were bad dreams he would rather not revisit. But clearly, he had thought about both, analyzed both, a lot. The company, he said, had sparked the interest of investors and, had it been allowed to continue and grow, would today be a publicly traded company on the Canadian stock exchange. As for Joe, Doug's own lay assessment was that Joe needed psychiatric help for his troubled mind. Joe, he believed, had either convinced himself that the company was on the rocks or disseminated that view for strategic reasons. Doug saw this as part of a grand plan that would put a homesick Lebanese-Australian man back home, where, buttressed by family, he had the power he craved.

Amcan was either tanking, or thriving, depending on who I talked to—my husband or my brother. Joe complained that the company was too small to force larger companies into a price war or to satisfy big customers, and that keeping paper stock on hand was extraordinarily expensive. He wanted to sell off the business because he felt it was treading water and Australia was beckoning to him. Doug, who did the selling, insisted that the company was doing really well. He was sure that Joe was up to something. By now, I was weary of trying to broker a peace between them.

In the last three months that Doug was with Amcan, Joe had set a sales target of $300,000. It was an impossible goal, set during a normally slack time in the industry. Doug pulled in $288,000 worth of business.

"Not good enough," said Joe. "We're shutting down."

Weeks later, Doug left. After two years, he had had enough.

Joe, meanwhile, would break a lease at one warehouse, then move to another and do the same. Joe talked to me of mergers, but it was all—I would learn too late—a smokescreen.

We had launched the business with about half a million dollars of our own money (from the sale of the restaurant in Sydney, savings we had accrued by living with Joe's parents, and remortgaging our house). But Joe said he had also borrowed money from his parents, that they had remortgaged one of their houses, too. Maybe that was all true, but given the deception that followed, I cannot be sure. Joe did the finances and gave me an allowance to pay the bills.

Things were coming apart for Joe both at home and at work, but I had lost the urge to keep everything together at all costs. A part of me had begun to shut down. There had been too many physical insults, too many blows to my pride.

My husband once shoved mango into my face, a humiliation that Hannah witnessed but thankfully does not remember. She was about two and sitting in my lap as we shared the fruit, and Joe and I were talking. This was just before we moved to Canada. I was voicing a criticism but trying very hard to sugar-coat it. Joe just took the fruit and applied it to my face while slowly turning his hand this way, then that.

He had, on occasion, mimicked what I had just said—like a child taunting another in a school yard. In our skirmishes, Joe knew which buttons to push. One day, soon after Cedar was born, we argued about my family, whom he called "scum." That was the kind of language he would employ, and this day he used the word over and over—to great effect. I remember standing at the top of the stairs, shaking my fist, him in my face and me screaming at him to stop using that word, and I kicked the wall behind me so hard my heel went through the drywall. I was embarrassed and ashamed, angry at myself for losing my temper and at him for counting my loss of control as a victory for him. Part of my emotionalism was rooted in lack of sleep—I was getting up every night with both Hannah and Cedar. But as the girls grew older, the sleep issue resolved itself. A sour marriage is not so easily fixed.

I was tired of the wars and I recognized that I was not myself. I saw a doctor at a walk-in clinic but did not reveal the physical and emotional abuse—my marriage, my thinking went, was my mistake for me to fix. She suggested medication. I passed on that option. I knew I was down because of my marriage, and covering it up with drugs was not going to help anyone. But I did like my doctor's advice: Draw up a list of things that once made you happy and do them. Competitive baseball was near the top of that list so I joined a team almost immediately, and, at first, Joe was supportive.

I loved baseball. Sports had always been an important part of my life and it felt so good to be back in the game. Women unhappy in their marriages sometimes have affairs, but I had neither the opportunity nor—more importantly—the slightest inclination. Baseball was a safe and rewarding outlet. In high school, sports had kept me and all my friends out of trouble with alcohol and drugs, and sports would now do the same as I approached my late twenties.

My coach had children around the same ages as Hannah and Cedar, so that was a bonus. They would play in the bleachers while I played on the diamond. My father and mother would always come out to watch our tournaments. Joe never watched a game, not one. He complained that he needed downtime from work, and that meant golf. If I played more than one game a week, or played out of town, he resented it. The baseball season was all of six weeks in June and July, and my parents were always on standby as babysitters, but my playing was still an issue in our house. Ball brought in no income and took me out of the house; in Joe's eyes, the game had no purpose and he wanted me to quit. I refused.

I later discovered in some boxes a disturbing letter that Joe had written to himself. In this chauvinistic lament, he complained of having to iron his own shirts and how he came home and dinner was not always on. Joe was a chef! And we often cooked together, so the letter struck me as very strange. Who was this man? What planet did he live on? And why, oh why, had I married him?

One day he talked to me about some of the hurt I had caused him, and no doubt I had caused him hurt, as couples inevitably wound each other over time. The breakup with Brad had been wrenching for me, but also for Brad's parents and his sisters—especially his handicapped sister, with whom I was very close. These are very emotional people: When Brad's mother discovered that I was going to marry another man, she called my parents—whom she had met many times—in the middle of the night, weeping and distraught. It took me by surprise, all that hurt long after the fact, and I felt guilt that I had brought this baggage into my marriage. I could not talk to Joe about it—that would have been unfair, and neither was he mature enough to deal with it. Joe took personally my anguish, my pain and loss.

In hindsight, I should have dealt with all this first—and then got married. There was no hiding my hurt, and I told Joe how sorry I was. But he would use his hurt, in turn, to justify hurting me. The difference, I told him, is that I cannot be arrested for causing you hurt. His counter was to say that he likewise could not be arrested—because he had never hit me in the face. This was the nature of his apology. I never felt it was anything more than words and excuses, and that meant I could never forgive or forget the assaults and put them behind us.

One of our last attempts to repair the marriage was a weekend retreat in which couples who have managed to overcome terrible ruptures in their relationships help other couples. One man, part of a couple from California, having heard our story in full, turned to Joe and said, "Your wife deserves the right to feel safe and secure in your relationship. And you need to do this for your daughters. They watch how you treat and talk to her, and the last thing you want is that call in the middle of the night [our daughter in distress saying that her husband has just beaten her]. You don't want them making the same choice for a husband that your wife did." The American was clear: If I did not feel safe in my marriage, I should leave it.

* * *

By 2003 and into 2004, I had reached the tipping point. It was not like Joe treated me badly every day; it was more like months of indifference and then a blowup.

When Joe suggested that we just pack up and head back to Australia, I pondered that and initially warmed to the idea. Joe had looked into a baseball team I could play with in Sydney, and he talked about me finishing my helicopter licence. Once again, he was trying to smooth the waters to get what he wanted. Over dinner with my parents, I announced our decision to leave but two days later I realized how impossible that would be.

(My parents were immensely relieved when I told them of my change in plans. I later learned that my parents had cried all the way home from the restaurant—not because they would miss me but because they were extremely worried about me going back to Australia with Joe.)

I would be at the mercy of his family and without the support of my own. I was working three days a week waitressing at a nearby golf course and was offered a management position. I was also interested in going back to school and pursuing a career in social work (Joe could see no point in that either). I was finally starting to feel happy and settled (in spite of him) and had started to feel more my old self. All these were positives, so going back to Australia was not an option.

I loved the Hawach family, and were it not for them, I would have left Joe a lot earlier than I did. I remember fondly the ritual of having a late-night beer with Louie and gabbing about the events of the day. But I had, by this time, also grown weary of the Hawach family dynamic and the currents of resentment and backbiting that are perhaps inevitable when family and business (especially the restaurant business) intertwine. The work is stressful enough, the hours long enough, the pressure intense enough without family feuding to stir the pot further.

Joe, who could be fractious with co-workers, once went eighteen months without speaking to his brother, Eddie, over some work-related slight. I remember Joe telling me that his brother was "dead to him." I had the impression that the core problem was not serious—more miscommunication than anything. I had watched Joe and his cousin, Fred, experience numerous fallouts over the years (Joe and Pierre likewise warred), and it always seemed to work itself out somehow. Joe was always very judgemental of others, and he can hold a grudge forever and a day.

I could not imagine turning my back on my own brothers in this way. Eddie's wife, a woman of Italian heritage also named Melissa ("Melissa number two," they called her), got caught up once in the firestorm—a situation they had tried desperately as a couple to avoid. My attempts at mediation (Wednesday-night dinners for all the women in the family, renting movies) failed. If you ask any member of the Hawach family if they are close, they would doubtless say, and believe, that the connection is deep, deep beyond your comprehension. That may well be, but they also spend a long time not speaking to one another. All this lay in the back of my mind as Joe tried to steer a course back to Sydney.

"I can change," he insisted. No longer the blind optimist, no longer so desperate to please and gain my husband's respect and approval, I told him he needed to seek counselling and attend anger management classes.

The former—we took counselling together and as individuals at the Family Wellness Centre in Calgary—had no apparent effect on him. The anger management therapy, I later learned, he simply ducked. We were going to engage in what is called a "controlled separation." This was a counselling tool, with rules and time frames and controls, all designed hopefully to get the couple back together. But within a week of Joe agreeing to the separation, he gave me his ultimatum: "Leave the house and move in with your parents, and we are finished for good." This was in August 2005.

By October of that year, we had begun to discuss the terms of the separation agreement. We found a web site that offered a model agreement and gradually during the course of several months—over coffee, via e-mail—we would fill in the blanks and make adjustments as necessary. The financial arrangements came easily. It was clear that we were both trying to be amicable.

Joe was *so* accommodating, in fact, that I should have cottoned on. I was actually thinking, "He's changing. He has seen the error of his ways." And I remember later saying to Patrick, "If Joe comes back from Australia and wants to try again, I will feel obliged to try."

To which Patrick replied: "I know women who would sacrifice for their children, and I understand it. But you see things in Joe that aren't there."

It seemed to me there was still hope. Or was it delusion?

* * *

In any case, I was firm that I needed to be out of the environment of my marriage to be able to think clearly, but the thought of my marriage being over was still abhorrent to my head and heart.

Joe had even tried to convince my parents as well as his mother (during a family intervention to discuss the abuse with Joe) that if they all just left us alone, he could convince me to stay with him. My mother and father were stunned that he so totally missed the point.

Religion did enter the picture for a time. During that summer of 2005, Joe's mother stayed with us for several months. My mother had called Gladys because our separation was imminent and we worried about Joe going through this without family support. It was then that Joe said he had been "touched by God," and he warned me that separation and divorce were sins, just as it was a sin for me to leave our home. (Later, I would learn that the Maronite Catholic church teaches nothing of the sort.) If I did leave, he warned me, the marriage was completely over—no therapy, no hope for reconciliation. Such a stance seemed incongruous to me, for it cut off all hope for our relationship to recover. That was Joe, though. All or nothing. He also warned me that were I to consult a lawyer and divorce him, he would get a better lawyer and "crush" me.

Perhaps I had been threatened too many times. On October 30, 2005, Joe Hawach and I separated. The notion of moving back to Australia had finally triggered my leaving. It was like a line had been drawn in the sand. Two months beforehand, Patrick had seen me crying at the golf course where we both worked. He knew nothing then of my circumstances, but he did reassure me by telling me that he was about to get a more senior position, that his old one would free up, and that I was more than qualified for the job. Once I got over my fear (How would I support Hannah and Cedar?), I realized I had options.

I moved with the girls into my parents' house on Copperfield Gardens (a house I later bought), and Joe stayed in our matrimonial home until the following March, when he rented one floor of a house close by, to ease the shared custody arrangement.

* * *

As a single father, Joe was sometimes lazy about his children and did not always watch them carefully. One time, after we had separated, I was shopping in a department store in Calgary with my mother on a day when Joe had the girls. I was walking down an aisle when a little girl approached me from behind and asked me to buy her something. I was about to turn around and say, "I'm not your mommy, sorry," but I *was* her mommy. It was Cedar, wandering around the store by herself while Hannah explored the toy section. Joe, meanwhile, was trying on clothes elsewhere in the store, and it was twenty minutes before he showed up on the scene.

My mother was astonished at his cavalier notion of child care. When Joe arrived he was clearly embarrassed, and I wondered: What else is going on when I am not around? This made no sense. Did he think God was looking after them? I was angry but, typically, inclined to coddle him and worry about his feelings. I waited until I got home and sent him an e-mail. I told him that while I knew he loved his kids, part of loving them is absolute vigilance. I reminded him that a little girl had been taken from a store just days beforehand, and I said that today's incident was unacceptable.

I never knew what I would get from Joe. This time, I got "You're absolutely right. It will never happen again."

Who was this man I had married? Sometimes his behaviour baffled me. The business of the coins still confounds me. Hannah was born in the first month of the new millennium, and 2001 also happened to be Australia's Centenary of Federation. Every child born that year was eligible for a set of commemorative coins from then prime minister, John Howard. The form to get the coins came to me in the mail, and I filled it out, of course. I love Australia and I thought the coins would be a nice keepsake for Hannah. I put a stamp on the envelope, gave it to Joe and asked him to mail it. Weeks passed, no coins came, and I pressed Joe.

"Are you sure you mailed it?" I asked him.

"Oh yeah."

"Because," I said, "they only mint so many coins and I don't want to miss this."

Eight months later, I was cleaning out drawers, and there, staring back at me, was that letter. When I angrily confronted him, he just laughed and offered no explanation. I put it down to pure laziness or perhaps indifference.

* * *

Although Joe and I managed to agree on how we would share time with the girls without the aid of a lawyer, I did see a lawyer on my own—at my father's insistence. Knowing that Joe had both the wherewithal and the blood relations in the legal profession to wage a court battle, I agreed it was time. And I will never forget what the lawyer said when I mentioned that Joe was from Australia.

"If he ever decides to abduct the children to Australia, we've got avenues," said the $500-an-hour lawyer, a woman with a wealth of experience. She then moved on to talk about custody and division of property. The separation was painful and emotional enough, but this was like getting hit on the side of the head with a line drive.

Joe abduct the girls? "No," I said. Then, "I don't *think* so."

My father sat beside me and said nothing.

Then the lawyer asked, "Is there any chance he would take them to the Middle East? If he took them to Australia, we have recourse. But the Middle East, we'd be in trouble."

She might as well have been speaking Chinese to me, so foreign were these words and the crazy notion they conveyed. "No way," I told her. "He hasn't been there since he was two, visiting with his family."

No, I was certain that Lebanon was nowhere on Joe's radar screen. I could not have been more wrong. Almost a year before the abduction, I was given fair warning and missed the signs. My father, too, would lament not speaking up in that lawyer's office.

* * *

Joe had told me on several occasions that he was sorry for being such a lousy husband. He told me so in person, said so in e-mails. But he never, I thought, truly apologized or fully understood the trauma he had inflicted on me. For me, it was like he had had an affair: It broke something in me, it broke trust. He had been careless with me and my feelings while I was his wife, while I was pregnant, while I mothered his children. In lighter times, I would call him The Fonz (a tough-guy character from an American situation comedy called *Happy Days*, which was set in the 1950s and created in the 1970s). The Fonz was a leather-jacketed hood who could never bring himself to say the word *sorry*. "Sa-sa-sa-sa-sa-sa . . ." was as close as he got.

Sorry was not really in Joe Hawach's vocabulary either. He did once write me a long letter to say what a beautiful wife I was, how he had been so wrong, how he should never have hit me. What was odd was this: He never did actually hit me. Drag me, kick me, push me, choke me, humiliate me, yes. The letter sat in my computer inbox for the longest time. I told Joe that while the letter was very touching, it did not change anything: He still had to go to therapy, I was not moving to Australia, and, in fact, I would be moving in with my father and mother for a while—just to get some distance from him.

Then the letter vanished, like the man who wrote it. The anguish for me in the summer through fall and into the winter of 2006 was not that Joe Hawach had disappeared (or deleted that letter), but that he had taken my precious daughters with him.

6

The Command Post

The cute little house on Copperfield Gardens with the grey cedar-shingle siding and the porch where I spent so many hours with the girls ceased to be just a house from the moment I learned my babies had been taken. The call from Pierre Hawach had come in the small hours of July 19, 2006. By the following morning, the transformation of that house into a command post was well under way.

That day, I remember, was hot and humid, with no hint of a breeze. By dusk, "the team" had already started to form and begun to work. My brother Brendan and his partner, Krista (who slept at the house most nights between July and September and took time off work). My brother Adam and his then fiancée (now his wife), Shauna. My brother Doug and his wife, Celeste. My boyfriend, Patrick Lalande. Friends from my past, friends from the baseball team. Friends from all over. Mom and Dad.

That morning, before first light, Patrick called Foreign Affairs in Ottawa—because of the time zone difference, two hours ahead of us—and got in touch with Jean-Marc Lesage, who heads up the national government-funded program called Our Missing Children. He was very calm, very matter of fact as he took down the information. Caught up in a crisis like this, you just assume that everyone will be as shocked and undone as you are. What I would learn is how commonplace it is for kids to go missing—teenagers run away to the streets, pre-schoolers get lost in the woods, children of all ages get whisked off to another country by a mother or father. Children taken by strangers make the headlines, but such cases are actually rare—less than 1 per cent of missing children fall into this category.

Within hours, we had clocks on the wall at Copperfield Gardens with signs underneath to keep track of time zones in Canada, Australia and Lebanon. There was a huge map of Lebanon on one wall, with tacks showing the most likely locations for Joe and the girls. There were pictures of Hannah and Cedar up on the wall, reminders of what our mission was all about, along with ideas and possible leads. There were three laptops running, my brothers or their partners hunched over them, fingers flying.

Andy's wife, Simone, would later remark on the transformation of the house. "It was surreal. I remember walking in—this was eight hours after you got the call. And it was like you had set up *CSI* [an American television program about forensic investigators, called *Crime Scene Investigation*] or all your brothers had been working for the FBI all their lives. Everyone was at their stations. I would talk to you and you would start rambling—almost like you were talking to yourself—your mind going at a hundred miles an hour. And the telephone kept ringing. Every time it did we all caught our breath in case it was Joe."

* * *

By mid-morning on July 20, the second day, my family had all arrived in Calgary at the house on Copperfield Gardens, and we met that afternoon at Richard Bennett's office, where he introduced us to his colleague, Kelly Stewart. I learned that we would require her services to secure the custody orders as the two police officers had recommended to me earlier that morning when they took my statement. Richard also suggested that we retain Bison Security Group, a local firm of private investigators, to help us further. Bison, in turn, put me in touch with the Missing Children Society of Canada (MCSC). In every case, my first meeting with each group had the same shape and feel: I told the story of how a three-week vacation had morphed into a kidnapping.

Within two days, this ensemble of experts had formed into a cohesive team. Headquarters for the team was the Edy Dalton law office where the roundtable meetings took place, sometimes twice a week in those first crazy days.

The "roundtable" was not round at all, but a long rectangular table that would comfortably fit ten to twelve people. The walls of the boardroom are painted a rust colour. At one end of the room is a cabinet housing spring water, coffee, tea and other refreshments; the other end of the room has shelves laden with casebooks. A window runs the entire length of one side of the room, affording an eighth-floor view of the city and of new high-rise buildings going up everywhere in this oil-fuelled boomtown. From that vantage point, I could see the Imperial Parking Lot where I parked my mini-van on every visit. Sometimes, during long meetings, I would rise to stretch my legs and see if my van was still there and not ticketed or towed. It was always fine.

By day two I was shocked and surprised to learn in these roundtable meetings that while parental child abduction (as defined in Canada's Criminal Code) is a crime in Canada, that's not the case in Australia. (I doubted that Joe thought he had committed a crime, anyway.) In Australia, family courts alone decide such matters—not civil *and* criminal courts, as is often the case in Canada.

I knew nothing of all this. I was so naive. I had no idea how many rules had loopholes, how rules could be circumvented. By degrees, I would learn, for example, how hard it is—on paper—for a single parent to get into Lebanon in the company of two minors. (A Lebanese-Australian friend would later describe to me in detail all the hoops he had to leap through before being allowed into Lebanon with his children—including showing a death certificate for his deceased wife.) Joe carried an Australian passport, Hannah had an Australian passport and Cedar a Canadian passport. He had no letter of permission from the girls' mother to be travelling into Lebanon at a time of war. Did he use political influence (his uncle is a high-ranking official in Lebanon's Hezbollah-backed Orange Party)? Did he bribe officials?

I had so much to learn. I had the growing sense that I was being asked to climb a mountain but that clouds shrouded the peak and I could get no sense of how high or steep or treacherous the climb would be.

My brother Doug, meanwhile, was spending the first few days of this ordeal visiting all the printers he had dealt with during his time at

Amcan. He was sleuthing, trying to gather any information that might help. Doug also went with my parents to a restaurant that Joe frequented and where he used to play in late-night poker games.

The restaurant owner, Doug learned, had apparently heard Joe say that he was moving back to Australia for good. And when the man asked Joe about Hannah and Cedar, Joe claimed he had sole custody and that if Melissa wanted to see her kids she'd have to move to Australia. All this information was brought to the first roundtable meeting at Edy Dalton.

Our meetings during these first days involved a lot of old-fashioned tracking techniques through Joe's credit cards (which I only discovered by collecting the mail from Fast Freight) and other means that I was not privy to. We learned that Joe had been staying at the Jeb Ali resort in Dubai (the largest emirate in the United Arab Emirates) but was no longer there. My father, meanwhile, had contacted my uncle David in Boston (who used to be very involved in the hotel industry), and he began compiling a list of hotels in Dubai.

My dad bought a dozen calling cards and we split up the list among family and friends to call the hotels to determine if Joe and the girls were registered there. Bison was also using their contacts in Dubai to see if we could hire a lawyer there to get the girls returned.

By this point I had learned about the Hague Convention on the Civil Aspects of International Child Abduction. Countries that have signed the document have all agreed to an abiding principle: that when children have been taken by one parent to another country without the other parent's consent, those children shall, by law, be restored to their country of residence—where the custody hearing takes place. The beauty of the convention is that it can spare one parent a complex, costly and extended court battle in some other country.

Among the first actions taken by Richard and Kelly was to file an application with the Calgary office of the Hague Convention. The response was immediate and efficient. Within twenty-four hours, the Hague office in Sydney was aware of my case. Had Joe stayed in Australia, chances are good he would have been found and hauled into court to explain his actions. The Hague Convention on missing children is a powerful force, and Richard and Kelly would often sing its praises.

Both Canada and Australia are signatories to that convention. Countries in the Middle East, alas, are not. Still, because Joe had no ties to the United Arab Emirates, Darryl Stark at Bison Security felt that the authorities there would be quite cooperative. Nothing came of the Dubai lead but every lead was assiduously followed. The aim was to follow Joe's tracks, find him, and enlist all possible help to get the girls back to Canada—urgently.

At the first meeting with Bison Security, we met one of their investigators, Lovell Bowen, for the first time. The mother of three grown children, Lovell is a former Calgary police officer with fifteen years of experience on the force fighting organized crime and child abuse. She is now manager of the Bison investigations team. Along with her husband, Don, also a former Calgary police officer, Lovell became a regular in the command post on Copperfield. Both Lovell and Don threw themselves into our case, and with every passing day my sense of family grew wider and deeper. This was especially so after Lovell wisely urged that I get in touch with the Missing Children Society of Canada.

The MCSC is a non-profit charity with expertise in the field (they work closely with lawyers and police). With a $2 million annual budget, the Missing Children Society is the only organization of its type with investigators who will go to where abducted children are thought to be. Enlisting the help of MCSC brought Dave Chittick into our camp. Dave is a contract employee with the Missing Children Society of Canada but also runs his own small private investigation firm. Dave was that rare professional working on our side but not billing us in any way.

Dave would say there was no quarterback on our team, no single person calling the shots at the Calgary command post or at the roundtable. Looking back on it, I would say Dave—especially later on—was the one running the show. I made a lot of important decisions on my own, sometimes even ignoring the counsel of people close to me, but there were other times when I was so depressed and emotional, and I needed someone to be calm and reasonable. Dave was that someone. One of the most intelligent people I have ever met, always even and quiet and purposeful, he became the voice of reason. He would take everything in and he seemed to know how to cut away the trivial, how to separate wheat from chaff. He would always choose his words carefully and never said anything glibly. For Dave, the process of reacquiring my children was about making a series of pivotal decisions, and he did all he could to help me make the right ones.

I admired his humility. When I would praise him for his calm demeanour, he would reply, "What's required in these circumstances often is a counterpoint. People in your circumstance are emotional, understandably so. They don't always think things through. Sometimes my calm comes from not knowing what to do."

He may look like a throwback to another time. The suede sports coat, the brush cut, the blue jeans and stocky build all suggest Alberta redneck. But no, he has the manner and the bearing of a diplomat.

* * *

On the advice of Barbara Snider, case director in the international division at MCSC's Ontario office, I began gathering letters—from the girls' doctor, Hannah's pre-school teacher, my psychologist. These letters were to show that the girls' network was, indeed, in Calgary, and that the girls were loved and well cared for. For myself, I got a wonderful reference letter from Catholic Family Services—with whom I had been volunteering by mentoring a single mother. I also obtained a police check to prove that I had no criminal record. The Missing Children Society of Canada is well aware of the roadblocks typically thrown up by the other side. The letters, in fact, would eventually serve us well.

Rhonda Morgan, a former graphic artist and the mother of a teenaged son, helped found the Missing Children Society of Canada in 1986 and very much sees her work as a calling. In 1983, she happened to see on Calgary television a profile of three abducted children—two taken by strangers and one by a parent. "The mother of the parentally abducted children," she says, "cried so hard, from the bottom of her heart, that I was literally moved into action."

Rhonda started as a volunteer with Child Find Alberta and trained as an investigator under a South African police detective who had moved to Calgary and started his own agency. Child Find Alberta, though, was not interested in taking on full-scale investigative work. (CFA does some fine educational and preventive work, but not the kind of sleuthing done by the

Missing Children Society.) There was a need, and Rhonda set up an organization to try to meet it. She would become MCSC's executive director.

These days, Rhonda no longer conducts in-the-field investigative work of her own. Instead, she spends much of her time behind a desk working on grant applications. She suffers from a rare neuromuscular disease called primary lateral sclerosis, which affects her balance, her leg muscles, and even her facial muscles. Rhonda misses horribly the joy of the intense, but also intensely rewarding, work of helping people reunite with their children.

At our first meeting, Rhonda looked impressed (or was it overwhelmed?) by the information we had managed to gather just in the first few days after the abduction. Dave Chittick and Rhonda Morgan were used to sitting down with one distraught single mother or father while the proper forms were quietly and sombrely filled out and government agencies alerted. I, on the other hand, had an entourage. The first meeting of my family members, Dave Chittick, our lawyers, Calgary police and our private investigators featured a virtual roundtable of twelve people, and such meetings would continue week after week all that fall and into winter.

When I wasn't attending meetings with lawyers and private investigators and police, I was doing some intense sleuthing of my own. Some days, I would be sixteen hours at my computer. My time on the Internet in these early days was centred around learning as much as I could about the Hague Convention, parental abductions, Dubai and the United Arab Emirates. I also contacted the priest at the church in Calgary I used to attend with the girls and Joe to see if he might be enlisted to call Joe or his family and offer spiritual support. I racked my brain trying to remember every person I could who might be able to help me. I constructed a family tree with details on contacts, relationships to Joe and myself, and people who might be willing to help.

I went back into my old e-mails to try to find any clues or information that might help me know more about Joe's plan. I contacted mutual friends in Australia and in Canada begging for help. (Later on, I learned that a close friend of Joe's knew full well of his plan to take the girls into a war zone and although he tried to talk him out of it he did nothing else.) I spent desperate hours digging through all my packed boxes (from my move to Copperfield) looking for the girls' birth certificates, my marriage certificate, photographs and other relevant documents. This was a frantic and desperate effort to gather information so I would not waste any time when I was later asked for it by authorities.

* * *

A lot of amazing people had their oars in the water and were pulling hard in the same direction. But my Hannah, my Cedar, they were no closer. Some nights I went to bed wishing never to rise again.

And then I would fix on some small crazy detail about the girls, and I would use this as fuel to keep going. Was Joe making sure they brushed their teeth? Was he keeping up their immunizations? Of course not. Their mother had always attended to such details, but their mother was gone from their lives, maybe long gone. I have no words to describe how much I missed Hannie and Cedar during the 179 days they were absent from my life.

I took comfort, when I could, in knowing that I was blessed in one way: The girls had not been taken by a stranger but by a father who loved them (in his own twisted way). I knew that Gladys was with them and that they were being well fed and cared for.

Not once during this whole experience, though, did I ever contemplate giving up the hunt. Still, there were days when I wanted nothing more than to sleep and to tell everyone, "I can't take any more of this grinding emotion. I can't take one more step. I'm going to sleep. Wake me when the girls are home."

The one respite from all the worry and anguish was the university course I was taking in psychology. I was working towards a degree in social work and started a course in September that was slated to end in December. Family and friends would ask how I managed to study and focus with all that turmoil in my life. For me, the course was an outlet. During those two hours in class every week at the University of Calgary, I was surrounded by young people who knew nothing of my circumstances. I had no wish to be a house-mom for the rest of my days, and I wanted the girls to be proud of me. So I soldiered on.

* * *

On July 20, day two, Louie was on the other end of the telephone line, and he asked me in the course of our conversation, "Who do you think you are?" I thought of an Alice Munro short story called, simply, "Who Do You Think You Are?" The story (also the title of her award-winning short story collection published in 1978) in part explores the comeuppance in small towns meted out to people who are seen to be rising above their station. Louie's wife and daughters would never dream of talking back to him. In Louie's eyes, I had risen above my station.

The call took place in Richard's office. I had just stopped in to sign some more documents and drop off more money, and I had called Louie on my cell phone. He answered and said, "What do you want?" And, later, "Who do you think you are?"

You arrogant man, I thought. I was floored by his question. I was, am, and always will be the mother of Hannah and Cedar. And, damn it, I had every right to speak to them. Lack of sleep and the tone and absurdity of his question pushed me to the edge, and I responded with anger and frustration. Richard took the phone from me, and Louie became hostile and threatening to him.

"I'll take care of you," Louie apparently told Richard.

"Are you threatening me?" I heard Richard say into the phone.

It was a very heated and emotional exchange, with poor Richard taken off guard by my calling Louie out of the blue. But it was good that Richard was there (we believe that Louie may have thought it was my dad he was talking to). In any case, when Richard demanded to know where the girls were, Louie told him Lebanon. This was the first time that anyone had told us this, and this fact was included in our affidavit in the family court hearing that took place the following day.

* * *

One way to put pressure on Joe to surrender custody was through the courts—first in Canada and later in Australia. The first step was to file for custody in Canada, which we did on the morning of July 21, day three.

I met Kelly Stewart at her office on 4th Street in downtown Calgary—

the law firm of Edy Dalton. We huddled at 9 a.m. and prepared for court at 10 a.m.

I had never been in a courtroom before. It was like being in a bakery, a very crowded bakery: You would only be served when your number was called. We waited and finally we were called into the courtroom. Told that my daughters had been taken by their father into Lebanon, the judge—an older, female judge with all kinds of experience in family law—arched an eyebrow. She was incredulous. The vicious war there was prominent on all the front pages of Canadian newspapers. Especially shocking were the numbers of civilian casualties in both Israel and Lebanon, but particularly in the latter country. Human rights observers would later accuse both Hezbollah and the Israel Defense Forces of committing crimes against humanity.

Over the course of the next hour and a half, the judge listened as Kelly outlined my case. In the end, the judge signed the custody letter. Outside the courtroom, I hugged Kelly and we both cried. We had been quite sure I'd be granted sole custody of Hannah and Cedar, but actually getting it still felt like a victory. After forty-eight hours of sensing only loss, this counted for something.

At that point, a court official—a "court runner," as he is called—approached Kelly. I understood that Kelly would have to stand in line to get the document granting me custody. But this man, who had been in the court and heard our story, said there would be no need to line up, that he would get the document and bring it to us. My first thought was an irrational one. This man looked Lebanese. Is he working for Joe? Later, in a calmer frame, I was amused by my paranoid response. The man could have been Italian. He was just a sweet guy sympathetic to my plight.

The next duty was to go to the airport that same afternoon and wait for Air Canada Flight 228 arriving from Sydney via Honolulu. It was the flight that Joe and the girls were supposed to be on. They were not, of course. Somewhere in the back of my mind I prayed that they would be there but I had already called Aeroplan (I had used my Aeroplan points to purchase one of the girls' tickets) and was told that Joe had not made the change we had agreed upon before he left (the switch from a four-week trip to three). Here was one more loose end that could have been Joe's undoing had I just made that call before he left. July 21 had come, and we—my father and

I—were there to witness the fact that Joe had not returned—thus paving the way for parental child abduction charges to be laid.

It was at the airport that I got a call from a friend I've had since childhood, Stephanie. We spoke for a bit and she immediately drove out to the airport, where, after a great many hugs and tears from both of us, I told her the full story of what had happened. That same afternoon, a business associate of my father's happened to be at the airport on a stopover. When he met me, the first thing he did was write me a cheque for $1,000 towards my legal and other bills. I had never met this man. Friends and strangers alike were lining up to help.

The next step was to get the Canadian judge's ruling recognized in Australia. The Lebanese courts, too, would eventually come into play—although at this point we were only looking at hiring a lawyer there because we were told it was the only legal way to hire a private investigator in Lebanon. Two Lebanese lawyers we spoke to both promised, absolutely, that they would find Joe, serve him and win my case—for a mere $20,000 (U.S.) upfront before anything was done. Such talk put our legal process in Lebanon on the back burner for the time being.

In the end, over the course of almost eight months, we would hire eight lawyers in three countries. Child custody is an astonishingly elaborate area, and I would slowly learn all the *i*'s and *t*'s that would have to be dotted and crossed before everything was in order. I had simply assumed that I had rights to my own children, but once children are out of province or out of the country, everything gets complicated. Even had I spotted Hannah and Cedar walking the streets of Sydney with my sister-in-law, I was not legally entitled to embrace them and whisk them home. Papers would have had to be filed in court, police would have had to accompany me to procure the children . . .

Joe, of course, had the right—and still has the right—to contest the Canadian judge's ruling, but such a court battle will henceforth have to be fought on Canadian soil. In her ruling, the judge declared that "any peace officer, immigration officer, border control or customs officer or any representative or agent of Bison Security Group in any jurisdiction in which the children of the marriage might be found, is authorized and empowered to remove the children from the Defendant's care and return the children forthwith to Calgary, Alberta."

* * *

In my quest to get my daughters back, there were no off days. A laptop always beckoned. For a while I used my own, then—after we discovered Joe's spy software on it—the Calgary police took it for analysis. After that, I borrowed my father's, Krista's and Patrick's. I was researching international laws on parental child abduction, lining up all the dominoes on three continents that would have to fall just so before I could once again hold my daughters in my arms. Every one of us on the team was calling in every favour owed, playing every hunch, plying every contact. A lively network—of friends, family, complete strangers—began to form and exchange information over coffee, by phone, by e-mail. Night and day, the house on Copperfield hummed.

In the weeks that followed Pierre Hawach's call, an e-mail campaign aimed at spreading information about the girls' kidnapping bore fruit—a response that hammered home the theme of never giving in to despair. I was contacted by a woman who had been abducted as a child into Lebanon by her father twenty years earlier. Her mother, after a frantic five-month search, did eventually find her but was powerless to get the girl back or challenge her husband's authority in his place of birth.

In her poignant letter, this woman implored me to do everything I could to get my daughters back and warned me of consequences if I failed to do anything less than my utmost. Regardless of how much the left-behind parent has done to find abducted children and bring them home, those children always feel that more could have and should have been done. The child thinks, "You didn't try hard enough. If you had, you would have found me sooner." That thought, too, pushed me on.

It was like getting a letter from the future, sent by Hannah as a woman and tinged with sadness and regret. This is who she might become unless I found her and her sister. The woman's advice: "Never give up."

* * *

The Internet would prove an enormous boon in our search for the girls. For one thing, my brother Brendan used a tool called Invisible Tracker to see where our web poster was being looked at around the world, in which country, for how long—and even the viewer's computer address.

Of course there were false leads. They were as frequent as Elvis sightings. Joseph Hawach, said one e-mail correspondent, had been spotted on a plane flying to Calgary from Montana. Another witness was quite sure he was working as a baker in Edmonton. Joe, his mother and the girls had been spotted at a lake in Saskatchewan. Or was it the Wal-Mart? People try to be helpful, but child-find organizations like the Missing Children Society of Canada are driven to distraction by such assertions, since every lead has to be followed.

It seemed that the phone at Copperfield never stopped ringing. Friends, unaware of what had happened, would call to say hello and I would have to tell them my awful tale. With every telling, the kidnapping became more real. Everyone was shocked. My parents, who had lived with us for a time, were shocked, too, but to a lesser extent. At the time of the separation ten months earlier, I had finally confided in them and detailed some of what had gone on in the marriage. On hearing this, my father's advice had been to get a lawyer. My father had said he trusted Joe only as far as he could throw him—and Joe is a much bigger man than my father.

* * *

As the chess match between Joe and me unfolded, as the team and I plotted strategy, as the hunt for the missing girls took on its many forms, I felt the impact. Paranoia set in: I thought I was being followed, and we had the house checked for listening devices.

I had good reason to worry (and so, it seems, did Joe). One day early in August, someone on the team—one of my brothers—managed to hack into Joe's e-mail address and see how he was trying to redraft the separation agreement to his advantage.

Joe quickly discovered our snooping and he was so angry that he changed the password to my own e-mail address—effectively blocking me from using it. His response told me instantly that he had cottoned on to our eavesdropping. I had to spend an entire afternoon with some California-based official working for Yahoo before I could re-establish my e-mail account. It was just one more wild goose chase that the kidnapping would force upon me.

How did Joe know my password? He had, at some point, installed spy software in my computer that allowed him to monitor my personal and business e-mails, my bank accounts, every web site I visited, every printout taken, every stroke of the keyboard. Until I had the software removed, Big Brother had been watching. This revelation, coupled with the fact that my copy of the separation agreement had gone missing from my drawer at home, led me to think that Joe had keys to my house—and thus the opportunity to install listening devices. Small wonder I was hypervigilant in the wake of the girls' abduction.

When I mentioned all this spy-versus-spy gamesmanship during a roundtable meeting, my lawyers, the police and private investigators were all aghast. While they were pleased that I had not tried to hide the spying, I was roundly chastized for doing it and was made to promise never to attempt it again. John Hebert of the Calgary police was especially taken aback by my impatience (or was it my impertinence?). He warned me that it might take several years before I saw my girls again, to which I replied that if John were ever to arrest me for invading Joe's privacy it would—given John's pace—likewise take him several years. We made peace later, but this was a measure of my acerbic mood then.

One day I was going through some paperwork in the house and I discovered something Joe had written—a journal entry. He noted that he was reading *The Art of War*, a classic book on military strategy written in China by Sun Tzu in the sixth century. He was reading the book, apparently, to "beat me" during the separation. *The Art of War*'s thirteen chapters include "Laying Plans," "Attack by Stratagem" and "The Use of Spies." The book is still read by Western business executives and political strategists, and some Japanese companies make the book required reading for their senior managers. Australian cricket coach John Buchanan famously handed out excerpts from the book to his players prior to a match with England in 2001. My husband evidently thought the book might prove useful for his side in the battle between Joseph Hawach and Melissa Hawach.

My confidence in my own judgement and instincts had never been lower. For a year, my husband had told me lies, elaborate lies, and I had swallowed every one. A lawyer had tried to warn me about the possibility of the girls being abducted, and I had ignored her. For such naiveté, I was now paying an exorbitant price.

* * *

In those last days of July and into August 2006, the wound of the kidnapping still so raw and tender, I was given one more cross to bear. The girlfriend.

She worked in inventory at Fast Freight, and Joe had taken up with her. They went to church together, dined together, they had even gone to Las Vegas on a trip earlier in July (her name showed up on an airline ticket billed to American Express), though both she and Joe insisted they were just friends. When I found out about her in August 2006, I was actually glad that Joe had someone in his life and Hannah and Cedar seemed to like her. It wasn't the romance that would come to trouble me so, it was the way she inserted herself into my life. As if I didn't have enough duplicity to deal with, she added one more layer.

I was in the kitchen at Copperfield when she called the first time, just four days after Pierre had called with his dreadful news. She was distraught, and for all kinds of reasons. The police had apparently been in touch with her, asking questions about missing stock at Amcan and whether she had misled suppliers. Now they were asking her what she knew about the kidnapping.

She was really upset, and I sympathized. "I'm a nurse," she told me, "and I'm trained to pick up on these things. I just didn't see it coming. I must have been so focused on the children." (By "these things," she meant body language and other clues.)

She would call again, at Richard Bennett's office, still distressed. "My sister's a lawyer," she said. "Have you considered the Hague Convention?" I thought that talking to her would calm her, so I told her that I now had custody of the girls through the Canadian courts and that extradition orders on Joe were forthcoming. In hindsight, I talked too much. Naively, I had no idea how Joe's girlfriend would use this information.

When we got into Joe's Hotmail account, we discovered that this woman was passing on to Joe what she learned from talking to me ("I'll get more information from Mel tomorrow over lunch," read one of her missives to Joe on MSN). Once Joe twigged to the fact that we were reading his messages, he must have alerted the woman, for she stopped calling me. Only when I told Richard and the Calgary police about this did I discover from them that Joe's girlfriend was being investigated by the police for possible involvement in fraud and was being treated as a hostile witness.

"Why didn't someone tell me?" I asked them.

I was angry at myself for failing to exercise caution. This woman was in over her head, way over her head, and she was trying to make herself more important than she really was. If she was a nurse, as she claimed, why was she working for a freight company and, later, a Lebanese kebab shop? Joe had given her all our furniture as payment for her babysitting the kids, but why would he need a babysitter? He used to be so adamant that his time with the girls was very important to him, and I had taken such care never to be late dropping them off to him. Now I found out that he had, in turn, been dropping them off to this other woman! I had misread her. Why? In part, because in the days immediately following news of the abduction I was so manic. "Like a hummingbird on speed," Dave Chittick used to call me.

* * *

I was also extremely upset at what I saw as my own failure: I had not created a life for my children where this could never happen to them. More than distraught, I was disappointed in myself. I kept poring over the past, the what-ifs piling up like driftwood on the shore. I could have made better and wiser decisions. We could have done better, Joe and I. We could have been smarter. I shouldered much of the blame for our ruinous marriage, and it rests there yet.

What lingers is an old mentality from a bad marriage that says "Everything Is the Woman's Fault." Joe would justify things he did or said by laying the blame at my feet. If only I were a better wife or mother . . . I took responsibility for everything; he took responsibility for nothing.

I was not alone in my *mea culpas*. My father was kicking himself for taking at face value Joe's claims about expanding the paper business. "The alarm bells," he would later tell a friend, "went off in my head the first time

I met him in Australia. I saw how he conducted business. There was always someone angry with him—even his own brother. Money was his god. We were thin on cash at the time of the wedding, and Joe and Mel paid for part of our flight." I distinctly remember that I worked at the restaurant for one month without taking a salary and quit helicopter lessons for a month—all to pay for those flights. And Dad, of course, paid Joe back. For Joe to bring up the cost of those flights as some sort of unpaid debt was doubly galling.

"Then when he was in Canada," Dad continued, "he brought it back up again. In Canada, I signed for things he bought on credit—furniture, vehicles. There was no gratitude. As for all the talk of needing money to expand the business, all I had to do was pick up the phone and talk to the company he was supposedly going to merge with. I should have checked his story."

My mother, too, regrets that she missed the signs. After the separation, she and Dad would sometimes look after Hannah and Cedar, and Joe would pick the girls up at Copperfield. He would stay in the truck and avoid all eye contact with Mom and Dad, and wouldn't speak to them. He had already begun to sever whatever connection he had with my folks, as if paving the way for the dramatic disconnect to follow.

Mom, Dad, me: We all felt guilt. On the other hand, I was very grateful that my family never once reminded me of the fact that my own decisions had got me into this mess. The love and support they offered me never wavered, even when they did not agree with decisions I would make down the line. And there was never any question that the big decisions were mine to make. These were my daughters, and how to proceed was always, in the end, my call. Still, I was glad of all the help and wise counsel I got.

* * *

I was not the only one looking for Joe Hawach in the summer of 2006. Forensic accounting by HSBC Bank Canada would show that Joe had used a $100,000 business loan for personal spending, then defaulted on the loan. The bank later took the case to court and got a civil judgement against Joe—meaning that if he came back to Canada there could be a lien on his wages or he might have to declare bankruptcy. Certain of Joe's financial transactions, as well as Joe's taking of the girls, meant that police here and abroad had interest in the case. The government of Canada and its embassy officials in several countries increasingly got involved in the case.

Meanwhile, I continued to send messages to Joe but these were always met with silence. In one message, I alternately threatened and begged the father of my children. The e-mail read, in part:

"There are literally tens of thousands of people praying for Hannah's and Cedar's return—real Christians, not just the part-time ones like you. Prayer circles all over Canada and Australia. It is so powerful and you cannot fight God, Joe—not even with all of your dirty money . . . If one hair on either of those girls' heads is harmed, I swear to God I will scratch your eyeballs out . . . My girls are strong and they know what lies are—especially Hannah. She seeks the truth and knows when she is not hearing it . . . It is my FULL-time job to find them until the day I die. You think you have crippled me financially and emotionally. You have no idea how strong I am and how long I will last . . . Please let me talk to the girls. If you have one shred of decency, conscience, morality left in your body . . ."

* * *

Things like laundry and cleaning and cooking at Copperfield fell by the wayside, until my mother and Celeste took over those responsibilities. Celeste had given birth to a baby boy, Hunter, just seven months before (he was born on my birthday and I'm his godmother) so she had double duty. Before that, the house was a zoo. Friends brought food to us constantly (a woman who works with Andy once sent over twenty frozen packets of lasagne), but eating seemed to me a low priority. One night we all went out to a restaurant, where the food was extremely good and we were actually able to have some fun—and then a light switch flipped inside me. How can I be enjoying myself? I should be home, on the computer, looking for my children. I lost twenty pounds that fall.

My network of family and friends likewise suffered. Lynda, the wife of my baseball coach, was overwhelmed with grief and spent day and night on the computer, writing letters and speaking to family members in the

Vatican. The sister of Brad, my former long-time partner in Australia, was so distraught at the kidnapping that she established an e-mail campaign of her own Down Under. So many people were affected, and often it was me doing the consoling.

When the leaves started changing colour that fall, I remember willing them to stay on the trees. As long as the leaves were not on the ground, I could pretend that time was not passing. But as the weeks passed into months, I was not easy to be around. I was very demanding of myself and all those in my circle. I had a short fuse, zero patience.

To counter the pacing, the shortness of breath, the shaking and the rising panic that I would experience just before and after a prearranged telephone conversation with Joe or Sid Hawach, I would talk to my mother and she would help calm me. A psychiatrist who saw me in the weeks and months following the abduction remarked on my loss of appetite, my inability to sleep, my hypervigilance and increased heart rate, my nightmares and vivid dreams (in a recurring one, my daughters no longer recognized me), my breaking uncontrollably into tears at reminders of my children, my worries that I was being followed and my inability to trust anyone—even friends and lawyers and strangers genuinely trying to help me. The psychiatrist diagnosed acute stress disorder (as opposed to post-traumatic stress disorder). The symptoms are the same, but the former requires less time to develop (one month versus three). My own symptoms would abate somewhat in the fall as I began to see that my fears were irrational, but I still suffered from panic attacks. Places that triggered memories of the abduction—the Calgary airport, toy shops, kids' clothing stores—would send me into a tailspin, so I learned to avoid them.

"Well-spoken, interested and cooperative," the doctor described me in his clinical assessment, which he passed on to my lawyer, Richard Bennett. "She gave the impression," the doctor wrote, "of someone who wished to remain controlled in spite of intense distressing feelings . . ." As for my prognosis, he could not say.

"It is difficult to predict," he wrote, "whether the resilience that Ms. Hawach has shown to this point will continue to sustain her, or whether she will reach a point where she essentially collapses. This condition has been aggravated by her understanding that she has been victimized not only through a complex set of misrepresentations by her husband over many months, but also that his family have deliberately supported him in an ongoing way. We know that the ability of people to accept difficult things in their lives is more challenging when they believe that this is the result of conscious choices by individuals, knowing that harm would be the outcome. This is especially the case when it involves people whom they formerly trusted."

Where was I bound? Continued resilience, or collapse?

* * *

There would be times during the hunt for Cedar and Hannah when I would be asked by members of the team to make sense of something Joe had said or done. Part of any strategy is knowing what the other side is thinking.

"Well, you know him, you were married to him. What do you think?" someone would say.

"I don't know," I would often reply. In hindsight, I hardly knew the man. There was so much I did not know, so many mysteries.

In time I would come to understand the depth of my husband's deception and treachery. Mine was the primary name on our American Express card, which Joe had in his possession. Before he left for Australia, he had, unbeknownst to me, run up $25,000 in charges—electronic equipment, golf equipment, trips to Vegas, massive charges from many bars in Calgary (I wondered if he had been buying rounds every night, so monstrous were the sums). I had a devil of a time cancelling the card—in part because Joe had rerouted mail to Amcan (presumably so it would take longer for me to twig and cancel the card). By the time I voided the card, the charges had hit $38,000—including a $3,000 tab from a high-end bar in the Rocks (the historic heart of Sydney, close to the Harbour Bridge) and several thousand dollars paid to Positano's to clear debts he owed his father.

Joe had talked that summer about possible mergers with another paper company and needing cash to enable that by buying more paper stock. I had no wish to cripple Joe's business (for one thing, it still supported, to some degree, the children and me) and I therefore delayed demanding my half of the equity in the house we had owned and sold. I did not press my husband for alimony. What I wanted, and I was prepared to wait for it until a better moment in the business's fortunes, was my share from the sale of our house—$100,000.

I had proposed, and Joe had reluctantly agreed, that in the interim I be given $35,000—enough to cover the down payment for my house at Copperfield Gardens. The remainder of the money owed me was to be paid in monthly instalments. I was also getting from Joe a small monthly sum, an amount that was to be later deducted from my share in the Mountain Park house sale. The entire arrangement seemed fair and reasonable, and was achieved with more goodwill than most separating couples can manage. Or so I thought at the time.

Only later would I learn that talk of a merger, of his being a partner with Asia-Pacific Pulp and Paper, of expanding into northern Alberta, was all a sham. I had met him at the warehouse several times during the four weeks before he left, and he always met me in the parking lot. Later I realized why. Had I walked into the warehouse, I would have seen that he had sold off all the stock. The cupboard was bare.

I would look back at things that Joe had said or done, things that at the time made no sense. Now they did. These "aha" moments offered no satisfaction as every little facet of his scheming was made plain. The question I asked myself most often was this: How could I have been so blind as to miss all the warning signs?

Warning sign #1. After we were separated and I had moved in with my parents, Joe took me out to dinner and tried to convince me to rent for a few months. This made absolutely no sense to me and I stood firm. I had decided to purchase my parents' house for several valid reasons: The place was familiar to the girls and close to our community and the Mountain Park house, making visits with their father easy and convenient. I'm only guessing, but perhaps Joe thought that if I rented, he could at least delay forking over the $35,000 as down payment on my parents' house.

Warning sign #2. After I had made the down payment on my home, Joe tried to convince me to put the mortgage in my name alone. The mortgage was then in my parents' name, but they were locked into such a good interest rate that it seemed foolish to renegotiate. Nevertheless, Joe had meetings at the bank, got a new mortgage all set up and told me I just had to go in and sign the papers. The interest rate? A point and a half higher than what I was already paying. This from a man who hated (like everyone) giving banks a cent more than he had to and who was never late paying his credit card bill lest they charge him interest.

What was he thinking? Did he still hope that we could get back together? Was this about keeping my family at arm's length (later I would read that an abuser's greatest tool is to isolate his spouse from friends and family).

Or was this, as Joe would write in e-mails from Australia, about "crippling me financially" so I would feel I had no choice but to give in to his demands? I believe he wanted the house in my name so I would lose my only real source of equity when the banks he owed money to went after me and my house. This was one warning sign I heeded. But math alone, not suspicion, spared me that outcome.

Warning sign #3. Joe and I had created our own separation agreement, modelled on one we had downloaded from a Canadian legal site and modified ourselves. Part of the agreement stipulated that I was to get money while the girls were away in Australia in order to renovate the basement of my house on Copperfield as a playroom. Joe had told me that all the money from the sale of our matrimonial home on Mountain Park had gone to fund the merger of Amcan with another paper company. He had asked me to await the arrival of dividends from the new company in the middle of July. When Joe and Hannah called from Australia on July 15, I asked him if it was okay to cash the post-dated cheque that he had given me. The dividends, he said, had not come in yet. Could I wait a few more days? Eventually I went to the bank (I was still a signatory), where I was told that the account was overdrawn by $15,000—well beyond even its allowed overdraft. This made me very nervous, especially since this news came just at the time that communication with Joe and the girls began to drop off.

From the golf store where I worked, I had bought, at cost, clubs and golf bags meant for Joe's brothers in Sydney. Joe paid me with a cheque—but from an account for which I was responsible. Only when he was gone did it hit me: It was like he had reached into my back pocket and paid me with my own money.

Looking back, I could see this was all a calculated attempt at impoverishing me so I would have no way of financing a campaign to get the girls back. I had been robbed every which way.

Warning sign #4. I had also missed a huge—and no doubt calculated—change in his attitude. In November and December 2005, Joe and I began to talk about financial arrangements during the separation. He made it clear that were I to go to a lawyer, he would liquidate all assets, hire the best lawyer and leave me with nothing. I thought it wiser to skip the lawyers, to proceed amicably as long as Joe did what he said he would do—and that Hannah and Cedar would be least affected by this approach. Their mother and father, though separated, would remain on good terms.

And so it seemed we were. In the months following the separation, Joe made all the promised payments and he was extremely cooperative. He was patient and always listened to my concerns. I had actually started to feel somewhat guilty for leaving him. Perhaps he was, after all, capable of great change.

I could not have been more wrong. What I felt more than anything was disappointment in myself and my failure to see the signs. Yet anger, too, entered the mix. The emotional end result was that my judgement was clouded. Bad judgement had gotten me into this mess, and my hope was that good judgement would now get me out.

* * *

Those of us hunting for Hannah and Cedar could not always agree on how to proceed. Who to hire. When to make a move, when to bide our time. My house had become a command post all right, and a strategic war was unfolding between an estranged husband and wife. I kept calling meetings—brainstorming sessions at the Edy Dalton law firm, where Richard and Kelly worked. Through all this, my family gave me every ounce of their love and vast amounts of their time, but inevitably they got caught up in the Hawach/Engdahl crossfire. We fought.

I fought with the very people who were trying hard to help me. Just days into my nightmare, Calgary police detective John Hebert called me at home. He said he had a few questions.

"This restaurant you worked at in Sydney," he said. "Positani's? How do you spell that? I also need a phone number for Pierre Hawach."

I was furious. Why was I having this conversation about the spelling of Positano's and telephone numbers? I had put this information into my statement. It was all there. Had he not read it? I was getting really worked up, but at the same time I didn't want to bite the hand that feeds. So I handed the telephone to Patrick and let him answer.

I got along well with Theresa Garagan but John Hebert and I were like oil and water. Yet when it came time to establish extradition orders and lay charges against Joe, someone had to meet—twice—with the Crown prosecutor in Calgary. Who made these trips? Who waited around for hours to speak to that lawyer? John Hebert, on his days off. He has children of his own (really lovely boys) and I often felt guilty at the time that people like him were taking from their own family to help reunite me with mine.

Richard Bennett admired my guts and my perseverance—and told me so—but there were times when we, too, battled, in much the same way that my father and I battled. Mutual respect and affection only muted the skirmishes, never stopped them from occurring.

A major source of anxiety and tension—what Dave Chittick called "static"—stemmed from the enormous sums of money going out to pay for all our professional help here and abroad. A friend with experience of hostage-takings in the Middle East told us, "You got a million bucks? That's what it's going to take to get those kids back." He was not off by all that much.

To pay some of the initial costs of the search, my father had borrowed money from a wealthy friend, who then said to my father, "Jim, whatever it takes, I'll back you." It was like having a fairy godmother, to be given the freedom to make the best choices. On the other hand, this was a loan, not a gift, and every cent would have to be paid back.

By this time, the dragonfly had been fixed in our heads as a symbol of hope. I am not an artist or a craftsperson, but one day I went to a crafts store and came home with materials. My thinking was that each member of my family could wear a dragonfly bracelet or necklace or pendant—charities have latched onto plastic bracelets, especially, as a way of raising funds and awareness, and young people wear them almost like fashion statements. Working with me, my brother Brendan's partner, Krista, fashioned a little dragonfly pendant, and I saw right away that it was perfect and that any man or woman could wear it.

We returned to the store and got more material. Now we wove *H* beads and *C* beads into each pendant, one letter under each dragonfly wing. We made them by the hundreds, trying all different colours. Making the pendants gave all of us in the command post a focus, gave us something to do with our hands during all the downtime, which might otherwise have driven us crazy.

We would hand the pins out to family and friends, and, as the story of Hannah and Cedar continued to spread, people began to ask for the pendants and to e-mail me their dragonfly stories. A cousin of mine was in Australia and reading on the beach a story about the kidnapping in *Woman's Day* magazine (which mentioned our embracing the dragonfly) when a dragonfly landed on her. The wife of my baseball coach was working at her computer to organize a ball tournament to raise money for us when her daughter came in greatly excited because a swarm of several dozen dragonflies had settled on the back door. A friend in Australia walked into her office one morning and noticed something new on the staff fridge: a giant handcrafted dragonfly.

We could not keep up with demand for the pins, so my mother's curling team began to make them from kits we sent them. Eventually, we used up all the H and C beads in Saskatchewan and Alberta and started ordering them via the Internet. Those who got the pins often made a donation, but for us the key thing was to get the pins out there. To get the story told and have it circulate.

Another friend, on a whim, ordered black-and-white plastic bracelets that featured, on the black half, the names *Hannah & Cedar* flanked by dragonflies and, on the white half, the words *Help Bring Them Home.* My friend thought the abduction was a black and white issue, and thus her choice of colours.

We also made T-shirts to sell at fund-raisers. We put on the front of black T-shirts a huge, stylized purple dragonfly, with the letters *H* and *C* on each wing, and on the back the words *Thank You for Your Support!* and our web site: www.bringhannahandcedarhome.com.

During the baseball tournament fundraiser, a television reporter came out to the diamond with a cameraman to record an interview. My team had set up an information booth for the Missing Children Society, with posters of the girls, and pins for sale. The interview took twice as long as it should have because the interviewer, a woman, and perhaps a mother herself, kept breaking into tears. I found myself consoling her, and then it was my turn for tears. We finally got the interview done, and she and her cameraman left wearing dragonfly pins.

* * *

Other offers of help were pouring in, typically through a friend of a friend. One such contact—a Lebanese businessman whom I will call Paul, since he would rather not be named—offered me important contact numbers, including that of Lebanon's ambassador to Canada. The two were not necessarily friends; I had the sense that one owed the other a favour. Just using Paul's name led to a useful telephone chat with the ambassador in Ottawa. More importantly, he gave me a bigger, clearer picture of what was happening in Lebanon, politically and militarily. Who was fighting whom, and why. A very wealthy, very intelligent, very thoughtful international entrepreneur, Paul belonged to a group of capitalists who act in philanthropic ways. They call themselves A Small World (which must be a very private and informal group, for I could find nothing about them on the Internet). I see it as a kind of brotherhood, an international group of latter-day white knights.

We would get calls from mercenaries, one of them from an outfit that claimed to have rescued Terry Waite (an odd claim since Waite—the British hostage negotiator who was himself held hostage in Beirut for five years, ending in 1991—was not rescued but released). Stories circulated about families in Third World countries who hire security agents to get their children back, but then have to deal with ransom demands from those very same agents. An unwary parent can go from frying pan to fire in the blink of an eye. Despite the desperation that I sometimes felt, I was never tempted by the cowboy commando approach. Everything I did now was guided by a single concept: If I do this, or that, what will it cost my children? If I mention to the media the fraud charges against my husband, what will it cost my children?

* * *

Canada's Ministry of Foreign Affairs was eventually able to piece together the journey the girls had taken with their father. From Sydney, they had flown to Dubai, and from there to Damascus. There, Joe rented a car and they crossed the border into Lebanon on July 22.

So they were in Lebanon, but where? I sent many, many e-mails to Hawach family members in Australia—including all of Joe's siblings and Vicki, Sid Hawach's wife. Not one responded. I learned later through friends that Joe had asked his sister Janet to call our mutual friends and warn them that I may be calling and asking for help and that he would like them *not* to respond to me. How many others, I wondered, knew that Joe was taking his children into Lebanon during a war and made the decision not to get involved or "take sides." The term makes me sick. What about Hannah and Cedar? If Australia recognized abduction as a criminal offence, would that have forced the hands of all these people who meekly obeyed Joe's wishes and stayed out of it?

On August 8, I was in a repair shop getting the mini-van's windshield changed—the cracks were huge and the job long overdue—when I got a text message from Joe. "I will be in Sydney with the girls within the next ten days, be there before me."

He outlined three conditions that I was to meet before he brought the girls to Australia: I was to sell the house on Copperfield, put $50,000 in an Australian trust account, and fly to Sydney. Dave Chittick had taught me early on that during any communication with Joe or his family, I was to say "yes" to as many questions as I possibly could and to avoid saying "no" until we knew more about what they wanted.

I immediately forwarded the message to Dave Chittick, Dad, Richard Bennett, Darryl Stark at Bison Security and Patrick. A roundtable meeting at Edy Dalton was quickly organized, and a great debate ensued on whether I should go to Australia or not. This was one of those pivotal decisions that Dave Chittick talked about.

Many at that roundtable meeting were concerned about my safety on this proposed trip to Australia and were apprehensive about my going. My family and the private investigators with Bison Security all expressed fears for my safety. But Dave and I agreed. I had to go. A "parenting plan" that was supposed to have been mailed to me had never materialized and we had been led in many circles. Here, for the first time, was a concrete request from Joe. Had I refused to come, that fact would have been thrown in my face by the Hawach family and used against me.

It was at this meeting that we tried to figure out the significance of the "ten days" stipulation in Joe's e-mail. Darryl Stark twigged that ten days would mark almost exactly one month from when Joe entered Dubai from Australia. (The Dubai visitor visa is a thirty-day visa and Dubai authorities are incredibly strict regarding immigration and, in fact, almost everything. Dubai wants to establish itself as a safe place to do business in the Middle East—no easy feat. But they have done a very good job of it, and it boils down to how strict they are regarding their laws and the handling of those who do not follow those laws.)

Once it was established that I would go to Australia, we just needed to work out the details—like who would go with me and what security was required.

Finally, I needed to renew my passport (I had just noticed it had expired) as well. So we put everything in place and then made a call to Louie Hawach. I was on speakerphone and the entire roundtable was present at Edy Dalton. I was not going to make it in the ten-day time frame, and I wanted Louie *et al.* to know with certainty that I was coming and to know why it was taking so long to organize. I called Louie at the restaurant and told him that I had gotten Joe's message and that I would be arriving in Sydney in the next few days. (I left the date vague for security's sake.) Louie sounded very happy and relieved.

"Would it be okay," I asked him, "if I call you when I arrive?"

"Of course, sweetie," he replied. "I will organize an apartment for you." I told him I was having trouble with flights and that my passport needed to be renewed, but I was leaving as soon as possible. This short conversation set the stage for the next chapter in our story.

In the days when Joe had our daughters in hiding, the anxiety that I felt when I had to speak with Joe or his family made me feel nauseated. But when I got off the phone this time, everyone said I'd handled it perfectly. We were surprised at how pleased and relieved Louie was at the news that I was coming, and we were hopeful that was a sign of cooperation. On the other hand, "the apartment" comment made it apparent that Louie believed I had finally caved and was coming to stay for good. As usual, I broke the tension with humour.

"I should have asked him," I told the roundtable, "for a few of my old shifts at the restaurant to help pay for flights over. Then we could all go back to how things used to be!"

Then I went home and started packing.

7

Back to Parramatta

This would happen often after I returned to Canada with my new husband and daughter in 2003: I would be watching a film shot in Australia and whenever the scene shifted outdoors, with the sound of birds singing I would be transported instantly to the land Down Under. As much as the distinctive smell of a gum tree (which has always reminded me of Vicks VapoRub) or a song by an Aussie rock group heard on the radio, those distinctive calls vividly brought me back to the place I called home for nine years of my life.

Around Sydney, I would hear crimson rosellas, brush cuckoos, Australian magpies, noisy miners, galahs and cockatoos, of course. These are all common and listed in the bird books, respectively, as whistlers, sorrows, carollers, peepers and screechers. The cockatoo, especially, though gorgeous to behold (with its white body and bright yellow crest), makes the most obnoxious and aggressive squawking and cawing.

It was screechers of the human variety I heard most in Sydney in August 2006. I did a little screeching myself—especially when it became clear that I would not see Hannah and Cedar. We had, of course, been lied to. I did speak with Joe, but only on the phone from Lebanon, and one of those talks ended in a shouting match. My dealings in Sydney were almost exclusively with Louie and Sid, and they, too, generated fireworks.

* * *

I arrived in Sydney on Tuesday, August 22, with what we came to call Team Australia: my father, my uncle (my mother's brother, David, who lives in Boston) and Lovell Bowen. The two men were there to act as unseen observers. Likewise, Lovell came along as an extra set of eyes and ears—a veteran police officer, she is a trained observer who can pick up nuances and body language. There to satisfy security concerns raised back at the roundtable in Calgary, she posed as my cousin (known in my family as "Auntie" Leslie), a woman who does, in fact, exist—though I have never met her.

Lovell also stood in my father's stead, keeping his troublesome heart from too much excitement (he had his first heart attack in his late thirties). A woman, we thought, would raise less suspicion in the cat-and-mouse game that both sides were now playing. As a teenager, Lovell had worked for a Lebanese restaurant owner, and she remembered how he was inclined to discount women. We were confident that the Hawach men would likewise discount Auntie Leslie—perhaps to our advantage.

Through Bison Security in Calgary, we had also hired private investigators in Sydney to do surveillance for two days on the Hawach family residence—to see if Joe and the girls were actually there (though we very much doubted it) and to ensure that we were not being followed from the airport or being watched. I was still hypervigilant, still somewhat paranoid. Through all our networking and e-mail contacts, we had been put in touch with a retired agent who had worked for the Mossad (the Israeli intelligence and secret police), and he was telling us that Joe was already back in Australia—in Lakemba, a suburb in southwest Sydney. We wondered if that was true, and, if so, whether he might do us harm. It sounded a little far-fetched but since the warrants were taking forever to get linked to the Interpol web site it was definitely possible. The red warrants and extradition orders were in place and Joe's photo was on the Canadian Police Information Centre (CPIC) and the North American computer systems—but it was not yet on Interpol.

At the airport in Sydney, it was an eye opener to see the security team in action—with their phones and radios and security precautions. When we were all safely in the lobby of our hotel, the PIs gave us updates on what, if anything, had occurred during the twenty-four hours we were en route to Australia. At one point, one of the investigators excused himself to call back to his office. The name Hawach, he said, was ringing a bell.

"You're not going to believe this," the investigator said when he got off the phone. "I did surveillance on your house here in Sydney five or six years ago. I have photographs on file of you and your baby daughter leaving the house." The circumstances were nebulous—something about trying to serve Joe with papers over an unpaid bill.

There were not a lot of laughs on this trip. This moment of déjà vu was one of the few.

* * *

When Lovell and I arrived at Positano's Restaurant later that same day, the lunchtime rush had ended and Louie was taking a mid-afternoon nap in the shade on the back bench. His first words were not welcoming and he seemed hesitant even to let us in the restaurant. He took a deep breath, then said, "You were supposed to call me first."

"I just decided to come by," I told him.

He had already dialled someone (Sid, most likely) and now he said into the phone, "Melissa has come." Ten minutes later, Louie's brother was on the scene.

Sid offered no hello, not even a pretence of civility, but simply launched into a defence of Joe's actions and an attack on me. This whole fiasco was all my fault, apparently. "Why, when you knew Joe was in Dubai [en route to Lebanon], did you not go there?" Sid demanded to know. "Why did you even let him bring the kids here?"

These were absurd questions, unworthy of a response. By the time we learned that Joe was in Dubai (a purchase made in a duty-free shop using his American Express credit card told us so), he was long gone to Lebanon. As for "letting him take the kids," I had done no such thing. Joe had taken the girls "on vacation."

Sid was ever the lawyer and I was ever on his own little travelling witness stand. Once, during a conference call at the offices of Edy Dalton, Sid had even suggested that my refusal to sign the parenting agreement meant that Joe would have to stay in Lebanon, and, with no means of income, he would be forced to turn to a life of crime. Incredibly, it seemed to me that Sid was trying to make me responsible for what Joe had done—taken our daughters into an embattled land.

How I loathed Sid Hawach. He is a little loud man, fortyish, with salt-and-pepper hair, an average build and a big man's swagger. Sid, though Joe's uncle, is just a few years older than Joe. They grew up together, they're close. After the abduction, I asked Joe via e-mail and on the phone, "Who's your lawyer?" "Sid," he replied. But when "El Sid" was asked—by my lawyer in Canada, by me or by anyone else—whether he was acting as Joe's lawyer, he always denied it.

Day one in Australia with the Hawach family, and the intensity was already sky-high. When Sid lambasted me for not going to Dubai, I replied that for someone who claimed not to know what was going on he sure seemed wise to Joe's secret location and our private conversations.

Sid wanted me to sign the custody agreement, and I said I would sign *if* I saw my daughters. I had no intention of signing it, of course—though my team worried that I might, out of desperation, do just that. I just wanted to force their hand and perhaps at least get the girls out of Lebanon. On the other hand, I had not yet discounted signing the agreement until I had spoken to our lawyers and determined whether such an agreement would stand up in court or whether the courts would view it as signed under duress. I was not going to make a snap decision and Sid was in no position to offer any guarantees.

Sid wanted to know, and he asked the question several times, "If you were to sign the agreement, would you be signing it of your own free will?" As if this obscure point would matter some day in a court of law.

I finally said, slowly and quite distinctly, "What the hell does it matter? Free will? Free will? My children are in the middle of a war in Lebanon, I have not spoken to them or seen them in months, I cannot eat or sleep, and I have travelled to Australia on the basis of a text message. At what point will free will be back in my life?"

I told Louie—who was fully aware of the abuse I had endured in my marriage, and who had always supported me as long as I stayed in the marriage—that had Joe gone to counselling as I had asked, we might still be together. I explained how difficult it had been for me to split up my family, but that I would not live with a man who treated me the way Joe had. Nor would my daughters, I said, grow up believing that men were supposed to treat women that way. I might as well have addressed the wall for all the good it did me.

On and on it went, our exchange of barbs—like shots across a ravine in a Hatfield/McCoy skirmish. Nothing was resolved, though Louie seemed clearly taken aback when Lovell and I showed him a small stack of paper: Joe's American Express card bills (his card, but my responsibility), all the credit card debts that Joe had rung up before leaving Canada, a letter from American investigators sniffing around for Joe in connection with a New York stock deal gone sour, and copies of airline tickets—which clearly showed that Joe and his girlfriend had taken trips to Las Vegas and New York while running up $28,000 in charges. This news stunned Louie, and, for the first time, Sid, too, went quiet.

Louie pleaded for more time to think things through, and I pleaded for some time on the phone with Hannah and Cedar. He seemed surprised that I had not been in contact with the girls. Please, I begged him, arrange for them to call me. Or have them call the restaurant, I suggested, and I would return that evening. Louie seemed to find it strange that I would make the hour drive from my downtown hotel. Why did he not understand my desperation? How could he so misjudge that calculation: Could an hour in traffic somehow be on equal footing with the sound of my daughters' voices somewhere in Lebanon?

"Call me at nine this evening," Louie told me. "I'll let you know then if it's possible."

After Sid left, I told Louie that he could consult with Sid all he wanted in private, but I wanted nothing more to do with his brother. I said that Sid made me extremely uncomfortable and that I only wanted to speak with Louie.

I think that it had irked Sid, mightily, that we were talking back to him. At one point, when I was on the telephone the following day with Joe and voices were raised, Louie strayed close to me and Lovell practically shooed him away. That, also, did not go down well. In fact, there was enough tension and raised voices in some of the exchanges between Sid and Louie and Lovell and me that Lovell made it a point never to be too far away from me.

That night, we called the restaurant but Louie said there would be no chat with the girls on the phone. Louie said he had become extremely angry with Joe on the phone, trying without success to convince his son to let me speak with Hannah and Cedar. So angry that he broke the phone. I had some sympathy for Louie, and he for me. Could we come again for another talk, he asked, at 3 p.m. the following day?

It had been an exhausting first day, difficult and emotional every step of the way. Each time I cried, Louie would try to get me to stop, offer me something to eat. Sid, though, kept hammering away at me.

"She's a mother," Louie scolded his brother. "Of course she's going to be upset." *Upset?* Of the two Hawach brothers, one (Louie) apparently had no clue of the anguish I was in, and the other (Sid) sought only to exploit it.

* * *

If day one was about testy exchanges, day two began like a bad spy film. Prior to the 3 p.m. rendezvous, Dad, my uncle, Lovell and I watched the restaurant for about twenty minutes.

What we saw was a former associate of Joe's signalling down the street to someone else. The owner of the hairdressing salon next to the restaurant, along with a woman I did not recognize, stood outside—as if on sentry duty. All were on their cell phones and in strategic positions outside. What a circus.

Louie, meanwhile, directed Lovell and me to a certain table and he went off to get a phone. He was setting up a conversation with Joe, but with Sid *et al.* so close they could tape what I said. In different circumstances, I would have laughed.

On the phone, Joe sounded disturbed and I could tell something was wrong. He wanted to know if I was alone in Sydney, and he seemed pleased to hear that Auntie Leslie, not my father, was with me. Joe had always felt he could control me more easily when my immediate family was not there to support me.

Then he launched into his line of questioning. Had I sold the house (as per his demand)? What about Patrick? When did I start getting involved with him? He needed to know my answer, he said, so he could determine if I would lie about other things to be discussed.

I flared at this and lost my temper. The one human on planet

Earth least qualified to lecture me about lying was Joseph Hawach, and I told him so before informing him that I knew about his girlfriend and the trips to Vegas. I knew about this woman (the girls had told me about her), but Joe had always insisted that they were just friends. That, of course, was a lie. But this conversation about our relationships with others was absolutely absurd and beside the point. The girls were in Lebanon! We might as well have been arguing about why one of us left the cap off the tube of toothpaste while we were married. Then he switched gears. Wanted to know if I had a lawyer in Sydney, and, if so, he wanted me to have that lawyer contact Sid and "make an offer." In the circumstances, it was a galling, almost obscene choice of words. You make an offer on a house, not on the custody of your daughters. I gave the phone to Louie. Maybe, I told him, you can figure out what your son wants by his riddles.

The two spoke in Arabic for a time, and then Louie came back with his son's demands in a nutshell: Joe wanted sole custody of the girls and the charges against him dropped. Would he also like me to bring him the moon? I inquired of Louie. I was not foolish enough to grant him what Canadian courts had, the month before, granted me—sole custody of Hannah and Cedar. The criminal matter, of course, lay squarely in the hands of the Crown prosecutor back in Alberta. (The prosecutor, I later discovered, will entertain a proposal to drop charges—but only after a child has been returned; not before, as Joe was suggesting.)

Now the phone came back to me. Joe said he had been advised by a British lawyer that I did, indeed, have the power to drop the fraud and parental child abduction charges. When they were dropped, he said, he would return the girls. I then passed on my compliments to Joe's empty-headed counsel. You can't win, Joe warned. He said he had consulted lawyers, stacked the cards, and he would get what he wanted. I knew this much: If any lawyer had helped him plan the abduction of a child, that lawyer could be disbarred, and this information, too, I conveyed to my husband. Our sour conversation grew steadily more fractious and bitter, with Joe telling me that the girls were not even asking about their mother. They would hate me, he said, when he was done with them.

I could take only so much of this sordid business, and passed the phone over to the woman I was calling "Auntie Leslie." Joe would have known the name from Engdahl family chats, though he, like me, had never actually met her in the flesh. Proof that comedy and crisis can coexist, the first thing Joe did was give her grief for not coming to our wedding.

This marked Lovell Bowen's initial encounter with Joseph Hawach. Her first impression? "He's a bully," she told me later. "He's insecure and he's used to getting his way by bullying."

They spoke for about thirty minutes. The tone rose and fell, now reasoned, now shrill, but he was evidently more on the ceiling than not. Joe told her, "I can stay in Lebanon forever. Melissa is nothing but a whore. I tell the girls every day that their mother is a whore and they will hate her by the time she ever sees them again." Lovell kept an even keel, insisting that while dialogue should continue, Joe had to know that Melissa would never give up rights to her children. By the end of their exchange, Joe was interrupting her, yelling and screaming at her—about his rights as a father, about how he was in charge, how the girls were under armed guard, and how he was, by virtue of his many well-placed contacts in Lebanon, untouchable and unreachable.

Lovell remarked later on how the word *control* came up constantly in the language of the Hawach men (Joe, Louie, Sid): After the phone call with Joe, Louie tried a new tack. If I would sign over custody, he would protect me from Joe and make sure I saw the girls. I just shook my head. You couldn't even persuade him to let me talk to the girls, I told him. Who was he to issue guarantees? His son was a loose cannon, beyond a father's control or anyone else's. Trust me, said Louie. I'll arrange it that you and the girls see your family three months of the year.

Did they really think I would believe a word they said? How could they defend and protect a man who would put my girls—Louie's granddaughters—in such mortal danger? How could they put their own loyalties and agendas ahead of my daughters' safety?

When Lovell was done with Joe, Louie took the phone out to Sid. Eventually Sid came back and handed the phone back to Louie. "Fix your own messes," Sid told his brother, then left.

Thus ended day two. Another four- to five-hour marathon at Positano's. I was not sure at all I could take another like it. Still, we acceded to Louie's request to come back a third time the following day.

* * *

Thursday, August 24, 2006. I had had enough of being led around in circles. At the hotel that morning over breakfast, I told my three compatriots—Dad, David and Lovell—that it was time to force Louie's hand. After some discussion, we arrived at the following plan: I would tell Louie that I was going to Lebanon to find the girls and that if he *really* wanted to help me—as he kept saying he did—he could either come with me or tell me where to go once I was there.

At the restaurant, Louie looked a changed man. He seemed more relaxed than he had been on days previous, perhaps because he was growing more comfortable with all this madness. Louie actually laughed at my notion of going to Lebanon and told me that I would be killed over there. He was not threatening me or implying in any way that I was at risk from the family. His tone was matter of fact: This is just what happens in his homeland.

Playing her assigned role in the little drama we had cooked up, Auntie Leslie told Louie that she had tried, and failed, to dissuade me from going to Lebanon, and that she had alerted my father in hopes he could abort my plan. Jim Engdahl, she said, was at that very moment winging his way from Canada to Australia. (He was, of course, sitting across the street in hat and sunglasses with my uncle.)

I pleaded once more with Louie, told him I was not sure how much more of this I could take. That if I did not see my girls again soon I might die. My weight then was 118 pounds, the lowest I had ever been as an adult. I was trying to show strength but feeling awfully weak.

Sign, said Louie. Then you'll get your girls back.

Lovell stepped in now, telling Louie he was crazy to try to make me give in to their demand. This would mark the last exchange between Louie and Lovell and me. The meeting was loud and, in hindsight, almost comical. Positano's is a corner restaurant, one defined by all-glass sliding doors, which were open this day, so as conversation between Lovell and Louie grew louder and more animated, passersby began turning to see the source of all this commotion. Louie was hollering, something to the effect that Joe was crazy, that he would not listen to his own father, that Melissa must sign the custody agreement to end this whole fracas. To which Lovell replied, quite loudly, "You keep promising this to Melissa, and *nothing* happens!"

Louie did not take kindly to being yelled at—in his place of business, at that—and he began to kick us out of the restaurant, all the while threatening to break Lovell's legs. (Neither Lovell nor I took any of his threats seriously.) A scene from my little Christmas skit was being re-enacted, this time by Louie himself, but the emotion was real and heartfelt.

"Go ahead," replied Lovell, now herself in high dudgeon, voice raised so every patron, every person strolling by, could hear. "You, the guy who helped your son kidnap her children out of Canada!"

"I'm going to kill you! I'm going to kill you!" was Louie's frenzied response.

Even in that state, Louie would pause in his ranting to make it clear that it was Auntie Leslie, not me, he was angry with. Finally, he turned his back on us both and walked away.

* * *

Lovell and I then took a cab to the home of Suzie, Joe's younger sister. Seven years my junior, she had, I thought, a defiant streak. Suzie had once run off to Dubai with a boyfriend she'd just met and twelve years her senior—very much against the Hawach family's wishes. Indeed, at the time, the family had tried to enlist me to talk some sense into her. It put me in a delicate bind: Suzie is a very strong-willed young woman, and I admired that greatly in her, but romance had clouded her judgement. She was not a seasoned traveller, and she would be going to another country to see a man she hardly knew. I told her it was dangerous, reckless, and wouldn't help her get to know this man better. (Suzie's plan was to spend two weeks in Dubai, and I reminded her that anyone can be on best behaviour for two weeks.) It all worked out in the end. Married now, and with a newborn son, Suzie, I believed, was the one person in the family who would help me—and stand up to the Hawach men.

Her face lit up when she saw me, and her greeting was warm and effusive. Suzie wanted to help, but we soon started moving in different directions—she becoming more guarded, me becoming more emotional.

On her living room wall were photos of Hannah and Cedar, framed photos I had sent from Calgary, and seeing those pictures only brought more tears. I was appealing to Suzie, one mother to another, the two of us sitting beside each other on her couch, but my begging was getting me nowhere. Twice I got up and ran to her bathroom when nausea overwhelmed me.

"The same thing could happen to me," Suzie said. Her husband had apparently warned her that involving herself in this affair would be ruinous to their own marriage. Gladys—an intensely religious woman who had always hoped that one of her sons would become a priest—had once come between Suzie and her husband, and he was wary of another incursion by his mother-in-law. Suzie also claimed that the Hawach family, aware of her past clashes with them and knowing how close she and I were, had intentionally not kept her informed of Joe's whereabouts lest she disclose it to me. I did not buy it. Surely Suzie had to know where her mother was? And wherever Gladys was, the girls were too.

Then Janet, the sister who lived next door, came to the house and she finally agreed to go home and get Joe's cell number in Lebanon. My hunch was that Janet had gone to get the men—Sid and Louie. The ones with all the power. I did not much care. I was doing nothing wrong, just sitting in the house of my sister-in-law, a house that Joe and I had once called home. By this time I was calm, even numb.

Janet was gone a long time, maybe ten minutes, and when she returned she told us that the telephone number we wanted was at the restaurant and she text-messaged Jean-Paul. I had seen Jean-Paul earlier and he had shot me a look that I took to mean, "This whole thing stinks." Janet, I was less sure about. I worried that she was using her phone to record us. The next people to appear at the door were Sid and Louie.

That day in Parramatta as I sat on Suzie's couch, feeling as drained as I had ever felt in my life, Sid and Louie marched in and now stood across from me on the other side of the coffee table, both men trying to look imperious, Louie with his arms crossed.

During our exchange, Sid did not like being talked back to. Louie, on the other hand, appeared full of sympathy for my plight. The whole time I was in Australia on this doomed mission, he never spoke a harsh word to me. Where Sid was always at me, Louie was always soft. This whole thing bothered him.

Sid kept telling Suzie to ask us to go, and I could see by her tears how hard this was for her. I was about to leave in order to spare her, but something turned in me. I wanted her to say the words, to own up to the fact that she was showing me the door and buckling to her father and uncle.

"I'm so sorry, Melissa. I guess you'll have to leave," Suzie said, finally.

"You better get yourself a good lawyer," was Sid's parting advice to me.

"And who shall I have my lawyer contact?" I replied, and again, Sid denied that he was the Hawach family's lawyer.

"You're on very thin ice," I said. Later, I wondered whether he, Australia-born, would have understood my Canadian metaphor.

Both Sid and Louie are short. At five-foot-seven, I am taller than both, and Lovell—who is five-foot-six—likewise towered over them. Now these two tall women and two diminutive men gathered at the door. Sid slammed the inner security door behind us as we exited, and Lovell did the same with the outer metal screen door. This infuriated them, and they stormed down the pathway.

"You're a piece of work, you are," Lovell said, turning to square up to Sid.

"I won't take that from you!" he yelled at Lovell.

"Come on, go your best lick!" Auntie Leslie replied. She was now sitting on a fence, patting it to drive home the taunt, absolutely calm in the face of Sid's rage and Louie's hysteria, and hoping, secretly hoping, that one of them would take a crack at her so she could enjoy repaying the favour. All their anger was directed at Auntie Leslie. This is all funny in hindsight. It was not funny then.

"I'll call the police," Sid shouted.

"I'll dial it for you," I offered.

Lovell is a grandmother, with grandchildren the same age as Hannah and Cedar. Her shock of red hair and freckles point to her Irish ancestry (she is one of thirteen children) but there's Pennsylvania Dutch and German blood flowing in her veins as well. And there she was, with me on the street outside Suzie's house while Louie threatened to kill her and Sid threatened to call the police. In her work and in her life, Lovell has had her share of crisis and tragedy, and it takes a lot to faze her. She is also skilled in self-defence and she was inwardly hoping that Sid or Louie would do something "to show what kind of men they are," she later told me, but also so she could land a few cracks of her own. Cooler heads prevailed, though. Sid pulled Louie back into the house, and we left.

Finally, Lovell and I went to the Maronite Catholic church where Joe and I had gotten married seven years earlier and where Hannah had been baptized. This church, just a block away, seemed the proper place to turn. Maybe a place of last resort.

Or was it? A woman working at Our Lady of Lebanon Church seemed entirely sympathetic to my plight, but when she brought one of the priests to speak with me, the first thing he said was "Are you willing to come and live in Australia?" He had been in hospital recently and shared a room with a Hawach relative, so he knew my situation—or at least one perspective.

I could not believe what I was hearing—from a priest. Where was the moral outrage? Did everyone here think it was perfectly fine for a father to abduct his children and take them to a country turned upside down by war? I just stared at the priest until finally he left.

The woman, though, was privately appalled. Her advice? "You lie to everyone you need to lie to, as they lie to you—to get your children back." This, I thought, is what real help sounds like, not the hollow stuff I got from Louie and Sid. I desperately wanted to believe that Louie intended to help me, and I had fooled myself into believing that he genuinely did care.

The words of this woman woke me up. She told me that many people in the Lebanese community would think that what Joe had done was wrong. She also said that no Lebanese mother would *ever* sign over custody of her children to her husband, and to stay firm on this because Joe's father would understand. In that moment I knew there were people who cared. (Later, on a second visit to the church, I spoke with the monsignor, who was also very helpful and sympathetic to my plight.)

So I called the priest back and told him I *would* be willing to come back to Australia—a lie that immediately paid a dividend. He gave the woman permission to put me in touch with Judy Saba—a Lebanese-Australian cultural psychologist who would turn out to be an extraordinarily useful contact and who would later offer me tremendous support and encouragement. On that day, though, I could not appreciate the gesture. Not yet.

Lovell and I then walked and walked, and neither of us said a word. Exhausted by the travel and the endless talks with Sid and Louie, all my hopes for seeing the girls dashed, I was beyond consoling. Just putting one foot in front of the other was a supreme struggle for me. It occurred to me that three more days like those I had just experienced in Sydney would kill me.

Lovell and I met my father and my uncle at the train station and we took the packed train east back to downtown Sydney. During the hour-long trip, I just held my father across seats and we both cried all the way. I was utterly drained. I suffered many low points during this whole ordeal, but this was one of the worst. That night I could not stop crying and I was violently ill several times.

Later, I would come back to that moment of betrayal by Suzie. I would replay her asking me to leave her house and I remember thinking: I never want my daughters, on the one hand, to know the right and true thing to do but, on the other, lack the courage to do it—even were their own mother to be the one opposing them. That, to me, is the truest testament to a parent. That when your son or daughter believes in something, they will stand up to you.

Suzie was not a child. She was twenty-five years old. And it hit me, and I gathered strength from it: I was the only one who stood for something different in that family. I would never bow to the bullying or be swayed—as Suzie was—by cultural or political or family influences. And even if I had to wait until the girls were sixteen years old to tell them all this, it mattered in some spiritual or psychological way for them to know that I did stand up to the intimidation.

* * *

There was one more card to play. The mother-to-mother appeal had failed miserably, so a father-to-father chat was the logical next step. My father decided on the afternoon of August 25 that he would not be able to live with himself if he had come all this way without speaking privately with Louie. I worried about such a meeting spiralling out of control, but my father assured me he would stay calm and see what information he could extract from Louie.

Dad wanted me to go with him, and, at first, the prospect literally sickened me, but I later agreed. Dad called Louie to say that he had arrived in Sydney that morning, and could they meet to discuss a resolution to their kids' problems? He tried to make it sound light, extending the hope that these two older, wiser gents might be able to unravel the mess their silly kids had got themselves into. . . .

We met Louie at the restaurant later that day. My father did an excellent job of keeping his cool, and Louie seemed more forthright about releasing details—though none that actually proved useful. Louie told my father that someone from the Canadian consulate in Beirut had gone to check on Hannah and Cedar and that one of Joe's armed men had shot the fellow in the leg. We took this as a veiled threat since we were quite certain that such action would have had consequences and that we would have been told. Also, if the consulate knew where the girls were, surely they would have told us? In any case, we later passed Louie's statement on to our lawyers and the Calgary Police Service—who could find no evidence of a shooting. They dismissed Louie's allegation as a scare tactic.

At one point I got upset and left the restaurant, in part because I really was emotional, in part because of a prearranged plan to give Dad and Louie some time alone.

I had noticed in the restaurant a man I knew, sitting with a female companion. I had also noticed the owner of the hair salon eyeing us. They were all eavesdropping, watching, and I went up to each one in turn to let them know that I knew exactly why they were there.

Now I went back to where Dad and Louie sat talking, and I stayed standing as I confronted my father-in-law. Gone were my weakness and frailty of the day before. I had had a good night's sleep—twelve hours. I'd had a massage at the hotel, swum in the pool, run on the treadmill and listened on headphones to heavy metal rock music (White Zombie, a '90s band that took its name from a horror film released in 1932). The hard-core songs got me going, plus I had my father with me. In any case, I felt a surge of strength and I gave Louie a blast.

I told him I was not going to have my daughters grow up in an environment that was so bullying and manipulative. I told him that his son was a coward hiding behind his daughters and using them to try to control me, and that I would never sign over custody of the girls to Joe or his family. I had just heard Louie tell my father that if I were simply to sign the custody papers and come to live in Australia, "I'll control him. I won't let him hurt her." Dad was having none of it.

If you want me to trust you, I told Louie, show me that you do, in fact, have some measure of control over your son. Get him to do the decent thing: Let me talk to the girls on the phone. It galled me so much that members of the family knew where Joe had my children and got to speak with them—but would not help me do the same. Did they believe that their rights superseded mine? I had loved these people, I had helped them, and I continued to be overwhelmed by their betrayal.

"Louie," I finally said, "you're never going to get it. You're not going to understand. We come from different cultures and you may not understand what I'm saying but I cannot sign these papers. I know it doesn't make sense to you because you think 'If you want to see your daughters again, just do it.' You have to understand that I am their only role model. I'm their mother and if I give in to the bullying by you and Joe and Sid and this family, I am teaching them that this is how the men in their lives are allowed—*allowed*—to treat them. I'd be condoning it, and I won't do it. And if it means it takes me years until I see those girls again, then I'll wait those years but I'm going to be somebody that they can be proud of. I will not bow down to this."

Louie did not say a word. He looked ashamed.

This second visit bore no relation to the first few. Gone was my beseeching and pleading manner, gone were the tears. I was now angry—really, really angry. Louie, too, was very different. The arrogance and dismissiveness I had observed in our last visit had vanished. He was clearly upset and he even cried at this meeting.

My father now stood up, put his arm around me, and we left the restaurant. We were standing on the street corner, waiting for the light to change, when Louie came out of the restaurant and asked me if I needed money. I just looked at him.

Louie Hawach's anguish was genuine. He did not want this conflagration, which was on the brink of becoming a very public and shameful humiliation. The Hawach family, long-time supporters of Our Lady of Lebanon Church as parishioners and donors, would have its name besmirched in the press, dragged through the mud, as a private family spat became fodder for the tabloids. Neither did Louie want Gladys—who did everything for him—babysitting Hannah and Cedar in Lebanon for who knows how long, not with their big house to run, the restaurant to manage. At the time of my separation from Joe, Gladys had come to Canada and she therefore missed the convocation ceremony when Pierre graduated from law school as well as Janet's twenty-first birthday. There were major milestones being marked in the Hawach family, and Gladys was missing them—because of Joe.

On busy Church Street in Parramatta, as cars and pedestrians passed us by, I looked into Louie Hawach's eyes. The best he could come up with in the course of three days were offers of food and now this offer of money, but nothing in the way of genuine help.

"All I want is my girls," I told him. "I don't need your money."

Louie looked sad, then he walked back inside.

* * *

Whether at the roundtable at Edy Dalton, the command post on Copperfield Gardens or the breakfast meetings of Team Australia in downtown Sydney, we were *always* discussing strategy. We all knew that only smart decision-making would get the girls back.

In those three days at Positano's, part of our aim was to feel out the family, to give them some breathing room should they choose to help. Often, if you push too hard too soon, the defences shoot up quicker and with more vigour. We were still hopeful and wanted to give Louie and his family an opportunity to do the right thing. Once it was established that the family would not be assisting us, we began to get a little more aggressive. Going public, talking to the media to put pressure on the Hawach family, was an option we had put on the back burner. Now we decided to turn up the heat.

Before leaving Calgary, we—my lawyers, Kelly Stewart and Richard Bennett, and me—were interviewed by Gwendolyn Richards of the *Calgary Herald*. This would break the story for the first time in the media. But before we dragged the Hawach family into the limelight, we needed to be sure that the family was not going to help us, and we asked Gwendolyn to delay until we had spoken with the family. After all the gamesmanship at Positano's, we gave her the green light. With the war between Hezbollah and Israel raging, the story ran on the front page of the *Herald* on August

25, under the headline "Mom Fears Snatched Children in Lebanon" and was subsequently picked up by many other newspapers across Canada. Family and friends not directly involved were shocked and upset to read the account.

The trip to Australia—for all the anguish it caused—at least laid to rest any hope that the Hawach family was really interested in helping us. The trip also answered one of the many legal questions that had been gnawing at me.

Throughout our visit, Team Australia met with Mark Whelan, our family lawyer in Sydney. In a conference call with our lawyers in Calgary and our investigative team, we shared information. I learned at that meeting about the implications of signing the proposed "parenting plan," the one much talked about by Joe, Sid and Louie but never delivered.

After many discussions with Mark Whelan and the Australian attorney general's office, I discovered that were I to sign the document, even under duress, it would still render null and void our Hague application and we would be stuck in the courts, possibly for years.

This is what prompted Mark to call signing the parenting plan "a deal with the devil." My Aussie lawyer pointed out that the Hawach family had been constantly shifting the ground under my feet for the last two months and to sign a parenting agreement that would supersede the Hague application would take away the one legal process (the Hague application) that was protecting the girls and me.

The bottom line was this: If I were to do everything that Joe demanded (including his impossible demand of dropping criminal charges against him), then he would be free to travel with the girls anywhere, leaving me with no avenue of recourse. How could I trust that he would bring them back to Australia if I did as he asked? I could not take the chance. I wrestled with the idea of just signing the document and getting the girls back into my arms, but when I realized there was no certainty of that happening, I opted out. Joe's track record on trust had been irreversibly tarnished.

* * *

The trip was not all disappointment and grief. My uncle David has connections in the hotel industry and he managed to get us accommodations on a "security floor"—with adjoining rooms. My father, my uncle, Lovell and I would have drinks in the evening and tell stories. Sometimes, the head of the Sydney PI agency would join us.

Lovell, especially, had a wealth of very funny tales to draw on from her days on the Calgary police force. I had heard many of them before, and I would egg her on. "Tell the one about. . ." I would say, and she was off. What a nice break those evenings were from the awful dramas at Positano's.

We would laugh, too, remembering the getups my father and uncle had resorted to as they observed Positano's. Dad—who never wears sunglasses—sported a pair of $5 mirror glasses, a baseball cap, socks and sandals, and a camera around his neck. David, meanwhile, wore a tweed blazer. They were not trying to make me laugh, but they did nonetheless.

It's a striking thing about ordeals like this: There is tension, but not ceaseless or unrelieved tension. Even back at the command post in Calgary, I would sometimes laugh uncontrollably while watching the American television comedy *The Office*—about the blissfully unaware regional manager (the actor and comedian Steve Carell) of, ironically enough, a paper distribution company (Dunder Mifflin) in Pennsylvania and his eccentric staff. *The Office* remains one of my favourite programs.

I had brought with me on this trip to Australia new pyjamas for the girls and a special gift—a red leather photo album full of notes and cards, virtual love letters from family and friends. I held out no great hope that we would see the girls, but if we did, this photo album would be the first thing I wanted them to see.

Child-find agencies, such as the Missing Children Society of Canada, had advised us that often the first question a recovered child asks of her mother or father is this one: Why didn't you look for me? I had brought with me, then, evidence of all our hard work, proof of a long, elaborate and dedicated search. The photo album would also remind the girls of their life before the abduction. Happy pictures, I was told, trigger good memories that may help to diminish any of the propaganda or lies that the abducting parent may have told them.

The photo album, the loves notes, the PJs: All these gifts would remain under wraps and undelivered. Hannah and Cedar would not be seeing them. Not now, not yet.

On August 27, we—my father, my uncle, Lovell and I—all headed back to Canada, back to the command post, with almost nothing to show for our efforts.

The girls' pictures, meanwhile, had been added to the Missing Children Society photo gallery. When I saw Hannah and Cedar up there on the web site beside "computerized age-enhanced" photos of other children who had been missing for many years, it was a very emotional moment for me. What an abhorrent thought. That there might come a day when part of our search would mean age-enhancing the girls' photos to make them more current.

The entire team now realized—forty-one days since Pierre Hawach had delivered his shattering news—that we needed to steel ourselves for a longer ordeal.

8

The Journal

I had taken with me on that flight to Australia an eight-by-eleven spiral notebook, with seventeen colour photographs of Hannah and Cedar laminated onto the cover. From the start, at every meeting—in the Edy Dalton board room, on planes, at the house on Copperfield, the hotel in Sydney—I had filled notebooks with the details of every phone call, every thought, every new lead. But I was forever losing the notebook and having to replace it, so Krista and Shauna made a collage of the girls' photos and stuck it on the cover of one of my notebooks—to ensure I would never forget or lose it. And from that point I never did. I still have it. That book became my companion on every subsequent trip, and it contains a partial record of my odyssey.

The entry for August 22, 2006, reads in part: "We landed today in Sydney with great anticipation . . . We landed and it was full spy vs. spy . . . We met with Louie. He is guarded but well-meaning. Sid, on the other hand, I detest."

The entry for August 27, 2006, begins: "My dearest angels: I am writing this letter in hopes that you will be home with me soon. At this point, I have moments of great strength and then other moments I want to go to sleep and not wake up. I do not know how to breathe. I do not know where to put my feet. I am scared to let my brain think because I miss you so much."

"May God protect you," the journal entry ends, "and watch over you both until I have you in my arms again."

For me, it was back to the command post, back to the phones and my computer, back to looking for two precious lost needles in a haystack. I called Dave on his cell phone just before we returned to Canada from Australia and he remembers pulling over on Sarcee Trail, a Calgary freeway, to talk to me. He remembers how despondent I was, so he threw me a lifeline. Dave told me that in many child abduction cases, investigators know neither the whereabouts of the children nor the kidnapper's intent. Joe, we knew, wanted custody and he wanted control. In Dave's eyes, this case presented the usual pain and heartache but some encouraging and unusual benefits as well. There was regular communication with the abducting parent, who was not attempting to remove the mother from the girls' life—though he was trying, without doubt, to manipulate said mother. The kids were thought to be safe (though we did worry a great deal about the fighting in Lebanon), being well looked after (Gladys was with them), and we at least knew what country they were in. Dave was putting a positive spin on things, and that helped a little.

I was not buying everything he said. It was unspeakable what Joe had done, but I did appreciate the fact that my daughters were with their father. For that much, I was, once more, thankful.

* * *

On several occasions that fall, I was part of conference-call conversations involving Sid Hawach and Richard Bennett at Edy Dalton. We were discussing the "parenting plan," but the subject of Lebanon also came up and I was unsettled by what Sid said. He painted pictures with his words about "all of the bodies on the ground over there. It's no place for two little girls. You're in a corrupt, lawless country. Over there, everything is for sale for a price. It's madness."

He and the other family members claimed to be concerned about the fate of the girls, but I had to wonder how hard they tried to prevent Joe from taking them there.

Sid and Louie Hawach in Sydney and Dave Chittick in Calgary had spoken several times on the telephone that fall, looking for a way out of the impasse. All these conversations were taped, and I listened to every one. I got a chance to admire Dave's smooth manner, how he always struck the right notes of sympathy and understanding without suffering foolishness. He is not your average investigator. (He has a degree in Canadian and European history and worked for seventeen years, including four as a claims investigator and seven as a fraud investigator, with the Workers' Compensation Board of Alberta.)

With Louie, Dave tried to put things in perspective, to reduce this whole calamity to its bare-bones essence. He explained that Joe and I separating was a mutual decision, just as Joe taking the kids on vacation to Australia was a mutual decision, but that Joe taking the girls to Lebanon was a unilateral decision. Louie snapped at this remark. He hated being told things and did not take kindly to a Hawach being criticized.

With Sid, Dave played the role of the good cop, taking the high road and offering sympathy. ("My job," Dave likes to say, "is part investigation, part social work, and part hand-holding.")

What Sid said about Lebanon continued to unsettle me. Hannah and Cedar were there, and I prayed they were not in the thick of it.

Another related thought occurred to me around this time. I had seen firsthand Joe's stubbornness and his violent streak. I also knew that even as little girls, Hannah and Cedar were both headstrong and independent. Joe loved his little girls and they adored him. But they were at an age when they would not question or challenge him yet. I knew for certain that as teenagers, they would stand up to him and confront him—in every way. And I knew what he was like when challenged. Though Joe had never harmed or threatened the girls, my fear was that if the months turned into years, the girls would get from their father what he as a husband had given to me.

* * *

By August 2006, thirty-seven-year-old Patrick Lalande was more than just a friend and co-worker and command-post regular. I had been working part-time for more than a year at a nearby golf course, where he was then assistant manager (he's now the food and beverage manager at the facility). I would talk a little about my marriage, and Patrick would patiently listen. This was in the spring of 2005.

He likened me then to a frightened and cornered wild animal—watchful, fearful, not inclined to trust. He would say little, offer no advice, just hear me out as I described my ruinous marriage and impending breakup. Often Patrick and I would be working together on a Saturday night wedding, and once the meal has been served there's not much to do until the wedding party leaves. He and I had time to talk, and, little by little, my story was told. In the months that followed, we became good friends and by August 1, 2006, Patrick had moved in with me. I knew it would happen eventually but the kidnapping had sped up everything and, in a way, forced our hands.

It was too soon, we both knew that. I did not want to make the same mistake twice—forming a new relationship when the old one had not been properly dealt with and put to rest. Yet the move made a lot of sense, not least practical sense. I had already been alone for the past couple of years in my marriage anyway. Patrick had watched me for a long time and supported me as I mourned my marriage. I never had that time after breaking up with Brad, and I think it made a difference. It seemed wrong to cut Patrick out of my life just because I had stronger feelings for him than friendship.

He is a good-natured man and is rarely in a bad mood. He has boyish good looks and, like all the Lalandes, a big dimple on his chin, and a medium build that served him well when he played football and hockey (baseball, he insists, is not a sport).

Patrick had studied the hotel and restaurant business at a special school in Montreal and had worked in Banff after coming out west in 1991. Those who work for him—he oversees a staff of eighty at the golf course—often remark on his professionalism and his sense of humour. When you have a staff that large, there is a dynamic you have to contend with, and he understands it.

When I first met Patrick, he was a smoker. I did not approve. I had never dated a smoker and was not about to start. Nor was I keen on the restaurant culture, which fosters a lifestyle of late nights, copious amounts of alcohol and long sleep-ins.

"I know you like the pub," I told him early on, "but there's no room for it in my life as a mother. So, no hard feelings but . . ."

"Give me a chance," he told me. Patrick has made some huge lifestyle changes. He has quit smoking—almost entirely, though our adventures in the Middle East would occasion a relapse. If Patrick needs incentive to quit, perhaps the fate of his parents offers some. His father, who had smoked in his youth then quit, died several years ago of lung cancer. His mother, a smoker to the end, would fight off cancer only to succumb to emphysema (in October 2007).

The abduction of the girls had left me extremely vulnerable, and Patrick was immediately and heavily involved in the command post. My brother Brendan and his girlfriend, Krista, were living at Copperfield and it seemed natural that Patrick, too, belonged there. Where would I be without him? My relationship with Patrick had a storm-tossed beginning, but I see calm waters ahead.

Patrick is smart and steady and open. He lets me be me, he makes me feel safe, he brings me flowers. An avid golfer himself, he does not mind my playing baseball, at all. Even if it's not a sport.

I can have a really bad day, be really down and I can say things that do not make a lot of sense, and it's not brought up again. Not everything is ticked off against you. Patrick does not keep score, and, after marriage to a scorekeeper, that is such a relief.

Patrick grew up in Montreal, and you can still hear the Québécois accent in his voice. He also works part-time recording French commercials and French telephone messages for corporations. Patrick's father used to call a certain airline just to hear his son say in his mother tongue that "This call is important to us, so please, stay on the line." Like many veterans of the restaurant industry, Patrick works long hours and drinks a lot of coffee. Caffeine is his fuel.

That fall, Patrick sold the house in Signal Hill he had shared with one of his best friends and put the money towards some of the major expenditures associated with regaining the girls. Had he not done that, I would almost surely have lost the house on Copperfield. "You didn't sign on for this," I told him during the early days of the command post, offering him an escape. "We can still be friends. Nobody in his right mind expects you to go through this with me." Indeed he did sign on, and in every way imaginable.

Patrick told me that he had already thought the matter through and that he considered the girls and me his family. He is a man who is utterly loyal to his friends and dedicated to people who need help. I had already seen at the golf course how open he was to his staff, how his counsel was both valued and wise. He got approached a lot. I was lucky to have him, as a friend and lover and ally.

* * *

Patrick never warmed to the house on Copperfield. He found it cramped, so one day in October we took a break from the command post and went looking for another place. We walked a golf course outside the city but the price of houses made us shudder. When Patrick sold his house, there were only about 400 houses on the market and buyers were lining up to pay the absurd asking prices. Patrick had cashed in, thinking he would rent for a while until the housing market cooled down. I had the same notion. I didn't want to forgo hiring a good lawyer in Lebanon, say, because I lacked cash. So selling Copperfield made sense. But where would we live?

By chance, we spotted a house in the country on a small acreage. The property had just come on the market and the owners were apparently anxious to sell. We drove out to see it, admired the playground. A few days later, an agent took us inside the house and we walked the land. I could see Hannah and Cedar being happy here, and that thought alone made me cry. The house needed some fixing, but not a lot. With a member of my family who treated the purchase as an investment, Patrick and I pooled our funds and bought the house.

Now we had to sell Copperfield. The agent handling the sale had organized a fund-raiser for us at the golf course. One weekend that September, a snow-pitch baseball tournament was likewise held to raise cash to fund the search for the girls (snow-pitch baseball is played with a rubber ball and every hitter starts with a two-ball, two-strike count to speed things up). The weather turned foul and my entire family descended on Copperfield for the weekend.

Patrick cancelled all the planned showings for the house, but it was too late to call off the Friday open house that was just ten minutes away. The house was not clean, there were maps of Lebanon on the wall, missing children posters up everywhere. The house was not exactly fluffed and prepped for sale, but that night, sell it we did.

On December 10, Patrick oversaw the move with the help of five burly First Nations guys. I was elsewhere, hunting for my daughters. Sooner or later they would come to a house they had never seen.

My mother stayed at our new house in the foothills for a long time—before and after Christmas. She was painting walls, wallpapering, cleaning and organizing. One day she saw two deer on the lawn and she could visualize the girls playing there, in the backyard. My mother is a strong person and she was just so positive. Her friends were lighting candles, holding vigils every night, and a church group had formed a prayer circle to encourage the safe return of Hannah and Cedar. My mother and other members of my family decorated the girls' room downstairs, they busied themselves preparing for the return of the girls and there was no hint of looking back. And if the Engdahls did now and again fear for the future, they never voiced that doubt.

Every day from my mother came some new call or e-mail with another story to inspire me and pick me up. These were notes expressing her love for me and the girls (Mom had always been very close with Hannah, especially), her support, her counsel. And I know this steady flow of messages helped my father when he and I were in Lebanon. My mother and father have this amazing connection after thirty-seven years of marriage. They do make fun of each other and each has annoying little habits that drive the other crazy, but they have a really special relationship. The whole time Dad and I were in the Middle East, my mother held it together for us.

About a year before, my mother had started to have health issues that increased in intensity when her own mother suffered a stroke. Mom was going through menopause and, for the first time in my reckoning, seemed to be struggling. When I realized on the morning of July 19, 2006, that I was going to have to call and tell my parents this excruciating news about the girls, I knew it would help my mother in her own battles. It would pull her out of her own funk because one of her children needed her to be a rock again—and that is pretty much what happened in the weeks and months that followed.

All that fall, I would get e-mails from strangers as well as from family and friends. "I don't know if you'll get this," the message would typically begin, "but I just want you to know that I'm so proud of you . . ." Such correspondents had no idea of the impact these notes had on me.

I, too, was a big believer in the power of intention, the power of positive thought, how willing something to happen can actually make it happen. From the day the command post was established, no one ever said "*If* the girls come home . . ." It was always *when.*

Likewise, another e-mail contact gave me hope. Her name is Jacqueline Pascarl and her story bore some resemblance to mine. This Australian woman's six-year-old daughter and nine-year-old son were kidnapped in 1992 by their father, a Malaysian prince, and taken back to his homeland. Efforts by Australian diplomats to have the children restored had failed, and the children were guarded twenty-fours a day in a royal compound. Only as adults, in 2006, were the son and daughter finally reunited with their mother.

The message from Jacqueline was optimistic. She said she had seen a picture of me in one of the newspapers, and she knew just by looking at my face that I would get my children back.

I felt this great power. I had stopped believing in coincidence: We had, throughout our campaign, observed a pattern. We would meet one person who would introduce us to another and that person would pass us on to someone else, and that person would end up figuring prominently in our campaign. The world seemed to be loving the girls home and I knew, just knew, that the right opportunity to get the girls would come along and that I would know enough to discard the wrong choice. What I felt was a powerful sense of destiny combined with a heady notion that I would, sooner or later, succeed.

My psychology textbooks talked about "locus of control," defined as "the extent to which an individual believes that . . . an outcome is contingent on [his or her] own behaviour or personal characteristics rather than being a function of external events not under [his or her] control or simply unpredictable." I had also purchased the movie *The Secret*—about shaping your destiny by your thoughts and intentions—and my family and friends all watched it together with me. Elite athletes have their own version of this phenomenon. After an amazing performance, a winning pitcher may say, "I was in the zone."

I was also feeling increasingly strong. I did not cry in meetings, for example. I wanted clear, rational thinking and I did not want those helping me making decisions just to make me feel better. It bothered me to see people getting upset or emotional. I could by no means make this claim in the summer of 2006, but by the end of that fall, I was comforting those around me more than they were comforting me.

* * *

After getting home from Australia, and at Patrick's urging, I decamped to Banff for a few days in early September to decompress. I needed a break from e-mails and reporters, from airports and the disappointment of all those bouts with my in-laws. From the mess my life had become.

It was while I was there that my father called me about a promising-looking e-mail that had just arrived. The girls had been spotted!

The last thing I did before leaving Australia was to get in touch with a reporter in hopes that a story might put a little positive pressure on the Hawach family. The Australian newspaper also ran the photo taken at the Calgary airport—a cheery close-up of me flanked by Hannah and Cedar. An Australian mental health worker who read the story sent me an e-mail to say that she had seen the girls in a north Lebanese village, and that they were happy and healthy. The woman had been in Lebanon as part of her training.

I cried when I heard the news, but I was also skeptical of the sighting. So much false information had come our way and I had learned to be steady and protect myself by not succumbing to highs and lows. Was this one more trail that led nowhere? Also odd was the health worker's statement that she was contacting us against the advice of the Australian Federal Police, whom she had at first alerted. Perhaps the police were checking her story for themselves, or going through "proper channels."

Thank God she did contact us. Theresa Garagan and John Hebert at the Calgary police force got in touch with her, and everything checked out. Now we were excited. For the first time since the girls had been taken, we knew where they were, and we knew that they were safe and well away from the fighting. On the other hand, what were we to do about it? Were they still there, or had they moved on?

I did, though, e-mail this woman to thank her. I told her that she was an angel and that knowing that Hannah and Cedar were well had lifted my spirits.

Her reply was very emotional. "I knew those girls were well mothered," she wrote, "and that their mother would never have abandoned them." This was the story circulating in the village to explain why these beautiful little girls were here alone with their father, who had no doubt planted the tale. The woman assured me that the girls were very happy and very much loved, as children are in the Lebanese culture. Her only worry was that the family who had hosted her had been asking questions about the girls, and, in the feudal system that still operates in Lebanon, might be vulnerable to retaliation from people sympathetic to Joe.

Finally, from this woman I learned of a conversation overheard in a village café suggesting that Joe and the girls were about to move closer to Beirut, specifically a village called Ghidras—where someone in the Hawach family owned a house. By now, I was starting to think that we needed some sort of presence in Lebanon, maybe a private investigator. I was told, though, that PIs are illegal in Lebanon so I put the thought on hold. Later we were told that hiring a PI through a lawyer has the blessing of authorities. We checked out a number of lawyers in Lebanon who all promised results but their payment requirements were more than suspect and we continued to be disappointed.

* * *

From the command post in Calgary, I went on working my borrowed laptops, virtually scouring Lebanon looking for the girls' whereabouts. Were they in school perhaps, and, if so, which one? I compiled a list of all the English schools in and around Beirut and sent them the following letter:

"Dear ———:

"The matter that I am contacting you on is a rather sensitive one. I am searching for my two daughters, Hannah (five) and Cedar (three) Hawach. We lived in Canada with their father, Joseph. He had taken the girls to visit his family in Australia during their summer holidays and abducted them into Lebanon about four days after the war started there on the 22nd of July through the Syrian border.

In Canada, parental abduction is a criminal offence and there are now charges against Joseph on Interpol, and the children are flagged with a yellow alert to be returned to Canada. While I would be comforted to know that they are attending your school (as I believe that he has enrolled them in school) I have been tentative in contacting any schools looking for them for fear of tipping Joseph off and him taking the girls further underground. My main reason for contact is to find out if the girls are attending your school and whether they are okay or not. I have attached some information regarding the children and photos as well as some contacts if you require further confirmation. I understand the necessity for due diligence and great care. I do have sole custody of the children here in Canada for what it is worth.

I am a mother who is desperate to find her two little girls. It has been over ninety days since I have seen them and I rely heavily on the good hearts of strangers around the world to help me and to help them.

Please find it in your heart to let me know if they are there . . ."

* * *

We tried every possible avenue, no matter how remote. In September, Patrick wrote the head of the Maronite Church of Canada at his headquarters in Montreal, and the bishop called back. I was in my psychology class when he called. He said he had been moved by what he called "the humanity of the situation." Two little girls in a war zone. He said he would try to speak with his counterpart in Lebanon.

At the end of that month, Patrick flew to Montreal to spend several hours with him. The bishop spoke English but French was his stronger suit, so Patrick laid out the whole story in great detail in French and left him with a thick dossier and all the important contact numbers.

A woman now living in England contacted me to say that she had been kidnapped as a girl by her father into Lebanon and she wanted to help me in any way she could. Elizabeth sent us maps of Lebanon and contacted a friend who works in Lebanese TV to see if that person had heard anything about Joe and the girls. Joe had apparently contacted a mutual friend of ours in Calgary (the friend immediately notified my family and the Missing Children Society of Canada) and said something about attending university in Beirut. Elizabeth tried to verify that claim through her friends in Lebanon.

For a time that fall, a prince of Dubai (I gather there are many) was involved in trying to retrieve Hannah and Cedar. A prominent restaurateur in Calgary—my friend Stephanie knows him, as do business associates of my father—put us in touch with the prince in hopes that he could help.

My father was in Dubai in early October and he and the prince met to discuss my situation. The prince and I also spoke on the telephone and corresponded by e-mail. Although he's a real gentleman, the prince's first thought was perhaps inspired by the long history of tribalism in the Middle East: an eye for an eye. "We'll just take Gladys," he said. "We'll trade her for the girls." When he realized that wasn't our style, he moved on to other possibilities.

The prince owns two houses in Lebanon, and he has useful contacts there. Many people throughout the Middle East want to move to Dubai because of its wealth and the business opportunities flourishing there. What if, the prince suggested, one of his staff were to approach Joe with a business proposal? Something that would tempt him—and the girls—into Dubai. The plan never really got off the ground. The prince's man did, indeed, locate Joe and they had a meeting but Joe was apparently very suspicious and wanted to know how this fellow got his name. The prince, meanwhile, heard the same rumour that we would later hear: Joe had acquired false papers and was heading with the girls into Syria.

* * *

The roundtable at Edy Dalton continued to meet, though not with the same frequency as we had in the summer. Kelly Stewart would get out a whiteboard and we would all brainstorm as she listed what had been accomplished so far and what still needed to be done. We worked well as a team, but sometimes we clashed.

Richard has some health problems (he's in the early stages of a chronic and disabling disease), which I blamed for our occasional tiffs. At one meeting, I brought up the case of an American woman (another left-behind parent whom the Missing Children Society had suggested as a useful and supportive contact), and he blew up at me. "What relevance does this have?" the old bear wanted to know. I left the room in tears, and when I returned I told everyone at the table, "I *will* be heard at these meetings!" I said it for my own sake as much as for anyone else's. Later, I hugged Richard and we moved on.

Dave Chittick would report on his most recent discussions with Louie or Sid Hawach about the "parenting plan." It had evolved from an Australia-only arrangement into something equally unacceptable—Hannah and Cedar living six months in Australia followed by six months in Canada. We began to wonder if Louie and Sid were somehow negotiating with Joe. Bison Security had hired private investigators in Australia and was looking to do the same in Lebanon. Detectives Theresa Garagan and John Hebert of the Calgary police would describe the most recent postings about our case on Interpol. (When Global TV came out to the house to conduct an interview late in August, I had no one around to support me. My parents had gone home, Patrick was at work, so Theresa very kindly agreed to come out and, metaphorically at least, hold my hand.) Richard Bennett was pursuing legal counsel in Australia and Lebanon, and he had also contacted various embassies in the Middle East. I had prepared a little "travel kit" for myself—just in case: photocopies of all our Canadian passports, Hannah's Canadian citizenship card (because she had an Australian passport), all the documents I would need for crossing borders.

Patrick and I reported to the roundtable on hits from our worldwide e-mail campaign and the flyer drop we did in Calgary neighbourhoods with a Lebanese population. (The flyer drop also covered the neighbourhood where Joe's girlfriend lived, and since she had the girls a great deal back in the summer, there was the chance that someone had seen the girls or Joe and had heard a telling comment.) Dave Chittick passed around copies of a Missing Children Society of Canada poster that was being widely disseminated in Canada and Australia. One plan discussed (though never implemented) was to circulate an Arabic version of the poster when, and if, Lebanese courts recognized my Canadian custody order. There were also fund-raising efforts under way to help with our rapidly escalating expenses and to lift the profile of the case in the media.

We all agreed that my trip to Australia was not the failure that it seemed. As a team, we always looked at what we had gained and what we knew now that we hadn't known before. We had, for one thing, a more complete picture of the family's involvement. We had also made important contacts and had many face-to-face meetings with our lawyers; we had a bigger understanding of the total picture. We also knew by then that we were definitely in for a long haul (even longer than first anticipated), so I could steel myself somewhat. We knew, too, that we needed to put the negotiations with the family on the back burner. We could focus our larger efforts elsewhere (without discarding the family negotiations as an option).

Dave Chittick and the lawyers on our team now wondered if a new round of legal, political and diplomatic pressure might be the next logical step to get the girls back. So we turned our attention to the courts and the embassies—in Canada, in Australia and, later, in Lebanon.

9

May It Please the Court

On Thursday, November 30, 2006, our lawyers in Sydney—Anthony Cheshire and Bill Madden—put Louie Hawach, Sid Hawach and Pierre Hawach on the stand in the Supreme Court of New South Wales. It is a desperation move to drag your in-laws into court, and I took no pleasure in engineering it or in watching it.

Essentially, I was suing Joe and Gladys Hawach for taking the girls to Lebanon and thereby causing me post-traumatic stress. International Social Services Canada (ISSC)—a non-profit agency that links social service agencies worldwide and helps to resolve individual and family problems resulting from the movement of people across borders—told me that such a move was unprecedented. My lawyers in Sydney likewise said they knew of no other case where in-laws became embroiled in this way: using medical trauma inflicted on a left-behind parent as a means of launching a suit against relatives of the abducting parent.

It was a lot of work. Dave Chittick and I spent countless hours creating a detailed evidence log for the benefit of our Australian lawyers. My hope was that this second trip to Australia would bear more fruit than the first one in August. If we were successful in court, my thinking went, we could nail down the location of Hannah and Cedar. Under oath, it was hoped (though I held out no great hope), that the Hawaches would be compelled to reveal what they knew of his whereabouts. At the very least, the lawsuit would ratchet up the pressure on the family, who were all paying a mighty price for Joe's indiscretions. Pressure the family, we thought, and the family might pressure Joe to come back from Lebanon.

There were two inches of snow on the ground and the temperature hovered around the freezing mark when we left Calgary. Sydney was sunny and a perfect 22 degrees. Both my mother and father had come with me this time, and we looked on from bench seats at the back of the court as all three Hawaches claimed not to know the current whereabouts of Joseph, his mother and the girls. In a grilling that went on for about ninety minutes, they seemed not to know much of anything at all.

As is common practice in courts in both Canada and Australia, each of the three men, in turn, was put on the witness stand. None was permitted to hear the testimony of the others until he had already testified himself (under oath, of course). Louie went first—while Sid and Pierre were excluded—and was permitted to speak in Arabic through an interpreter. (I'm speculating that Louie made the request just to add the cost of translation to my legal bill. His English is fine.)

Louie was apparently unable to remember even mundane matters, and lob-ball questions from Anthony Cheshire ("When is her [Gladys'] birthday?") got answers suggesting that a great fog had descended on him ("I don't remember."). It seemed to me that the judge (called an assistant registrar in this Australian court) and the interpreter were trying hard not to roll their eyes at some of these responses.

Asked, during a series of questions, if Joe was looking after the girls, if the girls were going to school, if Gladys had been to see Joe, Louie said he did not know. Asked five times in various ways, "Did Joseph tell you that he was with the children?" Louie Hawach wouldn't give a straight answer. When the lawyer for the Hawaches objected to Anthony Cheshire's persistent questioning, the registrar—clearly impatient—ruled that the question was in order, that it was not being answered, and that it would go on being asked until it was.

Questions to Louie about money elicited a range of responses. He said he knew nothing about a transfer from Amcan in May 2006 of $242,395 (Canadian) to Chamted Pty. Ltd.—a Hawach family account (forensic accounting undertaken by HSBC Bank Canada and research by my lawyers in Sydney determined that Chamted has a registered business address at the Hawaches' main residence.) Louie claimed to know nothing of Chamted (on the same witness stand, Pierre Hawach would later testify that he had heard "briefly" of Chamted Pty. Ltd.). Louie likewise said he knew nothing about a debit paid in June 2006 on my and Joe's American Express card to Positano's of $5,895, but he did agree that a debit on our Visa card to Positano's of $2,656 in August 2006 was partial repayment for a debt owed to him for support he had offered his son and Amcan. As for a $47,040 transfer from Amcan in June 2006 to an account in the name of E. (Louie's formal name is Elias) and G. (Gladys, presumably) Hawach, Louie said that this was partial repayment of a loan he had made to Joe. All of these transactions—from Joe to his father—occurred while Joe was still in Canada.

Questions about money were important for all kinds of reasons. Anthony Cheshire asked them, in part, to try to show that Joe was being helped financially by someone in Australia. Anthony reasoned before the court that day that Joe had to be using a bank somewhere in Lebanon, and wherever that bank was, Joe (and the girls, of course) might be close by. My lawyer was also having this fact read into the record: that Joe—after he had left Canada, and obviously without my consent—had continued to use credit cards in our names all over the place. In Dubai, in Melbourne, in Sydney. There were about eight reporters at the court, so my lawyer was making these points very much in a public way.

Sid took the stand next, after walking in with a swagger. The arrogance and the smiles soon faded. My lawyer would ask him questions, and Sid would object to their relevancy—until the assistant registrar had to remind this lawyer that the court had already ruled such questions relevant. My lawyer reminded Sid of what Sid had told me when we met in Sydney late in August—that Joe had been given legal advice on how to take Hannah and Cedar to Lebanon—and when asked if he had indeed said that, Sid responded by challenging my lawyer.

"How is this relevant?" Sid asked.

"Because I want to know who that barrister is," replied Anthony Cheshire.

"Well, you might want to know a lot of things," Sid came back, "but that's not what I came here to consent to—that's not what I consented to. And I'm not—I did—just to satisfy you, I did not tell her that, right?

I don't—I don't believe I told her that and in any event I wouldn't know which barrister he uses . . ." After repeated questions by my lawyer concerning the identity of said barrister, Sid finally told the court that he thought Joe's lawyer was a man named—Brian. He could muster no last name.

Sid offered the court a bizarre explanation for why no Hawaches in Sydney knew the whereabouts of Joe. Joe had apparently told him that two thugs had visited my husband in northern Lebanon and threatened him with harm—an allegation, Sid said, that was later corroborated by Sid's brother Jim, who lives nearby. According to Sid, Joe had told him that the thugs had been hired by me, a claim that my lawyer immediately rejected for the record. The Hawach family, it seemed, wanted the court to believe that Joe could not tell his own family of his location in Lebanon because he feared for his personal safety—because his wife in Canada had hired "thugs"! If one thinks about it for just a second, the claim unravels. If my "thugs" could find Joe, and therefore the girls, wouldn't you think that my thugs would also tell me their location (thereby sparing me this very costly lawsuit)?

Sid's most consistent objection to Anthony's queries was that they were not relevant to the whereabouts of Joe and Gladys. Sid also said—for the record, and contradicting what Joe and Louie had told me on numerous occasions—that he was *not* acting as Joe's lawyer. The court, though, did get a taste of Sid's ego. "I refuse to answer that question," he said at one point. "You're fishing, aren't you?" he replied to another. And my favourite from the day, "Don't insult my intelligence."

When called upon, the last to testify, Pierre was clearly nervous, and it seemed to me that he tried to answer as best he could without divulging much.

Part of the court process was what is called "discovery of documents," which involves an exchange of information between the two sides. Among the information we did get were two cell phone numbers in Lebanon. When I later called one of them, Janet Hawach answered. It seemed clear to me that she, too, was likely involved. She apparently knew where the girls were and had travelled there to see them, which infuriated me. Joe's sister had access to Hannah and Cedar, but their own mother did not!

When we supplied the second cell number to the Canadian embassy in Lebanon, they apparently tried it and got Gladys on the phone and when questions were asked about the girls, a male voice in the room (Joe's, I'm guessing) could be heard saying, "Hang up the phone! Hang up the phone!" I had thought, naively, that if I could just speak with Gladys, mother to mother, I could reason with her. For the same reason, I had bombarded Janet and Suzie with e-mails all that fall, begging them to let their mother know that there were options, that she could drop the girls off at the Canadian embassy. I told Janet and Suzie that I'd had worrisome dreams about Gladys (who has a heart condition and is dangerously overweight), warning them that the stress of this ordeal was hard on her, too. I never gave up hope, never stopped sending messages. I continued to believe that one of them would hit home.

Neither cell phone number worked after that first try. The Hawach family, as far as I could see, had done just enough to satisfy the requirements in the discovery process, then proceeded to shut things down.

Outside the court, clutching in my left arm a sheaf of missing children posters with Hannah's and Cedar's photos prominently displayed, I told journalists that the loss of the girls was an absolute torture, but that I was also now feeling a firm resolve and determination. There were tears, of course. My voice trembled as I spoke. But another side of me was revealing itself, the side that was now urging me to grit my teeth and clench my fists and do what had to be done to get my girls back. "I will find them," I said outside the court. "I know without a doubt in my mind that the girls are coming home."

* * *

While we were in Sydney, I hooked up with Sherry, a Canadian friend living there who introduced me to friends of hers—several former soldiers who had served in elite Aussie and Kiwi regiments and their boss, a man I knew only as Frank. We had by this time hired a private investigator in Lebanon, but I had grown frustrated by him.

In the beginning, Muhammad was not slow to produce results. He had provided quite a bit of information on local schools, the residences owned by Joe's uncle and the shrine that Gladys would frequent (a bronze statue of Our Lady of Lebanon draws many pilgrims to the village of Harissa, twenty kilometres north of Beirut). But it appeared that Muhammad had hit a wall and it was getting dangerous to have him so blatantly watching Joe. People at the resort eventually came to know that he was watching. Given his substantial fee, I wanted a detailed daily report of the comings and goings of Joe and the girls and their schedule. Did the girls, for example, leave the resort Monday to Friday every morning at the same time for school and return at the same time? What school? Where? We were not getting this information and were therefore open to other possibilities.

I was impressed by Frank's references, his credentials and his knowledge of human psychology. I felt comfortable hiring him to assemble a team of men to do surveillance on Joe and the girls. This was not something they normally did. It was hardly charity on their part (I agreed to pay their travel and accommodation costs), but, on the other hand, they would not have the insurance coverage normally available had a government or corporation hired them.

At that point, none of us had any idea how the story would pan out. It wasn't as if we had tried the courts and now we would let the military boys enter the picture. It was all a fluid process. Right up to the point where I got the girls back, I never lost faith that justice would prevail and that the Lebanese courts would deliver my daughters to me. Still, I knew this much: Had I stayed home and hoped for Interpol to do the job, Hannah and Cedar would still be a world away.

In our hotel room in Sydney, and with Frank's help, we filmed a video. In the short clip, I am seen offering my assurances to Hannah and Cedar that these men are my friends and would do them no harm. Should the girls and I not be able to hook up right away, the thought was that the video—along with some photos and comfort items from home (a familiar book and a stuffed animal)—would reassure them and calm them down. The video was never used, though it was used against us, as you will see.

* * *

Much against the wishes of my family—who worried for my safety—I now set my sights on Lebanon. Dad, meanwhile, had flown to Adelaide to interview an expert in computer surveillance who claimed to have evidence that Joe had false passports and was planning a move to Syria. Was this genuine? Or one more false lead?

What an awful time this was for all of us. We were so emotional, so tired, but sleep would not come. And the thought occurred to me: Why am I everywhere but Lebanon? I was going to where the girls were.

I was tempted to fly right then from Sydney to Beirut, but cost, in part, stayed my hand. It was cheaper for me to fly back to Canada, gather myself (and all the necessary documents) and fly from there. In Calgary, my longtime friend Stephanie, and her partner, Jay, went to their bank and withdrew $10,000 (U.S.) so I would have cash in hand for this next stage. Family and friends kept on giving of their time and their money and their spirit. It made me feel like I was not alone, and it had the same effect on my family. If I felt strong, it was because I had all these people holding me up.

By December 13, I was in Lebanon. The past five months had been a kind of training period. Now the real marathon was about to begin.

10

The Jewel of the Middle East

There were many black moments in my whole ordeal. One of the worst occurred on July 21, 2006. It was the day that Hannah and Cedar were due back in Calgary after their "vacation" in Australia. Flight 228, Sydney to Honolulu to Calgary. We knew they would not be on that flight (not after Pierre Hawach's gut-wrenching call a few nights before), but we felt duty-bound to go to the airport and wait. Wait we did. There was a sense of futility and hopelessness about that act—watching all those passengers being greeted at the luggage carousel. It was especially painful to watch mothers hugging their young children.

While we sat at the Calgary airport, Israeli guns were pounding Beirut and Hezbollah positions all over Lebanon, but mostly in the south. Based in Lebanon, Hezbollah (also known as the Party of God) is a political and paramilitary organization. Depending on your point of view, it is either a resistance movement or a terrorist organization. Hezbollah's cross-border rocket attacks on Israel brought the Israeli army and airforce into Lebanon and over the course of thirty-three days of fighting almost 1,200 Lebanese were killed, almost 4,500 were wounded, and a million people were displaced. Among those who lost their lives was a Canadian major—Paeta Hess-von Kruedener—who was manning a United Nations observer post in southern Lebanon when it was hit by an Israeli bomb on

July 24. Three other unarmed observers, from Austria, China and Finland, were also killed in that incident.

Israel was trying to force Hezbollah's leader, Hassan Nasrallah, to return two kidnapped Israeli soldiers and to stop the rocket attacks. (Using a network of guerrilla posts and underground passageways, Hezbollah had rained down on northern Israeli cities some 4,000 rockets, mainly Katyushas.)

"If the soldiers are not returned," warned Dan Halutz, the Israeli army's chief of staff, "we will turn Lebanon's clock back twenty years." The damage to houses and apartment buildings, the Beirut airport, the Beirut-Damascus highway and the country's entire infrastructure—roads, sewers, waterlines, electrical lines—was enormous and would require billions of dollars to repair.

By early December, Israeli troops had withdrawn from Lebanon, but fresh evidence of the war remained. Bridges bombed out, buildings scarred with bullet holes, tanks and troop carriers on the streets. My father and I were met at the airport on December 13 by a Canadian consulate official who briefed us on the latest developments in Lebanon. I remember going over makeshift bridges fashioned from scaffolding and planks, while in Hezbollah-controlled sections of Beirut we saw barricades in the street and military checkpoints everywhere. Somewhere in this country ravaged by war were my little girls and the man they called "Daddy." I felt bound and determined. In the early hours and days of the drama foisted on me, Joe was the active one. I felt passive. Now at least, I thought, the distance between the girls and me was diminishing. I was closer, and that was something.

Lebanon is a tiny mountainous country on the Mediterranean Sea, long known as "the jewel of the Middle East" (for its dazzling beauty), "the Paris of the Middle East" (for its nightlife and popularity with tourists) and "the Switzerland of the Middle East" (for its reputation as a banking centre). I remember sitting on the terrace restaurant of our hotel enjoying the warm sun (it was 20 degrees that day) and admiring the blue skies and palm trees.

"You can understand," Dave Chittick observed, "why people fight over this little part of the world."

But where in this country that was forever being destroyed and rebuilt were Hannah and Cedar? Were they safe from the fighting? Were they under armed guard, as Joe had said?

It seemed like the cards were stacked in his favour. I spoke only a few words of Arabic and had only a basic grasp of Lebanese geography.

On the other hand, I now had allies. Many allies. We had been busy back at the Calgary command post. Some of the people who would play vital roles in what followed had come to us and volunteered their help. Between the headlines and the web site, we were not hard to find. Others, we found ourselves and put on the payroll.

There was the man we called the General, who had commanded men in the Lebanese army and had extraordinary connections. When told of our predicament, a friend of the Engdahl family doing business in Dubai told my father, "I think I've got someone who can help you," and he put us in touch with the man we would hereafter call the General. He became the paymaster at the top of a pyramid now forming, taking the considerable sums we paid him ($40,000 would constitute one instalment, and there were several) to hire others down the line. In Lebanon, everyone does a little business on the side. The General spoke in riddles, stayed calm when the stress was threatening to unravel us, and he and his entourage of cohorts seemed to have walked straight out of a John Le Carré spy novel. A naturally happy and generous man, brilliant and funny, the General was "a fixer." Were this episode in my life ever made into a movie, the General told me, he had some advice for the director: Al Pacino should play the role of the General. That's how he was. He tried to make everything light and funny.

There was the Lebanese private investigator. Forever sitting in his car, smoking cigarettes with one arm out the window, eyes shaded by sunglasses, this man proved in the end to be a great friend to our cause. Though Muhammad drove us mad by how painstakingly slowly he acquired information, he would, as you will see, provide a vital piece of information that led us directly to Hannah and Cedar. He came under pressure—from his superiors, I would guess—to ascertain further information so he began pushing a little harder on the resort manager and the guards. In the process, he made himself known, but what else was he to do? The other side now seemed to know who he was and what he was doing. We know this because people on the other side, we learned, had threatened him. Some days I wondered: What was the point of hiring this pricey spy to watch the other side when the other side was watching him? Were we being taken for a ride? Maybe Joe's spies were taking Joe for a ride. This was the lunatic world I had entered.

With Muhammad effectively neutralized, five other men (Frank's team) now entered the picture in mid-December, men from outside the Middle East but who were familiar with the rules of the game as it is played there. There were two security contractors who had previously served in an Australian army parachute regiment: Brian and another man. There were three New Zealanders who had previously served in one of that country's parachute regiments: David, and two other men. Brian and David were the ones I spoke to; the rest I hardly knew. Red-haired and fair-skinned, Brian—or Charlie, as we sometimes called him—had a young family of his own, and he felt a powerful connection to my plight. He used a ribald Aussie expression to describe our Lebanese PI: "We saw your local guy in the parking lot the other day. He stood out like a dog's balls." On the whole, though, I found Brian to be very reserved, very professional and unemotional, and last I heard he was taking courses in physiotherapy at university and weaning himself out of the security line. As for David, I understand that he is still in the business and would rather keep a low profile.

I did not know precisely what sort of work they had done in the Middle East, but some of it involved assessment. They were like many men I know, with pictures of family in their wallets. Never, at any time in Lebanon, were they armed, and I shook my head later when I saw them described in media reports as "mercenaries," with all that the word implies. I know only that these men were all fathers, and they were all kind.

I had flown into Lebanon with my father on Wednesday, December 13, stopping beforehand in Dubai to meet for the first time with the General. On arrival at the airport in Beirut, Dad and I were met by Canadian embassy officials and we checked into the Hotel Alexandre in Achrefieh, the Christian section on the east side of the city.

My first fear was that I would be spotted on the street and Joe would discover we were in Lebanon. I was quite sure the Hawach family had no idea I was there but I did worry about the consequences if they found out. Joe's uncle Pierre (a brother of Gladys) has a high rank in the Hezbollah-

and Syria-backed Orange Party, and with those connections it would have been easy for Joe and the girls to slip into Syria, a much bigger country, with almost no chance of our finding them. That was a constant threat from the Hawach family: "You keep pressuring him and he'll go to Syria." The world I lived in then seemed flat, and the risk was great that the ship my daughters sailed on might tip over the edge and fall into a great void.

I stayed off the street and out of sight—just quick dashes from a car to the Canadian embassy or to meet with Lebanese lawyers and court officials, and always I wore a handkerchief on my head and sunglasses.

* * *

A Canadian court is quite similar to an Australian court, since both are rooted in British common law. A Lebanese court, I would learn, is another creature altogether.

But my task in all three courts (Canadian, Australian, Lebanese) was the same: Remind the courts in all three territories that in this case, the mother—not the father—had legal guardianship of the girls. This was a fairly straightforward process in Canadian and Australian courts. But in Lebanon it was a great deal more complicated, especially because in that country the rights of the father typically far supersede those of the mother. Would Lebanese courts recognize Canadian documents establishing me as the sole guardian? In many Arab countries, Sharia (or Islamic) law rules, and men have absolute custody of their children. In most Arab countries, the courts pay scant attention to the rights of women, especially non-Muslim women.

But in Lebanon, I knew, I had a chance: There was apparently a precedent there for mothers winning custody battles, and our lawyers expressed optimism. On the other hand, Lebanese courts operate at three separate levels—the criminal, the civil and the religious. In my case, the civil court was the most important, but there was a real chance that all three courts could become involved (that would turn out to be the case). One court literally led to the other. We started in civil court, trying to win recognition for my Canadian custody orders. The Lebanese criminal court got involved when Joe's lawyers attempted to have criminal charges (kidnapping) pressed against me. Finally, the religious court got involved when Joe managed to introduce a custody ruling by a Maronite bishop. Could we win this battle in all three? How does one go about finding a good lawyer in an Arabic-speaking country (one that happens to have been just recently at war)? Finally, how would Joe react to litigation on what had become his home turf?

For my first seven days in Lebanon, the plan being discussed was this: Serve Joe with legal notice (by regular postings in Lebanese newspapers) and, at the same time, have the courts put Hannah and Cedar in secure, third-party custody. This was a concept that we had discussed for some time back at the roundtable in Calgary. Third-party custody, I would learn, is common practice in many countries: If one parent is going to be served papers regarding a divorce or custody proceedings, it is only logical that the children be taken into protective custody. If one parent feels cheated by the custody arrangement, that parent might be tempted to flee with the children. Third-party custody eliminates that possibility. There was no precedent for this in Lebanon, but the hope was that the police and justice system—if they agreed with our proposal—could keep the girls secure and comfortable while the courts made their decisions. The risk was that if Joe felt the grip of the courts, he might flee with the girls to Syria.

Our criminal lawyer in Lebanon, Antoine El Kozah, was a great find. In times of distress, a good lawyer is always a necessity, and in Lebanon we faced the risk that if we did not nail down Antoine's services, the other side would. Our great good fortune was to find Antoine, and to secure his services in time. We also had working for us the Canadian embassy in Lebanon, the Canadian government itself and, to a certain extent, the Lebanese government.

Judy Saba, the cultural psychologist to whom I had been introduced through the Catholic Maronite church in Sydney, corresponded with me regularly and sent a letter to the religious court in Lebanon in support of me. On many nights—she in Sydney and I in Calgary—Judy would counsel me on the telephone and keep my spirits up. She was struck by my love for the Lebanese community, and how I was not turning this abduction into a cultural issue. We both knew that what Joe did had nothing to do with his Lebanese blood and that parental kidnapping occurs in every culture and in every class.

In her office at the church in Sydney, Judy bravely posted the missing children poster of Hannah and Cedar—despite pressure on her to take it down. Judy trains the Australian police to understand Arabic cultural sensitivities, which made her a tremendous ally to my cause. What she told anyone who would listen was that there was only one side—that of the children—and they belonged back in Canada with their mother.

After Judy had put up the poster, a woman walked in, saw the photo of Joe and said, "Uh-oh. I went to school with him. He is the most stubborn person I have ever met."

* * *

I had not asked to be parachuted into a spy novel, but clearly I was in one. And just as clearly, someone was listening. The General would later inform us that the other side was eavesdropping on our Lebanese lawyer's telephone conversations. How did the General know? He just did. And who comprised "the other side"? That was unclear.

Dave Chittick had it right. In Lebanon, all three of us—my father, Dave and myself—felt the same way. Like Alice, we had fallen down the rabbit hole. A Lebanese friend in Sydney had given me this advice: In Lebanon, trust no one. Louie Hawach refused to go with me to Lebanon (when I asked him during that first trip to Australia), no doubt for many reasons, but at least in part, he said, because he feared for his own safety there (a claim I very much doubt). Sid Hawach had told the court in Sydney that the only advice he ever gave Joe was this: "You're living in a corrupt country, you're to trust nobody, and be careful. Be very, very careful."

Sid had warned Dave on the phone that I was not even to think about going into Lebanon, which he described as a lawless place ravaged by war. People coming to Lebanon often hire their own security—armed men to drive them around and protect them. At first, "trust no one" seemed like sage advice. Yet whenever we questioned a Lebanese person in Lebanon, especially a Lebanese man, they were profoundly insulted. This strange dynamic governed us our whole time in Lebanon. It would have been naive to trust everyone, yet we were painfully aware that showing distrust conveyed a stinging rebuke. We were walking a tightrope.

I'm not sure what lay behind this hypersensitivity to simple questions.

For me, it was perfectly normal to make inquiries upon meeting someone for the first time—someone I might have to rely upon for a very serious matter. How is it that asking a question can be perceived as a deep insult? Is it a kind of self-righteousness? A poetic sensibility? Were the Lebanese truly insulted, or is that how they played it? I never did understand. I once sent an e-mail to one of our Lebanese lawyers, thanking him profusely for his good work, noting that this concluded our business, and how much did we owe him? The word *business* provoked a furious response. This was no business deal, he roared back. It was about morality and humanity. Part of the problem is the English language, part of it is that e-mails are so easily misinterpreted. In any case, with the Lebanese of Lebanon, we literally and figuratively did not speak the same language.

Thankfully, the General and his brother George (an active member of the General's squad of cohorts) were always sensitive to my point of view, and I never felt I had to tiptoe around them. We did trust them; we had to. We trusted them with our lives.

11

So Close, Yet So Far

While in Lebanon, I kept a diary of meetings and events and impressions. The log, I think, captures the escalating tensions as each day bled into another, all pointing towards one decision. The right one promised to give me back Hannah and Cedar; the wrong one might prove disastrous.

* * *

Thursday, December 14. The Canadian embassy occupies the first floor of the Coolrite Building at 43 Jal El Dib Highway in Beirut. Outside the all-white building, set ten feet out, are massive concrete blocks and barriers—meant, I presume, to create a security perimeter.

We meet with the rest of the Canadian embassy staff to be updated on the situation within Lebanon. My father and I are impressed with the team at the embassy. They are incredibly helpful and make every possible effort to locate my children. In Canada, I had signed over to the Canadian embassy in Beirut power of attorney so they could act as guardians of the girls should they ever be turned in to the embassy. This was before I went to Lebanon and realized how impossible that scenario actually was. Embassy staff are very young but also incredibly intelligent and forthcoming with information and assistance. We learn that a lovely local woman who has been working with the Canadian embassy for close to a decade had seen the girls while visiting a friend at the al-Rimal Resort on the Bay of Jounieh, 15 kilometres north of Beirut.

This is not the first time we have heard the al-Rimal Resort mentioned as a possible location for Joe and the girls. Before even coming to Lebanon, back on September 19, 2006, we had received an e-mail from German tourists who had been staying at the al-Rimal (and who had been sent, by relations in the United States, our poster on the Internet of Hannah and Cedar). The tourists were certain they had seen the girls at the resort two weeks beforehand, and they said so in their all-caps message. At the time, it seemed like just another Elvis sighting. The note seemed so matter-of-fact, almost cold, and we had treated it as "misinformation"—a term I had come to use a lot.

The subject on the e-mail message read, "We saw your children," and the text read precisely as follows: "YOUR KIDS WERE SEEN WITH THEIR FATHER AT RIMAL BEACH RESORT, ZOUK MOSBEH, TWO WEEKS AGO." The sender of the e-mail (who, for whatever reason, forwarded the message to several others) did not respond to our inquiries—perhaps because he or she had no desire to get involved in our case. On the Internet, I was able to obtain a telephone number for one of the other e-mail recipients, and Dave Chittick did speak to this man's wife a couple of times. The man was elderly and, at the time, in hospital. Based on these conversations, Dave learned that they were of German descent with family in both Germany and Lebanon. They claimed to be unfamiliar with the sender of the e-mail and unable to provide any confirmation of the sighting.

We also know—thanks to our Lebanese PI, Muhammad—that Joe's uncle, Pierre Raffoul, owns a unit at the al-Rimal Resort. Muhammad discovered this by doing a land title search. When this information came to us in mid-November, the September e-mail from the German tourists suddenly took on a whole new importance.

When we meet with Fawzi Metni, the Canadian embassy lawyer, on December 14, we have good reason to believe the girls are at the resort. We get from Fawzi his thoughts on how to proceed in the courts and the name of a civil lawyer he can recommend. We then have an in-depth and lengthy meeting at Monsieur Metni's office with Roger Abiaad—the civil

My parents, Jim and Judy Engdahl. This shot was taken in Saskatoon shortly after Hannah was born.

Me with my brothers *(left to right)*: Doug, Brendan and Adam Engdahl.

Sharing a happy moment with Dad at my wedding in 1999. Behind are Rayanne, my maid of honour, and Joe's sisters.

Me, dancing with Louie Hawach, Joe's father, at the wedding.

Celebrating our marriage with Pierre, Joe's brother, and my maid of honour, Rayanne.

Joe on our wedding day, flanked by his mother, father and paternal grandparents.

Louie with Hannah at Positano's restaurant in Parramatta, a West Sydney suburb.

Me, Hannah and Joe in Australia.

My daughters, Cedar *(left)* and Hannah, on a plane to Saskatoon in the summer of 2006. We were visiting my family in Saskatchewan before the girls left on their holiday to Australia with Joe.

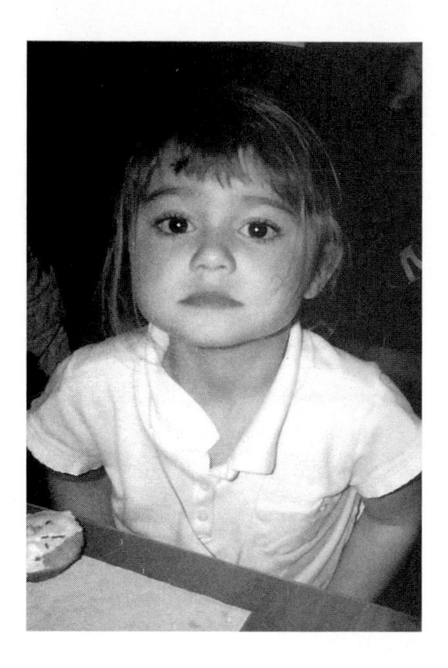

Left: Hannah at preschool.
Below: Hannah in the spring of 2006—before the girls left for Australia.

Above and *below:* Cedar in 2007.

Cedar and Hannah celebrating Christmas in Alberta, in December 2007.

lawyer recommended. The latter sits and listens to the entire story of the abduction, as told by my father and me. We have come prepared with all necessary documents—affidavits, police files, transcripts of recorded testimony. All Canadian embassy officials except for the ambassador are present at this meeting.

Later this same day, my father and I return to our hotel and receive via the Internet photos of Hannah and Cedar, photos taken by Brian within the al-Rimal Resort. Brian sent the photos to Frank (then in the Middle East on business) who, in turn, sent them on to us. I am thrilled to see the images: The girls are well, they are safe, and we know exactly where they are. This is the first I have seen of them in six months. What a jolt of emotion and pleasure to see photos of the girls biking at the resort. I am in tears at the sight—but I am also upset that they have been biking without helmets. Still, I feel one step closer to them. In good traffic, they are a 30-minute drive away. I say to myself, "Yes. Finally. This is concrete."

Hannah and Cedar are indeed, Brian reports, staying with their father at the resort on the Mediterranean Sea. There are no armed guards (despite Louie's claim back in Sydney that a Canadian embassy official had gone to do a welfare check on the girls and been shot in the leg for his trouble). Brian surmises, based on their daily routine, that the girls are going to school and after school they play in the resort's courtyard with two French-Arab girls being tended to by a Filipino nanny.

On the phone, Frank gives me an update on the progress that Brian has made but there is no actual assessment yet from my security team. They confirm the apartment number where the girls and Joseph are residing. They also tell us that the apartment we initially thought was theirs (through Muhammad's surveillance) is being occupied by another family.

* * *

Friday, December 15. My father and I go back to the Canadian embassy to get further updates (or to feel like we are). We don't know what else to do. The Canadian embassy is pushing for Interpol and the Sécurité Générale (the Lebanese border and immigration police) to act on the Canadian warrants for Joseph's arrest. Earlier, the embassy gave both organizations the apartment number that we had initially received from Muhammad along with the information that the girls had been sighted at the al-Rimal Resort. The embassy asked Interpol to investigate.

I am less than enthusiastic about Interpol. When Interpol finally attached a red flag to Joe's name and a yellow flag to the girls' names, Dave Chittick called the RCMP to learn more about the status of Interpol in Lebanon. He learned that the nearest RCMP liaison officer was in Jordan, and one of Dave's RCMP connections contacted him.

"What's your opinion of Interpol in Lebanon?" was the question.

"Don't bother" came the reply. Bison Security people worry that Interpol in Lebanon is corrupt, and that contacting them may actually hinder our effort.

Interpol may sound high and mighty, and I have the sense that it is a fantastic organization at the international level. But in Lebanon, as elsewhere in the world, Interpol is no more than local police acting on tips, sometimes from around the corner, sometimes from half a dozen time zones away. And those local police may be clean, they may be corrupt, they may be indifferent. Interpol apparently told Canadian embassy officials the following tale: They had raided said apartment and found it under construction and uninhabitable. Brian's own surveillance told him a family had been living in the apartment the whole time he was there. This confirms our suspicions that some police working for Interpol in Lebanon are on the take and not offering accurate information. This is a huge wake-up call for me. To this point, I have seriously thought that Interpol could, at any moment, reconnect me with my children. What a fool I was to think that.

That same day, my father and I return to Roger Abiaad's office to confirm that we want to retain him and to further our discussions of the civil process in the Lebanese justice system. He is friendly (his son went to university in Montreal, so there's a Canadian connection) and his retainer seems fair. We do not feel like we are being taken for a ride. He asks me if I have a boyfriend. ("You don't have to answer," he says, "if you don't want to.") "Yes," I tell him. "I'm in a relationship."

Roger knew the answer. He was just testing whether I would tell the truth. It may be that traditional Lebanese culture frowns upon a woman forming a new relationship so soon after a failed marriage and Roger wanted to see if I would "own up to it."

But his next question is mind-boggling—considering that he sat for two hours in our briefing meeting the day before. He asks me who my father is. He had thought Dad was my boyfriend! What had he been listening to the day before? How much more did he not understand due to the language barrier? Roger is a lovely man, but there are some things he just did not get. He actually advised me to go home for Christmas! I told him I would not be getting on one more plane without my children. The thought of being so close, then going home, was unbearable.

I continue suffering from back spasms—no doubt caused by stress and aggravated by the long flight. In the evening, I seek relief at the hotel from a masseuse. She is in her early forties, fit and blonde, as many are blonde in northern Lebanon. She, too, has a tale of woe to tell. She was married to an awful man who took their three sons to live with him and forbade any contact with her. He told them that he would not fund their university schooling if any of them visited their mother. She would take a cake over when one son marked a birthday and call out to him to come to the window of their apartment so she could at least wish him happy birthday, but her husband refused to allow even this. Now that they are older and finished school, her sons have reconnected with her. Her former husband, meanwhile, is now dying of cancer and his medical treatments are eating up what money he still possesses. When I tell her that I am in a somewhat similar situation (cut off from my children), she has this advice: "If you get your children, you run as fast as you can, trust nobody, and you get the hell out of Lebanon."

(A Lebanese woman from Calgary would later e-mail me virtually the same counsel. "Run, Melissa, run!" she said in her note.)

Later that night, Frank calls to tell me that Brian has been joined by the remainder of his surveillance team and after discussing the matter with them, Frank proposes a way of getting the girls back. The plan, to be executed on Tuesday, December 19, is to storm Joe's room at 6 a.m., subdue him, take the girls and drop them off at our hotel.

"What was being discussed," as Dave Chittick would later put it, "was—to use the language of the press—a commando-style operation." Frank's plan involves no weapons or overt violence but the potential for such, I think, is too great. No doubt the men know submission holds that could quickly subdue even a big man like Joe, but what if that goes wrong?

Surely witnessing their father being attacked would traumatize the girls—the reassuring video notwithstanding? There was too much potential for Joe and/or Gladys to be hurt and the girls to be scarred by the memory. I let Frank talk, then tell him I'll get back to him the following day. The more I ponder his suggestion, the less sense it makes and the more extreme it seems given the circumstances.

At 3 a.m. that night, Dave Chittick—after flying from Calgary to Frankfurt to Beirut—arrives at the Hotel Alexandre and we huddle as soon as he gets to the hotel. Dad and I bring him up to speed on our various meetings with embassy officials and the lawyers. At dawn, we all retire to our beds.

I told Dave (only a day before he left for Beirut) about the surveillance team we have in the resort. For a time, I didn't tell him—and that was a departure. I told Dave everything, but not this. I guess I felt that because I had not committed to anything yet, it was all right to withhold this information. Finally it weighed too heavily on me. The five-man surveillance team at that point was just that—a surveillance team. But I knew the potential was there for them to do much more for me and I needed Dave to know that before he left his family at Christmastime and got on a plane for the Middle East. I wanted him to know everything that was on the table. Yet I worried that he would not come, given the Missing Children Society's position on the type of action that I was contemplating. I would have sorely missed him. I knew my father and I would need his counsel. We were too close now and I was really worried about becoming too emotional to make decisions.

Thankfully Dave opted to come anyway (he knew me pretty well by that time) and had more faith in my judgement than even I did.

* * *

Saturday, December 16. The embassy is closed. We use the time for research on the Internet, to answer e-mails, fill in family, and recharge our batteries.

* * *

Sunday, December 17. Dad, Dave and I reconvene at noon and, for the next eight hours, discuss and debate what's to be done in the days ahead. What about deploying the men we've hired? Unlike me, Dad is all for using the men. "Let's let these guys do what they're capable of doing," is his advice. He is almost apoplectic that I am disinclined to use them in the way they have been trained and in the way that they themselves are strongly advising. With the men set to leave in a matter of days, my father warns that I am passing up the best, and maybe the only, chance to reacquire the girls. These are men with years of expertise and training and experience, and their boss has won over my father to his way of thinking. I feel pressure from both sides. My only thought is to delay. I need more time.

* * *

Monday, December 18. The three of us—Dad, Dave Chittick and I—meet for breakfast at 5:30 a.m. More discussion, more debate, no decision.

We take Dave to the Canadian embassy to meet with officials there at 9:30 a.m. The three of us start discussing the situation again. What to do? How to proceed? When?

We meet with consular secretaries Amanda Strohan and Mirna Karam. They tell us what help is available through the Canadian mission in Beirut. It is decided that Fawzi Metni will petition Sayed Mirza, the Lebanese prosecutor general (he is the equivalent of Canada's justice minister) for a meeting to discuss the case. It's important to know the prosecutor general's political leanings and alliances, and we learn what these are from Amanda and Mirna. Monsieur Metni is to be instructed to inform the prosecutor general that, to date, we have only made discreet inquiries about how the legal process in Lebanon might be used to get the girls back. My fear is that if Joe discovers either my presence or this strategy, he will flee with the children. Given that risk, I want the attorney general to have the girls taken into protective third-party custody while I pursue my other goal—to have my Canadian custody orders ratified in Lebanese court.

Frank continues to call. He says I have to decide what I am going to do because the guys have done their job on the surveillance and assessment side. I am wanting to hear something from my lawyers or the embassy that will help me make this decision. The pressure continues to mount. Frank and I exchanged messages last night, when he called me "arrogant" for rejecting his plan in favour of something far simpler.

"Your plan," I told him, "is more about your guys being home for Christmas. It doesn't make sense otherwise." In hindsight, I could have been more tactful. "Who the hell do you think you are?" was pretty much his response. I told him I would get back to him the following day.

With Dad and me in tow, Dave Chittick meets the aforementioned Roger Abiaad for the first time. Dave is not impressed. And I want facts, if not results. What I am getting from Roger strikes me as flowery double-talk.

Leaving Roger's office, I get yet another phone call from Frank. More pressure to do it his way. Dad tells Frank to call back in an hour. This whole day I am tense and introverted. Where is the sign? I need some omen, some direction, something to help me make this critical decision.

We all go back to the Canadian embassy where Dave and Dad and I continue to mull over what to do. Dad has not changed his position: Use the men. There is huge tension between us. He has done so much to help me and I am ignoring his heartfelt advice. Dave, though, takes my side. "You tell me," he says to me very quietly in Amanda's office that afternoon, "and I will stand by what you decide."

In the whole kidnapping ordeal, this is the critical moment of decision. Dave knows, as I do, that storming Joe's room could land us all in very serious trouble—charged with break and enter, forcible confinement, kidnapping. There would also be a huge risk of physical harm to Joe and the men and psychological damage to Hannah and Cedar. The kids would have been dropped off at the hotel, the security guys would be gone, and, as Dave later put it, "We wouldn't have seen noon" before getting arrested.

I know, from Brian's surveillance, that there are no men with machine guns guarding the girls. Had there been, we would have pulled back. No question.

And I examine my greatest fear: that the girls will believe what Joe has been telling them—"Your mother left you." Even if, I think, I get them only for a day, and hold them, Hannah, at least, will know how far I have come for them—no matter what happens later.

What is indisputable is that I cannot live with the "commando" option. It is not my style at all, and I felt certain that while this option ensures an exit strategy for the men, it is not the best plan as far as the girls are concerned. It's far too extreme. I struggle with my decision but in the end it is dead simple. I will trust my own judgement.

Once I decisively reject Frank's plan, I feel a huge change come over me. I laugh. I smile. Dave Chittick later remarks on it, says he has never seen anything like it, so quick and dramatic is the shift. I feel certain that a giant puzzle is now clicking into place and all my doubts are banished.

There is an Aussie expression, "Pull your head in." It means, "Get a grip." I am confident that I have, indeed, pulled my head in. I am dead certain that there is either a better way to get the girls back or now is not the time.

There, in the Canadian embassy in Beirut, Frank calls from somewhere in the Middle East, where he's on assignment. I give him my answer. No. You can send your guys home.

* * *

Tuesday, December 19. The phone rings at 5:30 a.m. I curse aloud. "Those guys," I think, "have gone against my wishes. They've grabbed the girls!" But no, it's Brian calling to say that they have discussed it among themselves. One of the men has gone home, but Brian and David and two others (I never did learn their names) are going to stay another day. What a great gift. Two of the men would later pay a very steep price for that gift, but we did not know that at the time.

Then Brian, who must have thought more about an idea I had broached the day before, asks, "Are you sure, Mel? Are you sure you don't want to just take your kids, and we'll just drive you?"

"Absolutely!" I reply. Brian says that he is willing to try doing things my way.

"But won't your boss be ticked?" I ask Brian. Frank, I well know, has other ideas. What we have in mind cannot be found in any mercenaries' handbook.

"Don't worry," Brian replies. "We've all spoken about it. This is the right thing. We know in our hearts we can't leave here without doing something to help you in some way."

Dad, Dave Chittick and I meet for breakfast at 6:00 a.m. It is decided that Dave and my father will go to the embassy. Dad, especially, still holds out hope that the Lebanese courts will help us. But I've been looking for a third option—neither taking the girls by force nor waiting interminably for the Lebanese legal system to recognize my rights. That can come later.

"Can you guys sneak me into the resort?" I asked Brian the day before. Now we're following through.

I decide to go to the al-Rimal Resort with the men around midday. I enter the resort, hidden under blankets in the back of Brian's van, its windows tinted black to further hide its human cargo. Like many resorts on the Mediterranean Sea, the al-Rimal is a pristine white compound, one you enter and exit only after meeting the approval of a guard who lifts and lowers the wooden security barrier.

Rooms at the al-Rimal Resort are comfortable but spare, with metal bunk beds and a tiny half-kitchen leading out to a living room. For some Lebanese, this is home year-round. And since this is December, it is cold inside and out. Gas heaters do a poor job of keeping us warm in Brian's apartment.

It makes little sense for a Westerner like Brian to be visiting Lebanon in winter, so he has casually mentioned to a security guard that he is awaiting a rendezvous with his wife. From Brian's second-storey balcony, I can see the beach and the fishing wharf, and the little park down below with a swimming pool. Palm trees offer shade to the landscaped rolling lawns, and rabbits in cages have been set near the playground to amuse the children.

My children. In the afternoon, peeking through plants so as not to be seen, I see Hannah and Cedar playing on their third-storey balcony. I can see them, hear them, but I cannot—dare not—go to them and touch them. I cry as I watch and, in a low voice, I talk to them. I remark on how long their hair has become and how both are tanned nut-brown from all that Mediterranean sun. No surprise, they look a little unkempt.

There is laundry about—Gladys has apparently been there earlier in the week. I look on with horror as Cedar climbs up on something that puts her over the height of the railing, then she steps back down again and I breathe a sigh of relief.

Later, I watch Hannah and Cedar come out to the courtyard and play with two other girls, the latter attended to by the nanny—just as

Brian has said is their routine. The four girls are collecting sticks. For one bittersweet hour, I watch them.

"They seem so fit, so active," remarks Brian, who has been watching them for a week and observed, correctly, that they run a lot and play hard. I feel a surge of pride, and of longing to hold them.

It seems absurd not to just take them. One, I am their mother. Two, the girls are not Lebanese citizens. (Joe has tried that route but was denied when he did not follow procedure. We know this, courtesy of the Lebanese ambassador to Canada, because the Sécurité Générale in Lebanon tipped off Foreign Affairs Canada that Joe had applied and then withdrawn his application. The stumbling block for him was that he would have had to return to the girls' places of birth—Canada and Australia—to make each application.)

That afternoon, I get a call from Dave Chittick. Amanda Strohan has updated them on the meeting between Fawzi Metni and the prosecutor general. The news is not good. The Lebanese prosecutor general, Sayed Mirza, has refused to comply with our request that the girls be placed in secure third-party custody. And he was certainly not about to recognize our Canadian court orders for custody, not until the Lebanese courts had decided. So the possibility of simply approaching Joe with a sheaf of court documents and some uniformed Lebanese policemen is off the table.

Following on discussions with my father and Dave Chittick, Fawzi Metni had also broached another subject in his meeting with Sayed Mirza. What if I were to call the girls and they came to me? The prosecutor general advised the embassy lawyer that I could face kidnapping charges.

Back at the Canadian embassy, we huddle yet again. The prosecutor general's warning about kidnapping charges has taken the air out of any plan to just call the girls and whisk them away. "Joe might file a complaint," Fawzi tells Dave Chittick. There is also the problem of passports for the girls. We have emergency passports for Hannah and Cedar, but Joe has their entry stamps in his own passports for the girls. Without those entry stamps, our emergency passports are useless. I cannot see a clear-cut path, nor can anyone else.

Christmas is close now, and Brian and the others are heading home the next day to be with their families. The general feeling is that this is no time for them to be away from their loved ones, a sentiment I share and fully support. Brian thinks chances are slim that Joe would move the girls over Christmas, though I still worry about him fleeing into Syria or elsewhere. The five men say their goodbyes in front of the Canadian embassy. One of them is visibly distraught at my anguish, but all of them are in a state. To a man, they feel they are witnessing a great injustice, one they seem powerless to right.

"We'll find a way through this," Brian tells me before leaving. "I'll come back, I'll continue the surveillance. You haven't seen the last of me."

That night, I break down completely, and all the emotion that I have been keeping in check for so long pours out of me. The dam bursts. This is, without question, the worst night of my life. "My guys," as I have come to call them, are leaving.

At that point, I trusted no one but myself to do what was best for Hannah and Cedar. Frank had proposed storming the apartment, which I had refused, so I didn't entirely trust his judgement. But there are degrees of trust, and given all the deception I had faced to that point, I did put some of my trust in these men. They did not seem fazed or bothered that I had turned down Frank's recommendation, but they did seem eager to find something I could agree to. More importantly, they represented what seemed my best shot at getting the girls back. And now the men were heading home.

Dave Chittick is likewise soon to be on a plane headed for home. I have seen the girls and will have walked away from them *because Joe might file a complaint.* That phrase keeps coming back to me. I am heartbroken, but I also feel cowardly, almost ashamed. I had my chance and I blew it. I am sure I have made the biggest mistake of my life and that there will be no second chance.

(In hindsight, I can see that I didn't truly fathom the danger that such "a complaint" potentially posed—or perhaps I didn't want to. Dave would later underline to me that a criminal complaint to the Lebanese police could have led to a criminal investigation, possibly criminal charges, a trial and even jail. Dave's very real concern was that the decision to go ahead with reacquiring the girls could have had life-altering consequences for me, my father and all the men involved.)

One crushing question weighs on me. If Joe takes the girls and leaves the resort for good or, worse, ferrets them into Syria (as I was warned repeatedly he might), would I be able to live with myself for failing them? I sob all night, sleep not a minute. It is a horrible night as well for everyone back home. They all know how close I now am to the girls, but I might as well be back in Calgary for all the good it is doing me.

* * *

Wednesday, December 20. Another early morning phone call from Brian. "Look," he says, "none us got our flights out as we wanted. We're here for the day. Are you sure you don't want us to sneak you in and drive you out? This is the last chance before we're all gone."

Brian warns me not to get my hopes up, to be prepared in the event the kids are not home today but gone for the holidays. If the chance doesn't present itself today, then we agree to reassess in the new year. As for all the snags in my plan—the risk of a kidnapping charge, the problem of no exit stamps—we will cross those bridges when we come to them.

It's decided. That afternoon, five days from Christmas of 2006, I will get a second chance.

I feel like I have been given a gift from God. The phone call is so unexpected. This is my sign, my omen. Sherry, my Canadian friend who lives in Sydney, calls me on my cell phone right after the call from Brian, and I tell her about the emotion of the night before, how I thought I had made this huge mistake and how I have been given this second chance.

It feels so right and I get this feeling that tells me I am on the right path. Sherry is still worried for me but she is happy as well that I have stuck to my guns and am doing what I think is right. Before I left Canada, I had confided in Lovell my worry about all the decisions I would have to make in Lebanon. Her words now come back to me: "Your mother's heart will know, Mel. Have faith."

12

"Hannie? Hannie?"

One minute I was in a John Le Carré spy novel; the next a Quentin Tarantino movie. At about 7 a.m., a couple of hours after Brian's phone call, we went back into the resort. All of us—Brian, David and their two compatriots—waited in Brian's room for nine long hours (what Tarantino's characters would call "downtime" before a hit or a heist) watching old shows on television.

We waited in that cramped, cold unit, me sometimes inexplicably hot and pacing, other times wearing either a blanket or David's jacket—a black, waterproof bomber jacket with innumerable pockets—to try to stay warm, all of us looking on while an episode of *Diff'rent Strokes* played out on the screen. This program from the 1970s and 1980s asked viewers to believe that a rich white widower in a Manhattan condominium had adopted two kids from a poor neighbourhood in Harlem. David would also try to take my mind off things by having me solve riddles or play puzzles, and often the strategy worked.

Dad, meanwhile, was at the Canadian embassy in Beirut, imploring them to take us in were I to succeed in getting Hannah and Cedar. The answer was not exactly no, but neither were arms extended—for many reasons. Embassy staff had been through a lot during Hezbollah's war with Israel as Canadian citizens scrambled to escape, and, contrary to Hollywood movies, the embassy is no sanctuary. If I did manage to get the girls but Lebanese police thought that a crime had been committed as the girls passed from their father's hands to their mother's, they would have entered the resort. If we got the girls, what then? The embassy option looked closed.

My father now had his own decision to make. "Do we bring the girls here and create an international incident?" he asked himself. Or should he call the General, the Lebanese national he had met in Dubai and who had offered to help us? My father called the General, who now agreed to come. In three days, he would be in Lebanon.

Back at the resort, the four men and I lunched on fettucine, pizza and chicken. It was a long, nervous day.

On the other hand, I felt like I was back on track. There had been other times on this long, terrible journey when I would feel an almost electric calm—perhaps a new "helper" had contacted me or some valuable new information had come my way. I would be in the shower and be overwhelmed by the feeling that I was getting closer, that my decisions were the right ones. Sitting in that room was one of those times. I knew with certainty that if Hannah and Cedar did not show up that day it would be for a reason and that by the grace of God I would be shown another way.

At 4:35 p.m., my long wait ended. One of the guys had been checking to see if Joe's rented vehicle, a brand-new black four-wheel-drive Suburban, had returned. Now the news came that he had arrived, that Joe was at that moment hauling groceries in both arms and Hannah was struggling to close the back door of his vehicle.

Almost immediately, I watched as Hannah and Cedar came out to the little park at one end of the resort. They were wearing mismatched track suits, their hair was unbrushed, and they looked dishevelled, as they had the day before. They were walking along the paved pathway towards the metal slides and swings, with their two friends and the nanny. I knew Joe's habits: He would be lying down on the bed, napping or watching TV.

I started to think aloud: What if Joe sees us from the balcony? What can we do to slow things down? Let the air out of his tires? Pour olive oil on the staircase? Jam the elevator? Or, I said, clearly trying to deflate the stress with humour, we could get Wile E. Coyote to drop an anvil on Joe's head from a great height. This is what comes of years spent with conniving younger brothers who liked to put soap on toothbrushes as part of their bag of tricks. But there would be no tricks this day. No guns ablazin' either.

As David and I walked up the spiral staircase to the sprawling park, we could have been a couple. Just a couple enjoying a walk under the trees as the sun began to set on the Bay of Jounieh. I was calm and focused and clear. We walked slowly, steadily, towards the girls, still some distance away. We took our time, even let fifteen minutes pass. The men had told me: Stay calm. No running, no sudden movement. Nothing, they said, creates alarm like sudden movement.

We had decided that David, not Brian, should walk with me. The nanny, a single woman, had earlier chatted with Brian and asked him if he knew of any unattached men in the area. Our thinking was that the nanny might be more easily distracted by seeing a new face. Brian, with his red hair and Irish ancestry, was the only fair-skinned one on our crew. All the others were dark and could have passed for Lebanese, and all wore red-white-and-green shirts with the Lebanese flag at the front.

Now we were five feet from the nanny. I wore nothing on my head, my blonde hair flying in the sea breeze. When the girls saw me, I wanted to look the same as ever. My focus was on Hannah, all on Hannah. Cedar, I knew, would follow her.

"Hannie? Hannie?" I called out.

She had this glazed look on her face. I was out of context, and six months had passed since she'd seen me. This was her mother all right, no question. But what was she doing here? Then, pure instinct kicked in.

"Momma! Momma!" she cried out, and she ran straight at me and launched herself up into my outstretched arms. Now Hannah was in my arms, and Cedar was right behind her, calling my name. "Momma! Momma!" I was not worried that Joe would hear or respond: His unit was far enough away, his window would have been closed in any case due to the cold, and besides, the Lebanese word for *mother* is close enough to the English. Little girls calling to their mothers was an everyday sound.

I said, loud enough for the nanny to hear and hoping she would be confused by this, "Hey, guys. You're going to come with me for a bit. We'll talk to Daddy after."

I was carrying Hannah, not Cedar. Everything was casual. We walked on, and at one point I wanted to switch the girls, put Hannah down to pick

Cedar up. Hannah, of course, was the heavier. But first I asked her permission. Things were going smoothly and I did not want a scene.

"Yeah, yeah," said Hannah.

In lifting Cedar, my cell phone slid from my hip and hit the ground. Nice and easy, David picked it up, and the four of us walked away. We were so casual. The nanny did nothing, said nothing, just stood there. No doubt Joe had made no mention of their circumstances—on the run, in hiding. It must have seemed to this woman a perfectly ordinary thing. The girls' mother had come along and taken them for a walk. What could be more natural than that?

There were no tears. The kids were as good as gold, and they were so happy to see me. It had been 174 days since I last hugged them. Everything we had planned for, had hoped for, all just came together at once. It was surreal, just surreal.

What I did not feel was any sense of victory or satisfaction that I had accomplished what Sid Hawach had said I could not. It was all so tentative, and at any moment, I knew, any feeling of a job well done—never mind the girls—could be snatched from me. Was it the Catholic in me? (Pride goeth before a fall.) Or was it the ball player in me? (It ain't over 'til it's over.) I would not be over-confident.

Now the speed of the film picked up—a lot. One of the guys had stayed in the stairwell, acting as lookout. Carrying Cedar and with Hannah holding my free hand, I and the two men now ran down the staircase, piled into the van with the tinted windows, and the van headed for the resort's exit. The girls and I were tucked in low behind the bench seat. After the guard lifted the long wooden security arm at the gate, we pulled away, but the guys in the back of the van eyed the gatehouse as we drove off. Guards had come out, which they do not normally do, and one was writing down our licence plate. The alarm had sounded.

Two minutes later, as per the plan, some of us transferred into a sedan, a regular car without tinted windows. I took to the back seat between Hannah and Cedar, scrunched down low so no one could see us, while Brian and one of the guys got in the front. It seemed like we drove a long time, close to an hour, in gridlocked traffic. Police cars would scream past with their sirens blaring, and we would all freeze.

In the car, the girls and I played. I had water for them, and books, and old routines to call upon. For as long as we would remain in the Middle East (and I had no idea then how long that might be), I wanted things to stay light for the girls. Whatever strains and stresses I would feel in days to come, I did not want them sharing my burden. We sang songs and played "I Spy" (a perfect choice, given the circumstances). I had a digital camera with me, so I could show Hannah and Cedar shots of Bumpy and Nannie (my parents), my brothers and their Canadian cousins. I had my iPod, too, so the girls could take turns listening to music. Finally, at dark, we arrived at our destination—an out of the way and empty parking lot at the Hotel Alexandre. Right behind us, another car, a big Suburban with tinted windows, pulled up immediately. In it was the General's brother, George, and Dad.

Dad was crying, hugging the girls and everyone there. But I was all business. I wanted out of that parking lot, fast.

"We're good?" Brian asked me.

"We're good," I replied, and the girls, Dad and I all piled into the Suburban—but not before Brian took a picture of the girls and me. Proof that they had done what I had asked them to do.

There had been no Blackhawk helicopter, no guns drawn, no commandos in fatigues, no grand escape. But our departure had not gone unnoticed, as later that day we would discover. Brian and David and their families would suffer terribly for the role they played in helping me, and I dearly wish it were otherwise. Till the day I die, I will be beholden to all five men but especially to those two fathers—who acted out of a father's instinct and no other. Four men had put themselves at great risk to help me regain the girls. Yet it was very much their decision and I was convinced—no matter what happened—they would never hold it against me.

Brian and David would have shared in my joy that day as I rode in the car and played with my daughters. Now it was Joe's turn to be "king-hit," to be taken by surprise. The Hawach family never saw me coming, never dreamed I would parachute into their war-torn homeland, find the girls and simply call them to me. Getting them was literally a walk in the park.

At that moment, even without knowing when and how we would ever get home, there was nowhere in the world that I would rather have been than in that vehicle with Hannah and Cedar. I felt such pure joy in being with them, but I also felt almost sick to my stomach knowing that their father was now feeling the same pain and loss I had felt. I would not wish that on anyone.

13

"What Have You Done?"

The first night with the girls was heaven. We slept three to a bed in a small, elegant cliffside villa up in the mountains overlooking Beirut, an hour-and-a-half drive from the city. Right away I could sense how high we were—the height of land and the fact of winter meant that it was much colder here than in the city below. The area was beautiful, a tourist destination with an ocean view, the sort of place that in different circumstances I would want to explore. It was so nice to cuddle with my daughters, to smell their hair, to watch them brush their teeth before bedtime, to bathe them—all the old rituals.

That night we called members of my family, and the excitement on the line from Saskatoon and Calgary was palpable. My mother got to talk to the girls, but Hannah would only talk baby-talk. I expected that. My own studies in psychology, plus information from the Missing Children Society, had warned me to expect it: The regression was caused by the huge transition as well as her confusion as she struggled to absorb what had transpired. After just a few weeks with me, Hannah was speaking normally. As for the trauma she had endured by being told that her mother had left her, this, I felt sure, would be resolved by time and psychological counselling. Cedar, meanwhile, seemed fine and spoke as normal. More importantly, we were reunited once again, and I could hold my girls.

Our unit in the villa featured an expansive living room, a half-kitchen, a huge hallway, a sizeable bathroom and two large bedrooms—one for Dad, one for the girls and me. The marble floors were cold but the owner, who was very sweet to us, brought in rugs to make the floors warmer and set up a heater. The power kept going out and we would light the gas burners on the stove to try to stay warm. The owner would call up to the room and ask if he could take the kids and Dad and me out for an afternoon meal of fried chicken (we declined, of course) or he would bring chocolates and cookies up to the room for the girls.

The area around us was strikingly beautiful—blue skies and mountains and cliffs. You could see Beirut from up there, where locals would refer to the city as "downstairs."

George had left his passport at the hotel office (sparing us having to register with our own passports), and the General would do the same at the next hotel. The law in Lebanon requires that hotel guests leave their own passports at the desk, but these brothers had called in all sorts of favours to enable this ducking of normal procedure in the interests of our security. No one, I was certain, knew where we were. I felt safe.

What I did not know then, and would only realize much later on, was that the General, his brother and virtually all those in Lebanon who would help us were members of the Masonic Lodge, or Freemasons as they are called. Here was one more stroke of luck in our favour. Claiming to be one of the oldest organizations in the world and thought to have millions of members, the Masonic Lodge is a fraternal and benevolent association. A long-time family friend in Canada—himself a Mason and the man who put us in touch with the General—is adamant that the latter would never have taken on the job, one that consumed him and his family and put them all at great risk, had the Freemason connection not been there.

I have known this family friend since I was two years old. His family and my family have vacationed together. He says that in North America, the lodge is a more casual organization. But in the Middle East and in Africa, he later told me, "The Masonic Lodge is much much more. Where you can't trust institutions that we in Canada take for granted, where Justice is on the take, where there's no security, the lodge is maybe the one thing you can trust."

* * *

Just before we went to bed that night, we got a call from Brian. He was in a departure lounge at Beirut airport, about to board a plane for home. He asked how we were, then he wished us luck and we wished him the same. Everything sounded fine.

The next morning, Dad got another call from Brian. He was wishing us a merry Christmas, making small talk. That was odd. Brian is not one for small talk, so Dad knew instinctively there was a problem. Besides, he had boarded his plane last night, had he not? A little while later we got a text message from Brian. Same thing. Merry Christmas. I said to Dad, "No more. There's something wrong here."

Then we got a call from Frank, head of the security agency that employed Brian and David and all the others. It seemed that three of the men (including the one who had left December 19) were safely out of the country. But the evening before, just minutes before their plane was to take off, Brian, the Australian, and the New Zealander, David, were seized by police. They were apparently under suspicion of kidnapping minors and, if convicted, faced three years in jail.

The Lebanese police had found on Brian's computer the video we had done. They had either themselves released it to the media or given it to the Hawach family, who released it. (Dave Chittick was surprised to learn that the computer had not been tossed. "I'm no commando," he told me later, "but it's a thousand-dollar laptop. It goes into the harbour and away you go." I was likewise astonished. I remember Brian driving the car in the minutes after reacquiring the girls, and he was telling David on the phone to chuck everything—the computer, the camera, my cell phone. It's a mystery to me why that message was not heeded. Maybe the message was garbled or never received.)

The video simply showed me addressing a message to the girls—telling them how much I loved them and missed them, how these men were my friends and Nanna's friends, how new books and Christmas presents were waiting for them at home in Canada. "Be very good," I tell them. "Be very brave and go very quietly. I will see you soon. I love you."

The press were soon calling this "an explosive video" and a tool of mercenaries now facing a long prison term for allegedly kidnapping the kidnapped children. More fuel for the headline writers. We had determined, on our side, to say nothing publicly about all this until Hannah and Cedar and I were out of Lebanon and on home ground. The other side, though (Joe's Lebanese lawyer), seemed more than happy to pronounce in the media.

At first, Frank was nice. "How can you help?" he asked me.

"What can I do? What do you want me to do?" I replied.

What he wanted was for me to go to the police and surrender myself and the girls into Lebanese custody while the courts decided our fates. I had not had even twenty-four hours with my daughters, it had taken me five months, three long journeys and a small fortune to retrieve them, and now I was being asked to voluntarily give them up? I knew that if Joe thought I was still in Lebanon, he would try to exploit his Hezbollah connections and have David and Brian used in a trade. He gets the girls back, the guys go free. The solution, as far as I could see, was to make Joe think that the girls and I were already out of Lebanon, and not to give up what I had fought so long and hard to get: Hannah and Cedar.

"You don't *know* what Brian and I discussed," I told Frank.

"Do something," Frank said, "or I'll do whatever I need to do. I'll turn you in and tell them everything I can. I'll trade you for those two guys in there." The threat was clear.

I knew this was too soon. I also knew that Brian and David would be angry if they thought everything they had done was for naught. Brian, I would learn later, had apparently told the Lebanese police that we had an escape plan and were long gone. He knew what would happen if the police discovered otherwise: All of us (the girls, Dad and me) would be used as a bargaining chip. In that scenario, David and Brian would get their freedom at our expense. Brian would have known that I would never surrender Hannah and Cedar. No, if there was to be a negotiation with the Lebanese police, best do it on the other side of the Lebanese border. I was not going off to any Lebanese police station any time soon. My conversation with Frank ended there.

We had spoken again to Patrick and my family and they were shell-shocked by the media explosion that had occurred. They tried to downplay it, but it was becoming clear that this was getting big. Not what I wanted—at all. How were we going to get out of Lebanon quietly when our pictures were about to be plastered all over the newspapers? Dad's cell phone kept ringing, phone call after phone call. I was doing a lot of pacing, and Dad was like me: mind racing, trying to form an actual picture of what was going on with the limited information that was coming in.

Then Frank called back. By this time I was hyperventilating. All civility had left Frank, and his language took a decidedly blue turn.

"Let me call some people," I told him. "I need to find out what can be done. I need some time here." Then I hung up.

Frank called back, irate that I had hung up on him. He warned me to call him back every fifteen minutes, "or I'll turn you in."

I did not see how he could possibly do that, but we did call him back as asked, offering him what information we could, my father now doing the talking. But along with panic came fear: During one call, Frank—whose manner had shifted again, the charm once more turned on—was asking me questions when he already knew the answers. I had the feeling he was stalling, keeping me on the line, perhaps so my location could be revealed. Again, I hung up the phone but in such a way as to make him think we had been cut off.

I would call him, apologize, say I got cut off, and repeat the procedure if I felt he was dangling me on the line. I was sure he had the technology to enable triangulation (in which the location of the cell tower is matched with that of the two callers).

Meanwhile, Frank had also been calling our new house in Calgary, going at Patrick as he had been going at me. Patrick had been very much involved in helping me and supporting me for the past five months, and he would go to roundtable meetings when he could. On the other hand, he himself felt somewhat on the periphery. He had a full-time job, the bills needed to be paid, the house looked after. But from the moment I got Hannah and Cedar back, a little hurricane began to blow, and Patrick was pulled right into the eye of that storm.

* * *

Frank called Patrick in the middle of the night. The first chat was civil. He said, "There's still time for Melissa and Joe to work things out. If Joe withdraws his complaint, the guys go home."

There were a lot of calls that week. Patrick would be up most of the night. He would sleep from 5 a.m. to 7 a.m., and take a nap after work. That was about it for sleep. On December 23, Frank called again. He was threatening. He was implying he had a lot of resources, that he had the means to give the girls and me up to the Lebanese police.

Patrick was tempted to dismiss Frank's threats and hang up, but he did not want to burn any bridges. That night, Frank gave Patrick a window of four hours. He had that long to get Joe and me talking, but Patrick told him the request was unreasonable. Frank even wanted Patrick to call the wives of the guys and tell them it was our fault, not his, that their husbands were in a Lebanese jail. Then the calls stopped.

Frank likewise stopped calling Dad and me in Lebanon. Brian and David were languishing in a jail cell and we were doing all we could to avoid a similar fate. There was absolute confusion on our side. Where to go next? How to get out of Lebanon? And when? I knew only that the men expected nothing from me, but I would help them in any way I could.

* * *

Only later would we piece this together, but Patrick was not the only one in Alberta feeling ripples because Hannah and Cedar were now in their mother's hands.

Dave Chittick's wife, Carolyn, drove a school bus at the time, and she started getting threatening calls—six altogether, after midnight over the course of two nights. The calls came from two males, one with a Canadian accent, who claimed to be Doug (my brother) and wanted to know about the girls and when Dave was coming home. Carolyn said she knew only that the children were safe and that Dave was in Frankfurt. The other caller had an Australian accent and claimed to be Brian's brother, though he never gave his name and that made Carolyn suspicious. The caller tried to convince her that Brian was going to be executed by the Lebanese authorities within hours if the girls and I were not turned over, and he tried to get her to reveal our whereabouts. This claim struck Carolyn as ridiculous. When Carolyn said she had no information and wasn't able to help, the caller said he was on his way over to the Chittick house to get her. He was screaming into the phone, and each call was more menacing than the one before.

"If my brother's wife can't be with her husband at Christmastime, then neither will you," he said. Carolyn hung up, but he called back, asking to speak to Dave. Again, Carolyn told him she knew nothing.

The following night it was Dave's turn to answer the threatening calls. "I want answers," the caller said, "or you and your wife will pay." He would demand information, and Dave would demand to know who the caller was. Thinking that the voice sounded familiar, Dave said, "Sid, is that you?"

The caller said, "Who's Sid? Write that down"—as if he were speaking to someone in the same room. When the caller asked Dave if Sid was his contact in Lebanon, Dave said he had no information to give.

"We're coming to get you," the man said.

"I'll be waiting," Dave told him.

All of these calls were reported to the Calgary Police and the RCMP, though none was ever traced. In the days following the calls, Carolyn worried as she drove her bus, looking carefully at every car and person encountered along the way. She was frightened to go home after her morning run, wondering if someone would be waiting there for her. But there have been no calls since the last one to Dave.

* * *

While I was in hiding with the girls, our Lebanese lawyers began to fight on my behalf in Beirut's courts. Gone was our original fear—felt my first week in Lebanon—that court action would alert Joe and lead him to flee Lebanon and take the girls into Syria. I had the girls now. Out the window, too, was any notion of putting the girls into "third-party custody" while the courts dithered about whether to recognize, or not, my Canadian custody orders. Such recognition still mattered a great deal, but for different reasons. If my lawyers were successful, there would be no question of my being charged with kidnapping. And secondly, odds were that Brian and David would be set free. If I had committed no crime, neither had they.

All the battles fought on my behalf in Lebanese courts were fought in Arabic, but the documents were translated and later came to me. And in the flowery language of the translator, I can see some universal truths being expressed. Mothers and daughters have a special bond, and that's true in every corner of the world.

"The defendant," reads one of the court documents prepared by my criminal lawyer, Antoine El Kozah, "is a Canadian woman, from a respectable family abiding by traditional family norms and customs, which resemble to a great extent the traditions and customs prevailing in Lebanese villages." The document goes on to record the facts of the case: that Joseph Hawach and I met, that "mutual love emerged" between us, that we got married and were "blessed with two children." And then, how Joe "deluded" me, "intending to deprive their mother Melissa ('a loving caring mother') [of] them."

The Lebanese court would later capture, not just the moment of my reconnection with Hannah and Cedar, but the maelstrom that ensued. Here is my lawyer, Antoine El Kozah, as recorded by the court translator: "When [Melissa] went to Rimal Beach Resort, where her two children are located, she saw them and managed to speak with them. Accordingly, both came to her and she took them with her, being the loving caring mother whose heart beats hundreds of times in absence of her two children and thousands of times when she saw them." He goes on to describe how Joe then went to Zouk Mosbeh Police Station and declared "a kidnapping offence. So, the whole world was mobilized and has not rested since. . . ."

At some points, court proceedings in Lebanon turned almost to buffoonery as the other side went to absurd lengths to smear my character. Where, I wondered, were the Christian Maronite values so highly regarded by the Hawach family? Where had their intelligence gone?

I, of course, never attended any of these court sessions in Lebanon (nor was I ever charged with kidnapping). But my lawyers and the General did keep me apprised of court proceedings.

One day, the General came back with the news that a woman (Gladys, almost certainly) took the stand one day and testified in religious court that she had come to Canada in the summer of 2006 because her son had told her that he was working flat out at the paper company and needed help looking after his daughters. The court was told that the girls' mother, meanwhile, was out every night prostituting herself. These remarks later found their way into Lebanese newspapers. How could Gladys say such a thing? Why?

Gladys had come to Canada not because Joe had asked her to, but at my mother's request. I had made up my mind that I was going to move out of the house and had confided this decision to my parents. They knew that I was going to counselling and trying to get Joe involved as well. Unbeknownst to both Joe and me, my mother called Gladys and asked if she would come to Canada so that Joe would have at least some family here during this difficult time. Gladys was only too happy to come: She told us that she had had a dream that our house was burning down. I kept waiting for her to go back home before I officially moved out to my parents' place, but it was becoming increasingly difficult as she moped around the house and her stay turned into months. I left the house that October but would have left earlier had Gladys not been with us.

So documents from Lebanon's religious courts now found their way into my custody case in the civil courts. Likewise, the criminal courts were eventually informed of the serious charges being levelled against Joseph Hawach by Canadian police, along with the extradition orders. Lebanese lawyers for the two sides—mine and Joe's—conducted in the Lebanese and international media a discussion of how this stalemate might be resolved.

I was in hiding in Lebanon, with the girls in my possession. Joe was in hiding in Lebanon, with the girls no longer in his possession. That much was certain. After that, reported facts got a little muddy. Joe's lawyer, Tony Tebchrany, told Nahlah Ayed of CBC-TV news during an interview in his office on January 10, 2007, that "We are ready to drop all the cases against her, and everyone involved with her, if the children are returned." By "cases," he meant, I presume, charges. The General, meanwhile, simply repeated to my father and me a warning we had heard often in Lebanon. Trust no one. You'll end up in the trunk of a car, the General said, with your legs and hands tied. Your father will become a hostage. This was reality in Lebanon.

Tony Tebchrany, apparently, had a rosier picture of Lebanon and a darker picture of me. "There are legal channels in Lebanon," he told the CBC. "But to hire a gang—even if she was in the right—she's lost that right." A gang?

Later, Tebchrany gave another interview to the same Nahlah Ayed in which he declared that I had used an illegal crossing to escape Lebanon undetected. "Melissa exposed herself and her life to danger, and she exposed her children's lives to danger, at a time when she didn't have to at all. She took a route that only criminals and smugglers take. These are very dangerous routes, which could be exposed to shooting at any moment from the Lebanese or the Syrian army." This lawyer claimed to be mystified by my leaving, and insisted that Joe and I were close to agreeing on shared custody that would have ended the dispute and seen all charges against both Joe and me dropped.

For the record: Antoine assured me there was no deal, not even close. All the time I was in Lebanon, there was no communication between me and Joe or anyone in the Hawach family. Our Lebanese lawyers had talked. That was it. Offers from the other side rang hollow, and they never followed up with anything. Antoine told me that the other side was just stalling, hoping for the judge to issue a warrant against me. Their version of "close to agreeing" was their promise that they would let me leave Lebanon if I allowed Joe to see the girls one more time. Fearful of an ambush, my lawyer never took this seriously even for a moment.

How, and precisely where, I exited Lebanon remains a mystery to me. Why I had come to such a perilous place, though—no mystery there. I had come to fetch my daughters, from Lebanon because that is where their father had brought them.

* * *

Due process in Lebanon's civil, criminal and religious courts continued through January, but in an agonizingly slow manner.

Meanwhile, "the whole world" had not mobilized in quite the way that Antoine suggested, but certainly many newspapers in Canada and Australia—I would later learn—gave the story major play. The newspapers did not always have the facts straight, but the tale of two young girls being kidnapped, first by their father, then (so it appeared to the press) by their mother, the use of "mercenaries" and the jailing of said mercenaries, the video, the backdrop of the recent war in Lebanon, the mother now in hiding with her daughters—this all made for lively telling. "Kidnap drama in Lebanon" ran the headline in the December 24 issue of the *Sydney Sun-Herald*, which also ran a six-month-old photo of the girls smiling from their airplane seats in matching tops, happily colouring away.

People noticed and remembered the story, in part because newspapers, magazines and television invariably ran photographs of the girls, my gorgeous little girls. Many mothers and fathers, I know, got heartsick reading the story and looking at those pictures. One photo, taken in Lebanon (someone in the Hawach family must have given it to the Australian press), shows the girls wearing identical orange summer tops. The Orange Party's colour. Hannah has turned to the side, so her bare left shoulder is facing the camera. She is smiling at the photographer, and holding Cedar's right hand in her left hand. Cedar looks rather elfin, wide-eyed and watchful. The photo is haunting. To me, it says, "We are sisters."

* * *

Aside from that first pleasurable night, the first week with the girls in Lebanon was hell. The General, who had arrived in Lebanon from Dubai a few days before Christmas, would come to our hotel, and he would look so tired. "What have you done?" his look said. "I've been away and now you want me to clean up this mess?" He never once said those words, but I was sure he was thinking them. The General was just head down, tail up, and let's do what we need to do.

We were now in hiding, and all communication, I soon learned, was governed by certain rules. At first, we were cautious about cell phone use. In time, caution would turn to paranoia.

Each of us had two or three cell phones, but every five seconds we would switch to another phone. We only used the phones to convey terse messages. The danger was constant that we could be "triangulated" and our precise location determined by the other side. Best was text-messaging: The incessant noise of the World Wide Web, it turns out, is a perfect cover. It was like chatting by a waterfall. No one could hear us.

But could they find us? During those first three or four days, I had trouble breathing and I worried constantly that there were people hunting for me and that I would lose the girls yet again. My panic attacks were of the full-blown variety and there were days when I thought I would pass out from hyperventilating. I would deep-breathe and think pleasant thoughts and my father would rub my back to keep the panic at bay until finally, after a week, the anxiety subsided.

I would play with Hannah and Cedar all day long, talk to them, just so I would be in their hearts if I lost them again. I knew what the girls were like, that they would be great, and they were. I knew that the first two weeks with me they would be happy and excited, and then Hannah, especially, would get cranky because the structure was not the same as she was used to. I had given Joe the same advice about the girls before he had left for Australia: A grace period of joy and excitement at all the novelty would be followed by a grumpy stretch, so strive for some routine (meal schedules, bedtimes) to help them feel settled. I braced myself, then, for the little meltdowns that I knew were coming, but in the meantime I pulled out a virtual chest of toys and games and distractions.

I had with me the red leather photo album I had taken with me on my failed expedition to Australia the previous August, with letters and notes from the girls' cousins and school friends back home, along with candies and books and cards, and we opened them all up as I tried to reconnect the girls with home.

Cedar would sometimes talk about her "other Mom." One of the first things she said to me when we were reunited at the al-Rimal Resort was "You're my Canada mom! You're my Canada mom!" Later, I questioned her about who this other mother was. What, for example, did she look like? "She looks just like you," Cedar would reply, "but she lives in our other house, where we used to make pancakes." In Cedar's accounting, that made for two mothers: the one she remembered and the one now facing her. Both moms were me.

"Cedar," I told her, "you can't really have a new mom. You have one mom, and you have one dad. There are lots of people who will love you as much. If, say, your dad got a new wife, she could love you just as much as a mom, but she's not your mom. I'm your mom, and your dad's your dad."

As I pieced together what their dad had told them, it became clear that the girls had been told this: Patrick had shown up and taken me away.

"Taken me where?" I asked Hannah. "Did I get on a plane?"

"No."

"So how did I go away?"

"I told Daddy on the plane where you were," Hannah said. "I told him we shouldn't get on the plane without Mommy." She clearly felt some sort of responsibility for being in Lebanon because she was not able to stop her father.

"It's not your fault," I told my elder daughter. "I'm sure you did. What Daddy did was wrong."

"Are you going to do to Daddy," asked Hannah, "what he did to you?"

It was a really good question.

"When your daddy took you away from me," I told her, "my heart broke into two pieces. And now that I have you back, my heart is one piece again. We can't do to Daddy what he did to me. That was wrong. I don't know how we're going to do it, but we have to teach him the right way to love and he has to say 'sorry' to us."

I needed to keep these concepts simple so she could understand them but I could not erase what her father had done. Hannah had been fed right-wing pap: that Baby Jesus would be angry to hear that a mom and dad had separated. But I asked her if Baby Jesus would want a mom and dad to stay together when the two were fighting all the time or when one was hurting the other. "No," she said. Hannah had been told by her father—or possibly her grandmother—that separation was a sin, that moms and dads who separate are going to hell.

Curious to know the Maronite church's actual position on divorce, in the fall of 2007 I put the question to my friend Judy Saba, a cultural psychologist living in Sydney. Here, in part, is her reply: "Marriage," she wrote, "is one of the blessed sacraments, so it is highly valued, as is family. Although the church does not advocate or promote divorce, it also does not accept or condone violence, abuse or unhealthy relationships." The church will, in its pastoral role, counsel couples about the commitment required in marriage, but it does not expect a woman (or man) to stay in an unhealthy marriage.

Divorce, Judy said, is viewed by the Maronite church as the only option left after support counselling and other interventions have been exhausted. The actual divorce is a civil matter. Once a divorce is recognized in a civil court of law, then, and only then, can the couple request an annulment from the church. Once an annulment has been granted, the man and woman are free to remarry within the church.

The real issue, Judy went on to say, is whether divorce is *culturally* accepted in the Lebanese community. In general, the community finds it hard to accept divorce. It brings shame on the family name and affects the marriage prospects of siblings. Stressing that it's hard to generalize, Judy nevertheless noted that blame for divorce is accorded differently along gender lines. If the son gets a divorce, clearly his wife did not care for him enough or accept his ways. If the daughter gets a divorce, she did not try hard enough or did something wrong. There is, Judy wrote, a lot of pressure put on women in the Lebanese community to "give in" and stay in a relationship.

"In the case of Joe's family," she said, ending her note, "I really believe that no one in the community would have accepted what he did, precisely because he endangered the girls." But in the response voiced publicly, many in the Lebanese community painted me as the aggressor, which Judy thought was rather sad.

* * *

My task, then, was to stoke the memories of the Momma the girls knew and of home. We would play in Lebanon the games we had played at home in Canada, like "Mother, May I?"

In the villa, I would stand in that massive hallway facing the girls, select one and then the other, asking each to take two baby steps forward or backward or sideways. They were supposed to say "Mother, May I?" before proceeding, or go back to the starting line. The goal was to be the first to touch Momma.

"Simon Says" was another variation we played, and, again, the child or mother who forgot to listen for the two magic words before obeying Simon's command was ousted from the game.

"Red Light, Green Light" was yet another spin on that old game, and we played it too. One of us would act as the "stoplight," maybe ten or fifteen feet from the other two, and facing away. The person playing stoplight could either allow movement (with the "green light" command) or bring it to a halt (with the "red light "command"). If the human stoplight spun around and caught someone moving after the stop command had been given, the one caught was out of the game. The goal for the two advancing was to be the first to touch the stoplight, and thus earn the right to play that role herself.

If the girls grew restless and wanted to go outside (not something I was yet prepared to risk), I would literally shake things up: Write down all our activities on separate pieces of paper and each girl would take turns drawing them from a hat. It was an exercise for me in the art of distraction with two energetic preschoolers confined to two rooms and a hallway.

Even on that first day, despite all the time spent playing, my thoughts were about getting home. Dad was working the phone, the text messages were flying. Richard Bennett, my lawyer in Calgary, had travelled widely through the Middle East while handling cases. He had contacts with the Israelis, both consulate officials and others working underground, and they talked about us getting through the Israeli border in some clandestine fashion. (Our case was now very high-profile, we clearly posed no security risk, and exit stamps on passports would have apparently not been an issue for the Israeli government.) The Israeli option, though, was eventually discarded: The border was too tense.

Finally, it was decided that we would leave by boat, but the cost became prohibitive (aware of our desperation, the contractor who had helped Canadians leave the previous summer had considerably jacked up the price), and the General was loath to trust someone outside his circle.

The General—who had in the meantime seen to the translation of our Canadian court orders into Arabic—had instead been negotiating with a fellow in the north who would take us out of Lebanon by water. This was not illegal (depending on the papers we possessed), but neither did I want to get stopped, questioned and possibly detained. I also knew that a cordon had been pulled tight around Lebanon's coastal waters as the navies of Israel and certain Western governments tried to stop arms shipments from entering Lebanon by sea. Four or five times we were told that today was the day, but then would come word of delays, unforeseen problems, rough seas.

My hair by this time was long and still blonde, halfway down my back. In preparation for the trip home, the kids and I cut it. Again, I made this exercise fun, told the girls we were going to play "hairdresser"—I did not want them to think it strange that I was cutting my hair. Thus trimmed, I would not stand out so much, and a scarf would hide the blonde hair.

Finally, the time came to leave. On Christmas morning, my father gathered the girls and me in his arms and said prayers (Hail Mary, the Our Father) and promised me that everything was going to be fine. George showed up at our hotel with warm jackets for the girls and red Santa hats.

We all drove down to Beirut in a Jeep, with one car in front and another behind—and with everyone on the lookout for checkpoints. Checkpoints are always on the move, but we did not worry too much about them—not on the holiday.

We waited in a parking lot near a big commercial hotel in Beirut, the Movampick, with its private beach and tourists everywhere, just twenty minutes from one of the three ports. The thought was to blend in with the crowd. We waited in that Jeep in the parking lot for an hour and a half while the phone calls went back and forth. Finally, we learned it was a no-go, that certain people were down there watching the port. Someone had been tipped off, and the other side knew of our plan.

Later, I wondered about those several odd "Merry Christmas" calls between Brian and my father (calls, I speculate, that the former was forced to make by Lebanese police). Did my father mention anything in their chat about a boat? Or were the ports being watched because the police had simply and logically concluded that fleeing by boat would have been our first option?

The dashing of the boat plan was upsetting to all of us, and most confusing for Hannah. "Why can't we just go home to Canada?" she asked. She would see a plane in the sky and ask, "Why can't we be on that one?" Later, she would understand that it was more complicated than that.

The "red light" had gone up.

Simon says, "Stay in hiding. Lay low. Bide your time."

14

"You Are a Very Dangerous Woman"

The General (and, to a lesser extent, George) were now our lifelines. They were our interpreters and providers, our protectors and advisors, our drivers and spirit-lifters, and they would become our valued friends. The General would bring his young daughters to play with Hannah and Cedar, along with an endless supply of Play-Doh and puzzles, books and DVDs and crayons. Though we rarely saw him, I know that George did much of the driving—to pick up documents and papers from the Canadian embassy and my lawyers—always switching vehicles and taking what the General called "longcuts" (never shortcuts) to avoid being followed back to us.

Whatever differences might have driven a wedge between my camp and the General's camp seemed hardly to matter. Their mother tongue was Lebanese, mine was English. I was Christian, they were Muslim. I was female, they were male. I came from a Western culture, they had grown up with Arab traditions.

During times when Dad and I and Patrick were dealing with Lebanese lawyers, I sometimes felt overwhelmed by the cultural difference. I wanted straight talk and I sometimes got poetic language in return. If I offered even a hint of criticism (was it because the challenge was coming from a woman?), I felt I had wounded them.

At one point we were told that one lawyer could handle my case at all three levels—civil, criminal and religious. Then we were urged to hire a religious lawyer in the Lebanese city of Tripoli—who was asking for a retainer fee of $10,000 (U.S.). And, by the way, we were informed, Joe's side had just that morning called that same lawyer, so we had better act quickly.

"I need some time to think," I said in response. The actual thought in my head was that none of this made any sense and, in fact, seemed highly suspect. I questioned Roger Abiaad, and he turned on me.

"Do you think we are like children?" he asked. "That we don't know what we are talking about?"

I was pushing against cultural and other boundaries, and at times I felt at sea. At times like this, Patrick was hugely helpful. He would get on the phone and talk to these lawyers, man to man and in French, to smooth over the rough waters. "You'll have to forgive Melissa," he would say. "She's been through a lot. She's emotional."

The communication problem, in part, stemmed from our lawyers' command of English—a third language for them. I heard, over and over, that these men were "like my father," "like my brother," "like family." But similes and metaphors did not cut it. (Besides, I already have a father, brothers, family.) I wanted concrete facts, and my Lebanese lawyers were not always forthcoming.

But with the General and his brother, there was none of that. Through the former, we found my criminal court lawyer, Antoine El Kozah, whom I really liked (though I never actually met him, except on the phone when we were back in Canada). This Lebanese lawyer was very thorough and kind and very matter-of-fact. Through the Canadian embassy lawyer, we hired the aforementioned Roger Abiaad, our civil court lawyer. Every Tuesday and Thursday he would meet with the female judge handling our case. We wanted the Lebanese courts to recognize the Canadian court's decision granting me custody of the girls, but in Lebanon there were all these delays: The judge was ill or away, translation of court documents was slow in coming. We were winning the battles but the war was taking forever. At one point, we were told this process could take two years.

It was important to win this battle because once the Lebanese courts recognized that I had proper custody of the girls, no one could say I had "kidnapped" them. Only when the Lebanese judicial system recognized my custodial rights could I say with authority that I had committed no crime. And neither had the men helping me. The sooner my custodial rights were recognized, the sooner Brian and David would walk out of prison. In the meantime, lawyers working for Joe were trying, without much luck, to show that the girls had been kidnapped by force. This despite the fact that no weapons had been used, and no one had been hurt.

One day the General came back with a report from Antoine. The other side had made a claim in religious court that I was an unfit mother since I had once worked as a stripper (!) and was out all the time drinking with my boyfriend. I found these accusations very upsetting, of course, but the General just laughed.

"This is good," he told me. "This is how desperate they are. We had five references to your good character from important people in Canada, from people within the Maronite church in Australia, and they're saying you're a stripper! The more they lie, the easier it is for us to prove our case."

The General had put out feelers and one of his contacts found out about a ruling in a Lebanese religious court. It seems that Joe and his mother had gone to see a Maronite archbishop in Tripoli. From what I understand, they told this cleric that Hannah and Cedar had been abandoned by their mother and, further, that Joe and Gladys were now fighting for custody of the two girls. It was all a masquerade designed to force the archbishop into a ruling (of course, he ruled in support of Joe). The ruling was later exposed and successfully challenged by my lawyers in the religious court, so the bizarre episode eventually worked in our favour.

None of this fazed the General. In Lebanon, a lot of people were referred to as the General, so he was one of many. It seemed that our side and the other side shared a great long history: They had fought together or against each other during the protracted civil war that raged in Lebanon from 1975 to 1990. Whatever game of spy-versus-spy they were playing, the participants were old friends. Or old enemies. The General was a veteran of these games.

He operated according to a code, which boiled down to this: Rightly or wrongly, family came first and loyalty to family was everything. My father and I had no experience of war or prison and the thought of even a few days in jail made us tremble. For the General, war time and prison time were just facets of his wide experience. Nothing rattled him. He never looked stressed out, and he could always manage to calm me or Dad with his humour and his sarcasm. George and the General were two of the kindest people I have ever met.

He would arrive and tell me, for example, that Hezbollah had posted my photo at the border, or some other crazy measure that the other side had apparently resorted to, and I was always so skeptical and full of questions. Always questions.

"Don't you know?" he would say while smiling, arching one eyebrow and lowering his voice to drive home the sarcasm. "You are a very dangerous woman."

Getting my father, the girls and me out of Lebanon and back onto Canadian soil was still going to pose a challenge, but in his play-by-play of the dangerous game of Melissa versus Joe, he was certain we were now winning—and winning on what was supposed to be Joe's turf.

"They feel like they're fighting ghosts," the General boasted. The other side would go to hire a good religious lawyer only to find we already had that lawyer under contract. The other side would have men at the port ready to nab us as we boarded the boat, but we smelled danger and pulled away. A dark sedan would pull up to the hotel, but the General would always know why the car and those in it were there.

A father taking his own children constituted no crime in Lebanese courts, but our lawyers were now introducing into the record in all three courts the fraud warrants against Joe and the civil judgement from HSBC Bank Canada against him. In Lebanon, as elsewhere, these matters represented serious assaults on one's character and credibility, so the court battles were starting to swing our way. We had held back the fact of these charges so as to avoid putting too much pressure on the family. Now we ratcheted up that pressure.

"We're in the driver's seat," the General said. "They're trying to catch up."

* * *

On Christmas Day we moved into a new hotel, one right in the heart of Hezbollah territory. The General reasoned that this was the last place the other side—which would have comprised Lebanese police as well as Hezbollah members connected to Joe's Lebanese uncle—would look for us. We knew they were searching for us, going from hotel to hotel and checking passports. We also learned that Canadian embassy officials were being monitored and, in some cases, being followed home because Lebanese police believed embassy staff were hiding us in one of their homes.

Ours was a small hotel, with laundry hanging from balconies, and eucalyptus trees growing in the courtyard below. We learned that during the fighting of the summer, people had flocked here to escape the bombardment and they would sleep hip-to-hip in the corridors. What was constant, the owner told us, was the noise of the Israeli guns and bombs.

The owner was a tall bearded man who always wore a kaftan. The girls thought he was Jesus. The owner had a wife and children who lived in another house. His own quarters featured a huge hot tub, and he assured my father that if he ever wanted "company" (female companionship), he would be happy to arrange it.

Now it was winter, we were the only guests, and the owner seemed happy to have us there. He and his staff were extremely friendly and kind and no questions were asked once they were told that we had a "social" problem—a Lebanese code word to describe a sensitive family issue best handled "in-house" and not by calling the authorities as often happens in Canada. Disputes and conflicts are rarely handled by police in Lebanon. Families and villages typically deal with these issues themselves. (Even so, there were risks involved in taking us in—which was why we rented an entire floor of the hotel. For the owner, the benefits of having us as guests had to outweigh the risks.)

We ate well and fell into established routines. In the morning, breakfast would be brought up for us: Nescafé coffee and Corn Flakes served on the balcony that was shaded by the canopy of trees rising from the gardens below. One day they brought up a toaster and peanut butter—my father's special request.

Then would come a lunch, prepared by a nearby restaurant and different every day. The girls and I love Lebanese food, so we feasted on *labneh* (a thick Lebanese yogurt for dipping bread), fresh cucumber and fresh garlic, *fattoush* (a salad of red peppers, cucumber, sumac, lemon and tons of garlic). Mid-afternoon, up to the room would come carrots for the girls and cucumber and celery and *za'atar*. And strawberries. My father, who would suffer horribly from stress and cardiac problems during much of our time in hiding, nonetheless still raves about the strawberries he ate in Lebanon (he fancies himself something of an authority on strawberries). "The best," he said, "I've ever tasted."

In the evening we would play "spa," the girls and I. The bathrooms had vaulted ceilings (as you would find in a spa) but they were also cold, so we would bring a portable ground heater in to warm the room and I would bathe the girls (they loved their baths), then put a towel on their heads and give them a massage—after they had paid me, of course, with their pretend money. These were things I had done in the past with Hannah and Cedar and I took comfort in grooming them, combing their hair, putting barrettes in their hair, rubbing them head to toe with baby cream. It's odd to admit, but I like them smelling really nice.

Hannah continued to process what had happened to her and her sister. She seemed not to be frightened, nor did she ever during our first weeks back together cry while asking for her father. Generally we shared this nice feeling of getting back together and finding each other.

My father and I would get daily reports through the General of our battles in the Lebanese courts, but victory continued to seem, if not elusive, then perilously slow. My father was down and sad, and there were times when I thought he was pressuring the General to get us all out—quickly. All my instincts, on the other hand, were telling me to be cautious, to go slow and to trust the General. I'd never felt more focused in my life.

15

Come What May

Twelve days into our time of hiding in Lebanon, on New Year's Eve, the General managed to set up an Internet connection for my father's laptop and we were thus able to read notes from family and friends at home wishing us well. For the hotel owner—who had no Internet connection—the hookup served to further cement us as valuable customers. Some days, the grateful proprietor would lock the front gate to the courtyard so that no one could enter and possibly see us in the lobby downstairs, and he would put out a great Lebanese feast for us.

The line of communication to home and the world kept me going through some rough patches, and even put a smile on my face.

Some of the players on my Calgary baseball team—who had been a huge support for me but who had clearly seen too many Hollywood movies—were sending me some lively advice on how to get out of Lebanon (submarines, helicopters and pilot friends of theirs figured prominently in their sometimes far-fetched but always well-intentioned schemes).

We heard via e-mail about a vision that Gramma Engdahl (my paternal grandmother) had had about us: Mel and the girls enveloped in a thick cloud of smoke and then just—poof!—disappearing.

I also went on the Internet and realized how big our story was. Reacquiring the girls and going into hiding in Lebanon had put pictures of the girls and me into newspapers all over the world. On the telephone, members of my family back home tried to spare our feelings by pretending that the story was not splashed everywhere, but we knew it was. I told everyone back home to stay mum, and to say nothing to the press.

The other side—Hawach family members and lawyers—was talking to the media, and I was not about to enter into a dialogue with them. Doing so would only add more fuel to a fire that was already out of control. In response to an e-mail that I had sent Dave Chittick worrying about a million things, one word of advice he offered was not to engage the media at that point. Our story, he suggested, should be told *after* and not *during* this situation. Dave was also trying to address some of my other worries (the other side—with all its political clout—was putting pressure on the judges ruling on our case, for instance). In his e-mail, which I very much valued and appreciated, I could see that Dave was trying to buoy my spirits without sounding hollow.

At this point, our story had run in local Lebanese papers and the woman who did laundry for our hotel brought up a picture of the girls and me—one I had left in a pocket. I was fearful that she would have seen the same photo in a Beirut newspaper. After that, I did our laundry in the bathtub and hung the clothes by the heater.

It is a strange feeling to plug your name into a search engine and see hundreds and hundreds of items coming up, along with all these photographs of yourself. One, a close-up in the *New Zealand Herald*, was taken on the steps of the courthouse in Sydney on November 30 as I took questions from reporters. Some people who saw the photo read intensity, even anger, into the photo but I do not remember anger. I just remember focusing on questions about my next course of action.

Another photo, taken on the same occasion and used by the *Sydney Morning Herald*, has me with my hand over my mouth. Again, others who have seen the image take it that I had just been given some shocking and appalling news. The truth is, when I am nervous I smile, and maybe I had no wish to be photographed smiling. It was an emotional day watching my in-laws on the witness stand being grilled by my lawyer.

Another photograph in the same paper showed the Engdahls (Mom, Dad and me) striding purposefully outside the Supreme Court, me holding a stack of the missing children posters. CBC-TV news later ran images of Cedar (giving her best 100-watt smile) and Hannah (bug-eyed and clowning for the camera) on January 10, 2007. The CBC story described how Melissa Hawach had "enlisted the help of several ex-soldiers to grab her two girls in a daring operation. . . ." The story also reported that I was wanted in Lebanon and could face charges of child abduction.

I closed the computer. It was too upsetting to read. The news was either just plain wrong or just plain dire, and the bloggers were sometimes slanderous in their judgements of me or my family. One Internet story about me provoked seventy responses, as correspondents alternately attacked and defended what I had done. This prairie girl had become a bone of contention.

* * *

Not every scribe or commentator had it wrong. Welcome support came from within the Lebanese community—most forcefully in the form of an opinion piece that appeared on December 30, 2006, in *The Age*, a newspaper in Melbourne. The author, Joseph Wakim, is the founder of the Australian Arabic Council and a former multicultural affairs commissioner in Australia, and he and I had spoken several times on the phone when I was in Sydney earlier that year. Judy Saba, the cultural psychologist in Sydney, had kindly put me in touch with him.

My parents and I were at dinner with Judy Saba when she called Mr. Wakim on her cell phone so that I could speak to him. His wife had died of cancer several years beforehand, leaving him to raise two daughters by himself. He and I chatted with a shared empathy; we had both lost loved ones. He moved me to tears when he suddenly asked, "Do your daughters sometimes visit you in your dreams? My wife does." In truth, I prayed every night for them to visit me. His question, so personal, made me feel deeply connected to this man and his sorrows.

Mr. Wakim had been holidaying with his daughters in Lebanon when the Israeli-Hezbollah conflict erupted. As they joined the queue exiting Lebanon at the border, along with hundreds of others, Joseph's youngest daughter whispered a question to him. She wanted to know—given the carnage in Lebanon—why some people were swimming against the tide: leaving Syria to enter Lebanon.

Joseph Wakim wondered whether he might have come close to that other Joseph, Hawach, during his crossing: "We might have seen each other in passing in the simmering heat on the one remaining unbombed border crossing via north Lebanon."

In his article, entitled "Why Melissa Hawach was forced to act," Joseph Wakim argued that the real victims in Joe's abduction were the children. Separating Hannah and Cedar from their mother, he said, was in breach of the UN Declaration of the Rights of the Child, passed in 1959, which notes that "a child of tender years shall not, save in exceptional circumstances, be separated from his (her) mother."

Joseph Wakim went on to praise me for never playing "the race card," for never trying to "dog-whistle to Arab haters" or in any way trotting out anti-Arab sentiments. I had, instead, described the warmth and hospitality I had experienced from the Hawach family during my marriage, and how the Lebanese culture loves and protects children.

Mr. Wakim admitted that while many community activists in the Australian-Lebanese community had instinctively defended their compatriot, Joseph Hawach, he, Joseph Wakim, was not among them. Mr. Wakim's parting comment was that Australia should have bilateral agreements with countries such as Lebanon so that international rights for the protection of children can be enforced.

Amen.

* * *

Some days I would lie on the bed with the girls and I would envision myself getting caught. I was no longer frightened by the prospect of jail. What frightened me more was thinking that the girls would grow up believing they had been abandoned by their mother. I had now dealt with that concern. Hannah knew the truth, and if the worst happened (Joe took the girls back), she could tell Cedar. Now, come what may. *Que será, será.*

Meanwhile, we three were reconnecting and making up for time lost. Via the Internet, we watched Treehouse TV (a Canadian channel that offers online games, activities, movies and colouring) and CBC Kids, another source aimed at preschoolers. Both programs reminded the girls of home. This added a new dimension to our play and allowed me to school the girls—addition and subtraction, spelling, teaching Hannah how to tell time and Cedar how to write her name. In a way, this time "in hiding" was a blessing. It was a gift to be stuck. Going home right away would have meant a distraction, and taken away from our intense and precious bonding. There would have been endless meetings with lawyers and police, visits by family and friends, a house to clean, reporters . . . All that could wait. For now, life had been sharply reduced to mother-and-daughter play.

There was one movie we watched three times and it seemed to resonate with us. It was called *Gold Diggers: The Secret of Bear Mountain*, about two girls on an adventure in a small town in California. One girl is a tomboy, an outcast viewed locally as a "bad seed." The other girl has just moved to the town after her father's death and her mother's remarriage to a man who turns out to be abusive to both mother and daughter. The girls form a fast friendship—while solving the mystery of the gold in the cave. Hannah and Cedar loved to pretend that each was one of the characters and we would watch the film while munching on a platter of cheese and cold meats with crackers, carrots, fruit and *mezze*, a spread of small appetizer dishes, and *markouk*—traditional Lebanese flatbread.

* * *

My father, meanwhile, was dangerously close to running out of his heart medication and was experiencing heart palpitations and other serious medical problems. The General, being the General, took the empty bottle and came back the next day with a new prescription, but my father's anxiety and paranoia would not be so easily relieved. He became convinced that he was a wanted man. His $5-a-minute cell phone costs were mounting: In the first three weeks of our hiding in Lebanon, the bill was a staggering $9,000 and would top out at $15,000. The Middle East has some of the most expensive telephone charges in the world.

My father had been a huge support and he had helped me in so many ways (the fact that his good friend had bankrolled our campaign paid testament to his character and reputation in business), but the past six months had taken a terrible toll on him—physically, psychologically, emotionally. My father is a dynamic man, one used to getting things done in a hurry. Being stuck in a room for weeks was hell for him. All he could think about was getting out.

My focus was on the girls, and while solitaire and music from the Internet kept Dad occupied for a time, he was growing increasingly agitated. He needed things to be happening and he even tried pushing the General—who is used to commanding others and is not a man to be pushed—into some sort of escape plan. I wanted out, too, but I wanted us out safely. The General would say vaguely in his idiosyncratic English, "We will get you out when the time is ripe. We must proceed always in a safety condition." My father and the several business associates back home he was consulting were all, on the other hand, of the same mind: Take the first opportunity. I had this uncanny sense that it would all work out, but that forcing and rushing things would be disastrous.

I look back on this time and I feel bad. The General was better at recognizing and assuaging Dad's anger and anguish than me, James B. Engdahl's eldest offspring. I was in survival mode and sometimes my response to his anger was anger of my own. If he complained to the girls about their squabbling and making noise, I would defend the girls with something like, "Back off, Grandpa." It seemed like I had endless patience with my daughters, but less with my father.

I was feeling very strong and I could not trust my father to make decisions that were safe for us. If he spoke on the telephone and I was not right there I would want to know later what was discussed and with whom. When the phone rang I would try to be right next to him, and that had to have been hard for him—being treated like he did not know what he was doing. My own father, an extraordinarily capable man, the president and chief executive officer of a mining company and a former vice-president of Barclay's Bank in Canada. But my children were at stake and I was shutting almost everyone out.

My father had been sleeping in his own room on one of the twin beds there, and finally, after seeing him so muted, I invited him to sleep in the king-size bed with the girls and me. In the evenings, the four of us would lie on that sprawling bed and watch English movies on satellite television. That helped bolster his spirits, but I knew he was still struggling.

He and the girls had colds, but not me. Going back to July when this whole thing started, I had not been sick—not once. I was so focused and intent, more so than at any other time in my life. I definitely had my weak moments when I thought we were up against an unstoppable Goliath—I felt it most acutely when the General would come back to our hotel room with reports of the other side's antics or what had been said in court. "How can we fight this and win?" was sometimes my question.

In the Bible, young David fells huge Goliath with a single stone from his sling. Faith and courage guided the boy, as I hoped they would us.

16

A Small World

By this time, Patrick had flown to Cyprus—that island in the Mediterranean just a few hundred kilometres northwest of Beirut—to be close. He arrived on the day after Christmas. His proximity offered a huge morale boost to us and it gave Patrick a closer vantage while he dealt—on the phone, in French—with Lebanese lawyers and all the other officials on our list. Doing that from inside Lebanon would have been extremely dangerous for him, given the proximity of Joe and his relations.

"We're close," Patrick would tell me on the phone. He would not say where he was, just as no explicit details were ever mentioned on the phone. Owing to the fear that someone was listening (and for a little comic relief), all of us had code names, though what they were I cannot recall.

"For God's sake, Patrick," I pleaded, "tell me where you are."

"Look out the window and you can see me," was all he would say. He would spend twenty-three out of every twenty-four hours in his awful, cramped hotel room—making calls or waiting for the phone to ring. In the squirrelly schedule that he now necessarily adopted, he would sleep one hour, then be awake for six.

Through friends of friends came another angel of mercy. A Canadian pilot arrived in Lebanon around this time (Paul, the Lebanese expatriate businessman who had helped me earlier in Canada, flew him in at his own expense), and they were discussing—with Patrick and the General—plans to get us out. The pilot, who had some previous experience of Lebanon, was working on various schemes, including a just-in-case scenario involving fake New Zealand passports. The General even took our passport photos in the hotel room but the thought of using a doctored passport made me sick to my stomach.

There was, meanwhile, some confusion (at one point I thought the General had a second pilot in mind) and communication got muddled. The General was keeping both Paul and his pilot on a very short leash. "When in doubt, trust no one," was, as always, his guiding principle. He was extremely nervous about any of these people coming to our hotel. Both our safety and his would have been compromised.

Through Patrick I learned that, back in Canada, Paul had been calling him to complain that the General was remaining very tight-lipped. It is in the General's nature to keep the circle small—so small it includes just him. The plan, as usual, was to hope for the best but prepare for the worst. All very nerve-racking. I felt so Canadian in those moments—forever the rule-follower. I knew I had to change my way of thinking if I was going to survive in this country.

Ideally, one needs quiet to ponder these momentous decisions, but quiet was sometimes hard to come by. The General would come back to our hotel room with some new reports about the plan to fly us out, and the girls at that moment, often as not, would be bickering.

"You see," my father would say. "This is why we have to get out."

I saw their behaviour as normal, an understandable consequence of their forced confinement indoors, and certainly not an excuse to seize on a plan that may or may not have worked. The plan to get us out by air gave us hope (Paul's gesture was kind and much appreciated) but it also bought us time, and the process of considering it taught us patience. The General never pushed us in his direction or gave ultimatums. He wanted us to be perfectly comfortable with our choices.

Paul, meanwhile, was getting frustrated and it was costing him to keep his guy in Lebanon. I was tempted to just latch on to this idea and a pilot who seemed ready to move. Paul had done so much for us but I was once more going on my gut. I would worry about mending fences afterwards. Had we gone with Paul's man, we may have been out of Lebanon weeks earlier, but all my instincts told me to sit tight and stay on course.

In the end, I decided that while the pilot could probably help us and I was grateful for his gesture, I would go with the fellow who had got us safely this far and who had risked his whole family to help us. The General.

Tensions had by now, weeks three and four in hiding, mounted considerably. After we got the Internet link hooked up, my father and I used MSN and Skype to communicate with our family a lot. Patrick was always waiting for news from someone and we were always waiting on news from Patrick. We had been told that our case had been brought up in the House of Commons in Ottawa and that Foreign Affairs Minister Peter MacKay was due to place a phone call to the Lebanese prime minister regarding funds that Canada had pledged to Lebanon. The minister had apparently promised to inquire about my situation to see what, if anything, could be done. Canada was obviously not about to withdraw its pledge of funds, but I was hopeful that some of the roadblocks that we were encountering could be lifted.

I (and other family members) had earlier written to Peter MacKay a number of times requesting assistance. We all received polite letters to say that parental abductions were a serious and continuing problem. Apparently you had to get yourself into a very tight and desperate spot before the minister of foreign affairs would get more active!

In Lebanon's civil court, meanwhile, we were encountering major challenges with the judge handling our case. Instead of telling our lawyer everything that needed to be done all at once, she would make Roger jump through a new hoop every time they met (when they met at all—many meetings were cancelled or delayed for one reason or another). Jean-Marc Lesage, head of the government's Our Missing Children program in Ottawa, likewise called this judge, pleading with her to tell us, all at once, what we needed to do to get our Canadian court orders recognized. She was forever sending us to get documents translated or certified.

Getting us all out of Lebanon was, of course, the other order of business. The plan was for the girls and me to cross the border by car into Syria with a certain commercial attaché (one more foot soldier in the General's small army) and to go from there to Jordan before flying out of Amman. By this time, I had convinced my father to go it alone—by plane. Still worried about his fragile state, I told him, "You can help us more from Canada than you can here." He agreed when he realized that separate arrangements for the girls and me to leave were also being made. We would all leave Lebanon on the same day. That, at least, was the plan.

I would learn that border crossings in the Middle East can sometimes be intense, hours-long experiences, while other times you just sit in your car as someone known to the guards takes in your passports and gets the correct entry or exit stamps—it can be over in minutes. The latter is what we were hoping for. The General would have either his men or like-minded men working at both the Lebanese border checkpoint and at its Syrian equivalent. The two checkpoints would have to be coordinated, but all in all this seemed a workable plan.

For many reasons, we would need such help. For one thing, the girls lacked entry stamps (that is, valid visas) on their passports and there were stop orders against them stemming from action Joe's lawyers had taken in civil court. I had obtained the girls' new passports at the Canadian embassy in Beirut. Usually, Canadian citizens got white emergency passports—like the ones that were widely issued to Canadians fleeing Lebanon during the war in the summer of 2006. We were there long enough that we got the actual blue passports. As for the stop orders, they were a civil issue in Lebanon and commonly imposed. All this we knew. What we did not know for certain was whether Joe's Hezbollah contacts (through his uncle) had posted all our names and photographs at every border crossing.

This last item was typical of the information that would come to us through the General—of course fuelling our paranoia. Whether it was true or just talk emanating from the other side meant to frighten or stall us, we will never know. I also wondered whether the fee being paid the attaché through the General meant we were worth more to him the longer we stayed in Lebanon. At one point, the attaché told me he had seen an Australian embassy alert suggesting that I was wanted by Interpol. Did he fabricate this to create more delays in our leaving? Perhaps there were other delays and this was the easiest way to get me to stop asking questions. (Obviously, he did not know me very well. I always have questions.) It was starting to feel like I was worth more kept in Lebanon than allowed to go home. These were my thoughts at the time, but it seems almost petty and ungrateful to voice them here. Without the assistance of the attaché and his family, we would have been lost.

Without help, we would have been easy targets at the Syrian border. But even with such help, we needed our other papers to be in order: all our court documents, in English and Arabic, as well as the Canadian court orders. Finally, my father had to live with the fear that if he were taken by members of the Hawach clan or Hezbollah as he tried to exit Lebanon, he might be used as trade bait. I would be forced to choose one of two options: freedom for my ailing father or keeping my daughters. One would come at the price of the other.

These were all real fears—or were they?

"You're living in a bottle, Mel," Patrick would say to me. Everything seemed to me magnified a hundredfold and in the swirl of rumour (Joe was preparing to take the girls to Syria) and fear (the thought of Dad in jail), it was impossible to say what was genuine and what was not, what warranted a lot of attention and what merited only a little or none at all.

* * *

Over in Cyprus, Patrick was living on caffeine and catnaps. He was like a machine, stuck in a lousy hotel room, afraid to sleep lest he miss a call, leery of having even one glass of wine for fear of being anything but razor-sharp. At his one-man call centre, the calls were always about the same thing: getting the four of us out.

Patrick was on the phone with Helen Harris at Foreign Affairs in Ottawa. He was putting out fires (some of which I myself had sparked) with my Lebanese lawyers. He was calling the Canadian embassy in Beirut. He was dickering with captains at a nearby marina about hiring a boat to get us out, or talking to a former minister of defence back in Canada about using an American helicopter. And every day, I or Dad had a hundred questions for him.

What's going on with the government of Canada? Why can't they get us out? What about that boat? That military chopper? Our conversations with Patrick were always to the point: "Any news yet?" We were hungry for updates. Dad slept beside his phone and the computer. A couple of times his phone service was cancelled (due to the huge bills accumulating so quickly), and both times we felt panic at not being able to contact anyone. Had someone inside Lebanon cut our cell phone service? Were they listening?

Patrick, who had often told me I was paranoid, now got a taste of that feeling himself. After seeing a suspicious character poking around the lobby of his hotel, he decamped to an even dingier place. He also changed his MSN handle—again for reasons of security. We were all now gripped by an overwhelming fear.

We paid the General, and his cohorts, a grand total of $180,000. I don't think we could have managed without him. But neither could I have managed without Patrick. One of his most impressive contacts was Helen Harris. Her proper title is Director, Program Development, Consular Affairs Bureau, but Patrick has another phrase to describe her—"woman of action." She was in Lebanon in the summer of 2006, helping Canadians to get out by boat.

"What a woman," says Patrick. "There was no bullshit. She'd tell you straight out. Yes, this is possible. No, not possible. She had a direct line to Peter MacKay's office. At one point, she had to get off the line to deal with another hot potato—the Myriam Bédard case [a former Canadian Olympic athlete charged in December 2006 with abducting her own daughter. She was later found guilty]. Whenever I used Helen's name, people paid attention."

This was typical of Patrick's dealings: Close to Christmas and still back in Canada, Patrick called Helen Harris and got the name of a boat captain whom Foreign Affairs had used—and trusted—during the 2006 exodus. Dad and the General negotiated a price to get us out: $50,000 to $60,000. I asked Patrick a dozen questions and relayed the information to the General, who nixed the deal when the captain jacked up his price to $250,000. The General thought we were being taken for a ride.

"That," remembers Patrick, "was when I decided to go to Cyprus. I thought I could organize transportation by boat from there in person. I'd be thirty minutes away from you, not thirty hours, and I could continue with all my phone calls. I became very selective on who I told what. Some days it looked bad."

Despite a huge effort, the boat option never materialized. The risk was too great, the price too high. Neither did the helicopter option, much to my father's disappointment, but not mine. I was certain that escape by helicopter—while fitting, in a way—was not going to happen.

* * *

The General continued to wait for precisely the right moment, the right "safety condition." The call to mobilize might come at any moment, and we all had to be ready.

Finally, on January 21, 2007, the call came.

We had been in hiding with the girls for thirty-two days. On that day, the General dropped Dad off at the Hard Rock Café in downtown Beirut, where he was picked up and conveyed in a very comfortable Canadian embassy car all the way to Damascus. Flying out of Beirut was decidedly not an option: The airport was being watched and we remained fearful that my father might be kidnapped by people sympathetic to Joe and used as leverage to get the girls back.

Dad crossed the border on a tourist visa, which is hard to get (in fact, we were told that the Canadian government had never before acquired a Syrian visa on behalf of one of its citizens). What terrified him on arriving in Damascus was that the flight the Canadian embassy had booked for him from Damascus to Frankfurt included a stopover in Beirut, and there was the risk that someone working for the other side would take him and use him to pry the girls and me out of hiding. Such leverage was very common in Lebanon. Jail time, Dad knew, would have killed him. The flight was thus rearranged. As much as my father loved Lebanese strawberries, he had had his fill of Lebanon.

That evening, I got a call from the Frankfurt airport. Dad was out.

One down, three to go.

* * *

Before leaving, my father and I had gone through all our stuff and separated it into what was necessary and what we could do without. We set aside everything that may have led to suspicion if we were caught—all pictures and letters, mail and phone numbers were either destroyed or left in a bag. (We laughed about the phone numbers later. We recorded in our respective notebooks all the critical numbers—for my lawyers, the General, his brother, embassy officials, etc.—but everything in a code so complex that we later had to brainstorm to retrieve it.) The owner of this hotel had had an escape strategy for us that involved a secret room at the top of the hotel, which is where he stored our bag (the General sent it back to Canada later).

My father's exit was fraught with emotion for him and it was almost entirely orchestrated by Patrick in Cyprus and his new friends in the Canadian government who were instrumental in their support of us.

Hannah, Cedar and I, meanwhile, were all driven towards the Lebanese-Syrian border at 4 a.m. that same day. I had packed snacks, bottles of water, changes of clothes, colouring books and crayons and a big alphabet book someone had sent from the Canadian embassy. *Chicka Chicka Boom Boom*, it was called, and it remains one of Cedar's favourites.

An hour from the border, we stopped for tea and cookies, and met with others on the General's team while waiting for friendly guards to take up their positions at each checkpoint. Many of the General's men were emotional and upset that a mother and her daughters had to go through all this. They knew what had already happened to us in months past, and maybe they had a sense of all that could go wrong in the days ahead.

Finally, the signal came. We all piled into the car and headed for the border. There we waited another thirty or forty minutes while the General consulted on his cell phone. But then it became clear: There would be no wave-through. With one of the General's cars in front of us and another behind, we waited, and waited. In the end, we learned that a person of high rank had made an unscheduled visit to this area, and extra police and security had flooded the zone. The General decided that crossing with tensions running so high would pose too great a risk. Much to my sorrow, we turned back.

The commercial attaché, a man I will call Mahfuz, lived close by and it was decided that we would stay with his family until a more propitious moment. The attaché, though, had decided it was time for lunch, and he took all of us to a sprawling, open-air Lebanese restaurant, with some 200 people inside and balloons and a playland for children. Boys were running around with hot coals for the shishas—tall water pipes that deliver tobacco flavoured with fruit or honey.

At first, I was paranoid, nervous and uncomfortable in the extreme, and I could tell that the General was likewise not happy with this arrangement. The two of us exchanged a look that instantly communicated all this unease. The girls and I had been in hiding for so long, and suddenly we were out in public and everybody was looking at us.

The General and his wife had helped me dye my hair black a few days beforehand, so I stuck out a little less now than I would have with my blonde hair. But what about Hannah and Cedar? Still, we were stuck in this now familiar cultural bind. To say no to the commercial attaché would have been to question his judgement. I would have preferred to stay in the car with the girls, but I decided to accept this offer of lunch. And though it was a fabulous lunch (barbecued chicken, fries, *labneh, baba ghanoush, hummus* and fruit), we were on our guard at all times: each time I or Hannah or Cedar went to the washroom, the General or one of his men escorted us there and back.

It was then decided that we would not seek a hotel for the night, but stay at the attaché's house. His, it turns out, was an ample and comfortable apartment with a big tiled kitchen and a balcony that afforded a view of the mountains. It was home to this man, his wife, and several of his twenty-something sons. Bright and airy and immaculately clean, the house was typical of Lebanese homes, with the walls covered in family photos and, on the mantels, glass ornaments and statuary and souvenirs of trips to African countries. The family's welcome was warm and instantaneous. The attaché had a kind and happy face, and his personality was the same. And he loved the girls: In no time, he had them on his lap, teasing them and joking with them.

My first thought, though, was a Canadian one. I didn't know these people at all. I had no cell phone (though the General would later give me one), so there was no way of communicating with Patrick or the General. Aside from the attaché and his sons, who were only around intermittently, no one in the house spoke English or French. And the soothing little routines the girls and I had established back at the hotel now suddenly seemed even more precious and I longed for them.

What I really wanted was a good cry, just to release some of the anguish and disappointment over the dashed chance at crossing the border. But neither did I want to appear ungrateful or impolite. My fears were soon allayed by the kindness of the man I call Mahfuz (it means *safe* in Lebanese). His sons brought out toys, and, though the boys' English was limited, they played with the girls. I was reminded that Hannah and Cedar are half Lebanese, and maybe that explained part of the warm and instant connection. That evening, at supper, Cedar sat on the lap of the youngest boy, who was in his early twenties, while she ate and she grew particularly attached to him. Cedar is like that: Once she warms to someone, the affection she issues is wholehearted and constant.

"The girls can sleep in my bed," Mahfuz later announced. We were their guests, and it was decided that the girls and I would have his bed, while he and his wife slept on the floor in the salon. I was overwhelmed by their hospitality.

That night, Cedar repaid Mahfuz's generosity—by thoroughly wetting his bed.

17

The Voice of Reason

From Mahfuz's house, we could see down into the streets of Beirut. Hannah could see the airport, and planes taking off, and she would renew her questioning.

"Why can't we be on that one?"

I always tried to hide my emotions from the girls, but one night at Mahfuz's house (we would stay there almost three weeks waiting for the General to determine the moment and method of escape) I was weeping and Hannah heard me. Our exchange went something like this.

"Why are are you crying?"

"I have a tummy ache."

"Oh. Are you scared?"

"Tonight, just a little."

We prayed, as we did every night.

"Momma," said Hannah, "I don't want you to think about Daddy. You let *me* think about Daddy because it doesn't make me cry." Then she did what I as a mother often do to get through a difficult time with a child.

"Do you remember the time last Christmas when we all went skiing, with Uncle Doug and Aunt Celeste and the whole family? That was a fun time. Why don't you think about that?"

The voice of reason, distracting me, taking my mind off things.

Offered to a mother by her six-year-old child. I saw so much in Hannah that night. What I was teaching her, she was giving back. It made me smile.

That same week, I was awakened one night at midnight by intense cramps in my lower back and abdomen, as sharp as labour pains. I have a high tolerance for pain, but this pain had me struggling to breathe and on the floor, rocking.

Hannah and Cedar heard me and both got up.

Hannah asked, "What's wrong?"

I told her I had a little pain, and when Cedar wanted more information, Hannah stepped in, again playing mother to me and rubbing my back.

"Cedar, Momma's not feeling well. We need to take care of her. Don't bother her."

I went to the medicine kit I had brought along with us and took four Advil before hearing from Patrick. (I had made him promise to call me, and I always slept with my phone close by.) I told him I couldn't talk and would call him later. Within twenty minutes, I was feeling a bit better. But now I needed the washroom, and Hannah held my hand as we walked there (all the while trying to be quiet since the whole house was sleeping). The washroom across the hall, though, was occupied. Cedar had propped herself on her throne and was happily singing away.

Hannah lit into her. "Cedar, I'm bringing Momma to use the washroom and you're singing on the toilet!"

"I have to take a big poo!" she said.

Hannah was livid. Cedar was oblivious. Momma had no choice: She had to laugh. The pain subsided and in the morning both the General and George showed up at the house. As soon as I was feeling better, I spoke with Patrick, who called my mother, who told my father, who called the General. Mom feared that this was a gall bladder attack, and had called our family doctor in Calgary. In a subsequent telephone conversation with me (when I was still in the Middle East), he wondered if I had suffered a burst cyst—a painful but not life-threatening event. His words gave me some comfort. But more than that, I felt a great pride in my eldest daughter. I had seen a different side of her.

* * *

There were no repercussions from Cedar's wetting of Mahfuz's bed. On the contrary, it occasioned laughter (and a plastic cover on the mattress).

"Don't worry," said the attaché's wife, whom I will call Fatima and who was ever gracious and generous. The three women of the house—Fatima, the African cleaning lady, this guest from Canada—developed a wonderful affinity for one another. Language was no barrier at all, just a nuisance. Sometimes Fatima would try to explain something to me while the African cleaning lady would join the game of charades, and, in the end, we would all burst out laughing.

We were strangers to them, but they took us in and made us feel very comfortable and at home. I was overwhelmed by their almost casual generosity. One of the sons would bring home a movie and make popcorn, buy art supplies and the girls' choice of cereal, and Mahfuz's granddaughter would play hide and seek with Hannah and Cedar.

The girl (a little older than Hannah) would hide in the house and insist—through translation offered by one of the adults in the house—that we count to 100 before trying to find her. (Hannah by now could count to seven in Arabic.)

"Are you hiding in Beirut?" I would tease the Lebanese girl.

"Okay, fifty," she would say.

The girls and I would have counted to forty when the girl would emerge from hiding.

"Are you sure you're counting high enough?" she would say.

Hannah, who likes order and clarity in her life, would storm off in a huff, her arms crossed.

"I'm not playing with you," she would inform the little girl, and the tiff was on. But then would come a change of heart, and Hannah would write love notes to the other girl and leave them outside her bedroom door.

Once again, as we had done at the hotel, we settled in. I would want to help the cleaning lady (who dusted daily), but that insulted Fatima. "But I miss this," I would explain. I satisfied my domestic urges by washing the girls' socks and underwear in the washing machine and drying them on the laundry line at the kitchen window. In time, Fatima grew more lenient and allowed me to help with laundry and dishes.

If the cleaning lady was always dusting, Fatima was always cooking: rice-and-bean casseroles, chicken schnitzels and, a Lebanese favourite, home-made French fries. Or she would order up fresh bread with *za'atar*. The windows were always open, and though Fatima smoked a shisha and one son smoked cigarettes (Marlboroughs), the air was always fresh thanks to the sea breezes off the Mediterranean.

We fell back on old routines, the girls and I. We played school, a lot, on the balcony, or read on the big sectional couch, the sort of furniture I would have bought myself. Occasionally, the girls would watch cartoons, though we were not about to interrupt Fatima's steady diet of Arabic soap operas.

Mahfuz was a confident, gregarious man. The cleaning lady adored him and the whole room lit up when he walked in.

"People think Joe Hawach is clever," he would say to me. "But I think he is stupid. He failed to keep you. And you are a special woman. You have come so far." Would he feel the same, I wondered, had I married one of his sons?

One night, Mahfuz, Fatima, the girls and I all went out for a meal of pizza—as normal an outing as could be expected, given the circumstances. On the way, Mahfuz stopped at a fruit stand and whatever the girls wanted (coconut this night) he happily obliged them. I would go to bed with the girls, often earlier than was normal or necessary, just so I could have my time with them. Hannah wanted to hear stories of babyhood—hers, mine, that of my brothers.

By now, the General had given me a new cell phone, and Hannah and I would play "Mine Sweep" and "Bounce"—simple video games in which the player's goal is to avoid virtually exploding. We became quite good at it.

The attaché's apartment was feeling like home. One night, one of Mahfuz's sons marked a birthday (his girlfriend had given him a six-foot teddy bear) and the boys just marched into our room at 9:30 p.m., roused us and announced that it was Time To Eat Cake. Proof, I guess, that they were feeling relaxed with us, too. By now, we had been guests in their house for close to two weeks. I joked with them often, remarked on how well I was eating and that I would be so portly when I got back home that no one there would recognize me. (Actually, that was a stretch. I had a way to go before regaining what I had lost during that first week in Lebanon.)

But if we needed reminding that we were not really at home, we got it on January 14—precisely one month before the second anniversary of the slaying of Rafiq al-Hariri, the former Lebanese prime minister after whom the airport in Beirut is named. Many Lebanese believe that Syrian agents had a hand in the murder, and the marking of his death had become an occasion to protest Syrian involvement in Lebanese affairs. The Orange Party, meanwhile, was organizing protests in an attempt to bring down the pro-Western Lebanese government. (Hannah later told me that during their time with their father in Lebanon, the three of them had attended an earlier protest.) We looked "downstairs" into Beirut and could see the tires burning in protest, and we watched on the news as hundreds of thousands gathered on the streets. The airport, the courts, the whole country, virtually shut down.

Finally, on February 10, my father and Patrick at home in Canada, the General with me in Lebanon: We all agreed. I had been in Lebanon for sixty-three days and it was time to start our journey home. We bade a tearful goodbye to Fatima, the cleaning lady, Mahfuz and his children. In the little bag that Mahfuz packed for us were Baby Wipes (moist towelettes). Imagine. A man who thought of things like that.

A now familiar convoy formed outside the house. The attaché's youngest son drove us in one car, while George and a friend led and the General and another man followed.

Beirut to Damascus—downtown to downtown—is a forty-minute drive. But when one hour became two, then three and then four, I began to worry.

18

I Spy

By this time, we had our ducks in line, or at least most of them. Through the Lebanese courts, and following the required postings in Lebanese newspapers, I had with me our passports and Canadian custody orders in Arabic saying that I was the sole custodian of the children and that I had the right to travel with them. "Research and information warrants" (issued for both Joe and me, these warrants come from the Lebanese judiciary and are executed by the police as a means of providing a judge with more information) are only valid for thirty days and they had by now expired. I was free to go.

On the other hand, the girls had stop orders (posted by their father) against them. This is very common in the Middle East: a wife attempting to cross a border finds the way blocked because her husband has had such an order placed against her. Lebanese officialdom was looking for us, and so were people working for the Hawach family. I believed that my own personal safety was an issue if we were to be caught, and the Engdahl family shared that worry. Besides, crossing any border is somewhat nerve-racking, and I wanted this one over.

I had packed a lot of treats and water for the girls and myself, and we would need them all. We had left behind most of our clothes—the last thing I wanted was baggage. We were travelling with the attaché's son through rocky, barren country, and while we encountered soldiers everywhere and lots of security checks, we flew through them without anyone checking our passports.

At one point, we changed into another vehicle—this one driven by Mahfuz. Possibly for security reasons, he was back in the picture. As we drove, Mahfuz (who always carried a gun, as did his son when he drove us) was telling me about all the Lebanese people fleeing into Syria. He seemed nervous, and I didn't know why.

Neither did I have any idea of where we were. You can drive from south Lebanon at the Israeli border all the way to the northern border at Syria in four hours. To repeat: Beirut to Damascus is a forty-minute drive. Were we driving in circles? One problem, perhaps, was that every time we approached a small border crossing, we found that it had been bombed out or closed.

Finally, all three cars stopped at a cheese factory, as I was told, and the men convened. Two men I had never seen before appeared in a tiny sedan.

"We're parting ways," the General told me. Then he said, "You and the girls are going to go with these two guys. They're family. We trust them." Mahfuz likewise assured me that "No one will touch a hair on your head, or the girls' either." He was fiercely protective of us. Still, I was puzzled by this shift. I had been sure Mahfuz would stay with us all the way to the border.

Another tearful goodbye. The General, George, all the men were crying, hugging the girls and me and saying, "Call us when you get to Canada." We would never have survived in Lebanon without the General and George and all their many contacts. We had been so incredibly lucky to have found these two.

But by this time, I was starting to get very confused. If the General trusted these men, then so did I. But neither spoke a word of English, and since I had gotten rid of the cell phone card as a security precaution, there would be no reassuring chats with Patrick or my family along the way. My fate, and that of my daughters, was completely in the hands of these two strangers in whose car the girls and I were backseat passengers.

We travelled a short way when one of the men, the one not driving, turned to me and, by sign language, asked me for our passports. He looked inside the passports, and, again, through mime—two hits of the bottom of his right fist into his left palm—asked, "Where are the exit stamps?"

We had no stamps. Of course we had no stamps. Why did he not know this?

We stopped at a small building in the centre of a gravel parking lot. It looked official, with a Lebanese flag out front. The passenger in our car got out, with our passports, and we drove off. At that point, I decided I was not going to worry. I was going to read books to my girls and keep them happy as we sat in a car travelling over a dirt road made muddy by recent rains. You could safely call it the middle of nowhere.

We stopped. I remember a man working on a metal roof. There were kids playing in the street, men on scooters, and the air was bracing and cold. We were led across a makeshift corrugated metal bridge and there, on the other side of the bridge, waited a young woman in her late twenties. She was pretty and smiling and dressed in a jogging suit. It felt good to see another woman. I was not frightened, but, on the other hand, no one had prepared me for this.

Were we in Syria?

"*Syria hahn?*" I asked her, but I got no reply. The driver of our car whistled and a man on a motorbike came straight to us and stopped. Hannah, meanwhile, was fuming because mud had stained her boots. To avoid the mud of the paths, we were—all three of us—invited onto the motorbike. Four people on a motorbike? Welcome to Lebanon. The girls loved this. The order went like this: Hannah, then the driver, then Cedar, then me. We only went about 60 metres, and at a snail's pace, but we did avoid the mud.

We finally arrived at a small house, and entered a room devoid of all furniture. Just rugs on the floor and cushions against all the walls. Again, this delighted the girls, who did somersaults and played on the cushions. It was warm inside, with a little oil heater, and fruit and *tabbouleh* had been prepared for us. Several men and the young woman smoked cigarettes and spoke in Arabic. Some sort of waiting game was in play here.

The young woman spoke some English and I also tried my high school French. They were asking me questions about my husband and my instinct was to say nothing. I did not know these people.

She said, in Lebanese, "*Na mas hahn.*" You'll sleep here. Was this supposed to be fun or amusing? Were they teasing me? Testing me?

"*La,*" I replied.

No.

"*Na mas Damascus.*" We'll sleep in Damascus thank you very much, I said, and was not comforted when they all laughed.

Then a man, a big imposing man in his thirties, pulled up in a pickup truck. He had a pleasant face, but he looked very tense. It was time to go. But where? And where was I? I had no clue. By now I was feeling both anxious and vulnerable: My bag was back at the car, and it had been a while since I had seen our passports. Still, I knew the General would never put us in danger.

I had been wearing a white scarf, called a hijab, and one of the two men from the little sedan—I took him to be the husband of the young woman—kept coming to me and rolling and re-rolling the scarf until it was just so. The General's wife had given me the scarf. Most Muslim women wear it the way this man wanted it: the long edge of the scarf across my forehead and just above the eyebrows, the ends pulled down and pinned under the chin, then draped over my shoulders. The problem was this: I had no pin and the hijab would not stay in place. My instinct was to tuck the scarf in behind my ear, but no, he wanted the scarf just in front. He was very, very carefully fussing with this scarf, as if the way it was arranged mattered terribly and might spell the difference between getting across, or not. Between flying home and languishing in a dark jail cell.

I felt a rising panic but I once more reminded myself that the General and his men would never have put me in a dangerous situation. The guy in the truck, though, lacked the General's charm and fierce protectiveness. He was all business. I had with me a small bag, with little more than Baby Wipes and the kids' storybook inside, but he did not want it on my lap. He wanted the bag on the floor. We were driving down a bumpy road, over this puddle and then another, on this drizzly miserable grey day. Houses along the road were modest, the children poorly dressed. Now and again a motorbike would pass and give a nod or a wave. Our driver kept turning to me, looking at me and saying "Shhhhhhhh."

Now and again, he would motion to me to re-roll the side of my scarf. I was to adjust my hair, my black, bobbed hair, and tuck it in behind the scarf, the scarf to cover the ears, never exposed. Again, that almost obsessive, fastidious attention to the scarf. I was not talking, just trying to keep the girls calm but they were getting antsy. We had been on the road now for five or six hours.

The driver pointed up ahead. Police. This moment was the most intense of the journey. The man wanted the girls' hoods up, but Cedar was having one of her meltdowns. The driver was miming angrily: Get that hood back up! Though there are a lot of fair-haired children in Lebanon, he did not want her blonde hair grabbing attention. He put her hood back on, whereupon Cedar screamed and had a full-blown three-year-old's tantrum. The driver went on saying, "Shhhhhhhh!," hoping that male authority would do the trick. It did not. I could tell he was scared. He made a sign: I was to put my hand over Cedar's mouth. I just shook my head. I thought, if we get pulled over and I get arrested, okay, but I am not going to cover my child's mouth to make her be quiet. If this was it, this was it. We were in God's hands.

The man signalled to me that a van up ahead was driving towards us. "Police!" he said urgently in English. But the van drove right past us and almost immediately we came upon a policeman sitting in a chair outside a small single-person shelter and holding a machine gun in his lap. He did not so much as look at us when we drove past him. It was like we were invisible, but for forty-five seconds I experienced a numbing, heart-pounding intensity.

Cedar was still screaming as we passed the policeman. What felt like a checkpoint, I now know, was the border. I kept my eyes forward, kept rubbing Cedar's back and saying "Shhhhhh, baby, shhhhhhh." We drove on and suddenly our driver turned to me and gave me a big smile and a thumbs up. He was a different person now, proof that he had been truly terrified—despite any and all precautions the General had orchestrated, there was doubt and fear all around. We were in the clear and now I knew we were in Syria. In that moment, I was both angry and glad I had not been prepped for such a crossing. I would never have agreed to a crossing that seemed so much like a wing and a prayer.

We stopped in a village near a fruit stand, and from a taxi that pulled up emerged one of the two men the General had assigned to us. He had our luggage and our passports and he, too, seemed as relieved and elated as we were. Now it was off to Damascus in a different cab—another three hours or more away.

The girls and I sat in the back and played "I Spy," we read books, sang songs. Hannah kept kicking the driver's seat, which the driver did not much like and he kept turning around to deliver withering glances. Both girls were by now really tired and hungry and they took turns having meltdowns, but by now I did not care if the driver was miffed. I went on singing, and sometimes the General's man—sitting up front with the cabbie—would offer to take Cedar up there and play with her.

Finally, after an hour of getting lost and the cabbie having to stop and ask directions, we arrived in the cold and the dark at our destination: the Canadian embassy in Damascus. I knew that the consul general's wife happened to have a sister who is good friends with an aunt and uncle of mine in Yorkton, Saskatchewan. Though I had never met these career diplomats, I saw Steve and Carole as family friends living in Syria, which made this a homecoming of sorts. We arrived, I said goodbye to our guy, then we walked into the embassy. Canadian flags everywhere, a picture of the Queen, brochures—Niagara Falls, the CN Tower—which the girls now went around collecting.

"Hello," said an embassy official. "I'm happy to see you."

Hannah had grown accustomed to hearing a lot of Lebanese spoken, often loud and expressive Lebanese. The language is so guttural that a speaker can sound angry even when he's not. My daughter looked up at me and said, "His voice sounds nice. Are we in Canada?"

19

Plan B

Inside the embassy and Steve's ample office, the girls helped themselves to candy canes and bottles of water. They were also playing with something on his desk but I cannot remember for the life of me what it was. In the courtyard outside was a huge maple tree with bright red leaves—obviously plastic and fake, but cool nonetheless.

I called Dad at our house in the foothills of Alberta. He was still in hiding and would stay in hiding until we were safely out of Lebanon. His worry was that someone would retrace his steps and perhaps learn of our own escape plans.

"How was it?" he asked. He meant the crossing.

"I don't know if I can quite talk about it. We didn't exactly stop at the Hard Rock Café and cross in a tinted embassy vehicle."

"I know what you mean," he assured me.

"No, Dad," I said. "No, you don't."

"That bad?" he asked.

"It wasn't what was discussed or what I was prepared for," I told him, not wanting to say too much for fear of aggravating his heart. "There were a lot of back roads and it took twelve hours."

From Dad I later learned that Plan A had been scrapped—for a very important reason. There had been a timeline, a little window, and, for whatever reason, we had missed it. Steve, meanwhile, had waited for us for hours in the free zone between Syria and Lebanon—all our visas in hand.

We had gone to Plan B.

Still, I was breathing a sigh of relief. We had jumped the biggest hurdle. Steve, then Canada's consul general in Syria, took us to a shopping mall and bought us all toothbrushes and shampoo. For the first time in months, I felt I could relax. We went to a Kentucky Fried Chicken restaurant and the girls frolicked in the play area.

We would be bunking at the Four Seasons Hotel—chosen for us by the Canadian embassy in Damascus. Much used by Canadians and less than a year old, it was the finest hotel I have ever stayed in. Hannah, Cedar and I slept in a king-size bed. We had our own slippers and robes, a bathroom fit for a queen and, of course, breakfast in bed: pancakes, muesli and fresh grapefruit, all wheeled into the room on a silver service. We pretended we were princesses, and, for a while, I actually felt like one.

Hannah and Cedar delighted in the little perks that grand hotels offer their guests—such as a complimentary shoeshine. We hung our mud-splattered shoes and boots in a bag on the doorknob and they came back in the morning immaculately clean and polished. We likewise left our laundry at the door in a bag, and the clothes were returned, having been washed, dried and folded.

My father had stayed in this same hotel during his night in Damascus. I was concerned about the cost (I had no credit cards, just $2,000 in American cash that the General had given me) but the hotel was incredibly well priced.

The next morning we went for a walk outside the hotel, where construction was under way on the high-end shops to come. It seemed that I was the only woman on the streets, and everyone was staring at me. Is this a street, I wondered, only for men? Am I even supposed to be here? Every man wanted to touch Cedar's blonde hair. The girls started to play on a swing set in the park behind the hotel, and soon there were five men watching us. Pretty quickly, I began to feel very alone, and very vulnerable.

Later I would read in a Canadian newspaper about Syria and how tourism there is growing as oil revenues decline. Government figures show that more than three million people—excluding the hundreds of thousands of refugees fleeing violence in Iraq—visited Syria in 2006, almost double the number who visited in 2000. The welcome mat may be out officially but I had the sense that Syria is much more conservative than Lebanon and that Syrians still view outsiders as curiosities. Canada's own government does not warn against travel to Syria but does counsel travellers to "maintain a high level of personal security awareness at all times." The Australian government advises "exercising extreme caution," while Americans are told simply and flatly: Do not go there.

Some of those I met in Lebanon (lawyers, embassy workers) would sometimes say to me during my time in hiding there, "At least this didn't happen in Syria." What did that mean? Then I would hear stories of children being detained in Syrian prisons with their mothers and fathers for long periods. "You don't want to know," I heard some say.

The story of Maher Arar, of course, was fresh in my mind as I walked the streets of Damascus with my daughters. He is the Canadian engineer who got caught up in the post-9/11 furor—a stopover in New York following a family vacation in Tunisia led to his being branded a terrorist, deportation by the Americans to his native Syria and more than a year of torture in prison.

Someone had told us that Damascus was home to a million stray cats, so the game the girls and I sometimes played on the streets was to count the strays. I felt a strange kinship with all those homeless cats, and home still felt a long way away.

The flight of the dragonfly was very much like ours: We would rise, then dip, pause and drop like a stone.

* * *

The next evening, Steve picked us up and drove us to the school where his wife, Carole, taught—at the kindergarten level—both Syrian and expatriate North American children. The 100th day of school apparently occasions a major, two-day celebration in Syrian primary schools, with "100" the abiding theme. Students had on display all kinds of collections (one pupil, for example, had glued on a board 100 different types of pasta). Hannah and Cedar walked wide-eyed about the classrooms full of arts and crafts.

We then went back to Steve and Carole's house and made dinner together. Their eldest son, a gifted athlete, was then sixteen and he was about to watch World Cup soccer on television. There was Canadian maple syrup in their house, Starbucks coffee (two touches that reminded me of home), and they had a lovely black Labrador retriever dog and a cat. There had been no pets at any of our stops in Lebanon, and the girls now fussed over these animals. The whole family was sweet and it felt good to be with them. Before we headed back to our hotel room, Carole helped Hannah and Cedar pick out games and books and puzzles to take with us.

That night, from the hotel room, I called Patrick. He had returned to Calgary weeks earlier, since it was costly to stay in Cyprus, even in his modest hotel, and at that point there was no guarantee when we would cross into Syria. The girls were asleep as we talked. Ours would be a marathon conversation.

Another snag, you see, had arisen, one that would strand me in Syria until it was resolved. By going from Plan A to Plan B, we now lacked proper visas to leave Syria. Our entry stamps—and remember, you cannot leave most Middle East countries without them—had been applied for by the Canadian embassy, had been approved, and were still waiting for us at the crossing point designated as part of Plan A. That night, it hit me: I was in Syria, illegally, and the girls and I were vulnerable. The thought of Lebanese jails for some reason did not terrify me, but Syrian jails did.

From my hotel room in Damascus I would call home and hear all this celebrating and cheering in the background. For me, the high-fives felt very premature. We were not out, not by a long shot, and I worried that word would get out that we were in Syria. Our friends, their friends, relations: How do you keep a lid on all those people? How do you stop reporters from issuing the news when they inevitably hear it? As bad as it was at times for us in Lebanon, Syria had the potential to be far worse.

I was angry, and I was still very much in survival mode. I could not let my guard down and I was so distraught to hear the breezy chatter emanating from members of my family in Alberta and Saskatchewan. The cold fear kept assailing me: that I would lose the girls all over again, this time for good. It is a parent's greatest fear, one I had lived with for some six months, and I could not shake it.

I also felt very, very alone. I thought someone was going to come through that hotel door and get me. Canadian embassy staff were evidently worried about me. Later I would learn that staff had been told to forgo attending a big conference in Egypt. The reason? Melissa Hawach was not out yet.

Patrick and I talked on the phone that night—my second night in Syria—for three and a half hours. "You really lost it that night," he would later say. "I knew right then I'd have to come to Syria. If I didn't, I was sure that just pieces of you would come home. I thought for one hour I was talking to a crazy woman."

The happy front I had been maintaining for the girls' sake fell away that night. I cried all the while I was speaking to Patrick and continued even after we said our goodbyes. More than anything, I felt extremely unsafe.

Patrick said he could hear the relief in my voice when he said he was coming. The following day he was in Jordan. But there he discovered that if my getting out of Syria was nettlesome, so was his getting in. The Canadian embassy in the Jordanian capital of Amman—well aware of the Melissa Hawach file—flatly advised him: Don't go into Syria, and don't do anything stupid. Patrick was told that Syria does not welcome tourists, and that getting a tourist visa involves sending one's passport to Ottawa, and a six- to eight-week wait that may or may not result in a visa (which would be good for one visit only, and that no longer than fifteen days).

"I'll do what I have to do," Patrick told the embassy. "I'll keep you posted." Then he walked out onto the streets of the ancient city of Amman. Patrick is an experienced traveller and he knows that in a sticky situation or when bureaucrats throw up roadblocks, you look for people in the know. Cabbies and bartenders.

20

Happy Valentine's Day

Later that day, a Tuesday, Patrick had lunch with a Jordanian taxi driver who knew a clerk at a certain embassy. Turns out a visa to Syria was available—if you knew who to ask. In many countries in the world, people like this cab driver and this clerk must continually weigh what they might earn by cooperating in such an illegal venture against the penalty they might face if caught. The rewards may seem to them substantial, and likewise is the penalty, but meagre wages in the Middle East mean that someone, somewhere, is almost always willing to roll the dice. And bartenders and cabbies seem to know who these gamblers are and where they live.

What made Patrick's situation even more challenging was that he wanted the stamp in a hurry. He needed it by Wednesday or Thursday, because the Middle East is pretty well shut down Friday (their sabbath, which is strictly observed) through Monday. Amman is an expensive place in which to loiter, and Patrick also worried that I was finally beginning to wilt under the pressure of this almost eight-month-long ordeal.

* * *

While Patrick wrestled with the visa requirement in Amman, we in Damascus were given shelter—yet again—by people we hardly knew.

Steve and Carole and their family welcomed us into their home, not as dinner guests this time, but as house guests. Even the black Lab, Simba, seemed happy to see us. Their gesture offered me immense relief: Their house was Canada to me.

And once again, as had happened at Mahfuz's house in Beirut, someone (one son—in this case, the second-eldest boy) was forced onto a mattress in his parents' bedroom while Hannah and Cedar and I got his room.

And, strange as it may seem, I was excited to be able to do my laundry and that of the girls. This most personal of labours had been mostly denied me for months and it felt good to have the job back. Each evening we all helped make dinner, cooperated in the cleanup that followed, and then Steve would help his kids with their homework while Carole prepared for classes the next day. I had heard that the families of diplomats respond to the constant uprooting by becoming a closer and more involved unit, and I responded to that. It was like cozying up to a warm fire on a cold winter's night. Being with what seemed a strong, but in many ways typical, Canadian family took the girls and me one more step in the direction of normalcy.

The girls were happy to be in a house that felt as close to home as they had experienced in almost eight months. The place was big and comfortable, maybe 2,000 square feet, with a central courtyard and a basketball net and picnic/barbecue area. The family's youngest boy would play with the girls on the computer and the youngest girl would colour with them, and all three children were generous with their time. This was just what the girls needed: hearing English and eating Fruit Loops for breakfast. It seemed like we were all in rehearsal for home.

On February 12, Patrick arrived in Damascus. The entry stamp (it had cost him $180) had done its work. We were all so excited to see him, and Steve and Carole made him most welcome. He had brought with him new DVDs for the girls, video games for the trip home, gifts from my mother (jogging suits, underwear and pyjamas for the girls, and clothes for me) and the thyroid medication I had done without for weeks. We all hugged and hugged.

I did worry a bit about how the girls would receive Patrick, given what Joe had told them, but there were no misgivings. The girls ran to him and welcomed him, as they would have any friend from home. That night, it was decided—by Hannah and Cedar—that they would sleep on foam mattresses on the floor of our ample bedroom while Patrick and I got its double bed. This followed a spirited debate between the girls over who was going to sleep next to Patrick or next to me, and finally it was decided the two girls would share the mattress and watch a movie.

* * *

Valentine's Day came and Cedar and I woke up early and made pink heart-shaped pancakes—decorated with sparkles and strawberries and topped with Canadian maple syrup—for Hannah and Patrick when they woke up. Carole had left us Valentine's plates and cups to round out the theme, and so we all enjoyed a special breakfast by candlelight.

Patrick had brought with him a small video camera and so we have on tape a long (no, interminable) and hilarious song that Cedar sang that morning in Damascus. The melody and the lyrics were entirely hers, made up on the spot, and it expressed her love for every person and object in Carole's immaculate white-tiled kitchen. All of us laughed heartily at Cedar's love song/rap song to the world.

In the days that followed, we walked around Damascus together. With Patrick at my side, no one stared anymore. Damascus ranks among the oldest continuously inhabited cities in the world (some say it dates as far back as 10,000 years before the birth of Christ), and its covered market (Al Hamidieh Souk) may well be the oldest in the world. Not many tourists go there, but now we felt free to explore the city and environs.

We travelled to an ancient amphitheatre built at Basra by the Romans and marvelled at its size and efficiency. The girls were dancing and playing on the stage, and so ingenious are the acoustics that Patrick and I could hear them perfectly in the upper bleachers of this dizzyingly steep theatre that once seated up to 15,000 patrons. Outside, fifteen men sang religious songs in harmony and it was impossible not to dance or clap to their song. At last, I felt I could clap.

We hired a guide and toured the site in a mule-drawn cart, all of us looking in amazement at the laundry hanging everywhere and the vitality of the place. Though this is a tourist site, and one of the gems on Syria's list of attractions, the people who had been living in the surrounding homes had no desire to move to new digs. So the government let them stay, and they add a lively, human dimension to an ancient site. On the tour, Hannah had learned about keystones—the central stones at the summit of arches—and the game as we toured the site was to count them.

In the ancient covered market, we picked out Syrian pyjamas for the girls—striking, long-sleeved, ankle-length garments. Hannah's in orange, Cedar's in green. Patrick suggested we pick out something for me, but I had to decline the giant feather boa that Hannah had her eye on. I also bought a big bag of *za'atar*, the Middle East spice mix that's slightly different in every country, to bring back to Canada with me.

We then bought new shoes for the girls, groceries so we could make make dinner for our hosts, a movie to watch that night. It all felt so nice, so normal.

21

A White (and Late) Christmas

On February 16, 2007, we bade Steve and Carole and their family a tearful, heartfelt thanks and goodbye. Hannah Hawach, Cedar Hawach, Melissa Hawach and Patrick Lalande left Damascus in a Canadian embassy vehicle bound for Amman, Jordan. Our passports, at last, were all in order.

The Canadian government had applied—through the embassy on a rush request directly to the Syrian government—for tourist visas for the girls and me. In the entire history of the Canadian embassy presence in Syria, I was told, this had only been done once before, and that was for Jim Engdahl. We had been told by the General that our photos were at the Syrian borders and on a special Syrian government computer system—the latter accomplished by an extremely wealthy family in Syria as a favour to Joseph's uncle. All this made me paranoid in the extreme, but for all that, the visas were granted without a single question. Not one red flag was raised.

Was the General's information wrong? Was this just a rumour launched by the other side? Was the General exaggerating the risk to justify his fee? Any and all explanations are possible.

Steve reassured us. He said that despite what we had been told, had there been even a hint of trouble with our visa applications, they would have been denied. Getting a tourist visa for Syria can be difficult and time-consuming. As Patrick had earlier been told, one typically applies from Canada by sending one's passport to the embassy in Ottawa, and it can take up to eight weeks to find out if the visa will be granted. No guarantees. Our Syrian visas, by comparison, were a breeze.

As for the nagging problem of our exit stamps from Lebanon and our entry stamps into Syria, Steve simply delivered our passports back to the General, who arranged for the correct stamps to be inserted.

At the border, none of us even had to leave Steve's mini-van. There was a half-hour wait, but these were the normal delays that travellers face in the Middle East and elsewhere. We were no longer in hiding, no longer fearful or watchful. We were, thank God, just camera-toting tourists.

The girls left with the teddy bears given to them by Mahfuz (it seemed he always had something for them—candies and treats and dolls). The teddy bears went inside the backpacks we had bought in Damascus—a Barbie model for Hannah, a Mickey Mouse one for Cedar. In Jordan, we were met by a Canadian embassy official who escorted us to our hotel for our one-night stay. There, we got a reminder of all that we had been through: We, the girls included, had to pass through a metal detector just to get into our hotel.

Next day, the same Canadian embassy official escorted us onto the plane, right to the roomy seats at the front aboard Lufthansa Flight 693, bound for Frankfurt, Germany. Our final destination: Calgary, Canada.

Every Lufthansa flight to Europe from Jordan stops in Lebanon—except the business-class flight. That, for obvious reasons, was the one we wanted. The girls' names had been assigned yellow alerts by Interpol, but thanks to the efforts of Jean-Marc Lesage and his colleagues at Foreign Affairs in Ottawa—who were working around the clock on our behalf—those alerts had been removed. German authorities had been alerted well in advance and I had a few telephone numbers of immigration officials there. Just in case.

In Frankfurt, we faced an eight-hour delay before boarding our plane home. A curious thing happened at that airport in western Germany: Tired and hungry, we had settled into a giant bench seat at a restaurant but I soon worried that the seat's lone occupant was feeling overcrowded by the four of us. When he shot us an annoyed look, I immediately moved the girls' bags onto the floor and out of his way.

The man, who happened to be a black man, spoke German but

enough English to get across his point: He followed Patrick, who had gone to exchange some money at a kiosk, and essentially accused us of racism. He thought we had moved the bags because of his colour.

My first thought when I saw him leave the table was that he did not like children, and, had he been there, a lively argument might have ensued. Later, I wondered about my combativeness. Perhaps it was because I still felt protective of the girls, and anyone not friendly to them was, by default, my enemy. We retreated to the plastic seats in a huge McDonald's restaurant and the girls jumped with other children in the glass-enclosed playground.

With us in Frankfurt was a Canadian embassy official, who did not leave our side until we were on the plane and headed home. He told us that it was his experience in Germany that children are to be seen and not heard. He was not surprised by the man moving or the ladies next to us shooting piercing looks at the girls every few minutes. The embassy official seemed even a little amused, as he was obviously used to it. What a stark contrast to the lavish attention and time our Lebanese friends had heaped on the girls every chance they got.

On February 17, we arrived in Calgary. There had been some debate among members of "the team" over whether the media should be alerted. I was dead set against that. I just wanted to settle in before the storm hit.

* * *

I did not realize that the storm had already hit—at Christmastime. Reporters had flown in from Australia, Calgary reporters had interviewed my old neighbours on Copperfield, one aggressive journalist had been at the land registry office pulling records in hopes of learning the location of our new house—not something we wanted broadcast to the world.

While we were still in hiding, the book offers and movie offers had flooded in. Where had all these people been when we were desperate to raise awareness and tell our story back in the fall? In Canada, the Missing Children Society handled media for us, but in Australia—where the story was even bigger—my Canadian friend living in Sydney, Sherry, helped Patrick find an agent who could take on some of this.

Sherry's sister, who lives in Toronto, had seen my story in the news and passed it on. A television producer, Sherry was a very important contact for me: This tough little blonde found my literary agent, she hooked me up with Brian *et al.*, she introduced me to Paul, the Lebanese businessman, and she was on the phone with Patrick—a lot.

Even before I touched down on Canadian soil, then, I had an agent (based in Sydney). I found myself on a stage under a blinding spotlight, but what I really wanted was dull normalcy: a quiet breakfast with Patrick, reading to my girls at bedtime, a chance to play centre field and maybe nail the runner heading for home. And some rest. I was absolutely exhausted.

When I was in Syria staying with Steve and his family, he brought home a printout of a news clipping suggesting that my Australian agent was in Calgary, that my return was imminent, but that if I did not show up soon the agent would be going home. I went ballistic and called my family. "What is going on?" I asked. "Why is anyone outside my family in Calgary waiting for me at the airport?"

Apparently a reporter and photographer from Australia, along with my agent, were in Calgary waiting for me. I cannot express in words how livid I was. Did nobody understand how much I did not care? It was not that I was angry about the Australian press being there: I had agreed to an interview and aimed to honour that commitment, there was a fee paid (and there was no denying that I needed it, with bills coming in fast—including a bill of more than $50,000 from my Australian lawyers). What had me fuming was that my return had been guaranteed—on a certain date. How could anyone have promised that?

I had not been on a holiday tour, nor was I bound to return home out of allegiance to reporters who had come a long way. I, too, had come a long way, a very long way—and then some. I felt like nobody understood that the girls and I were not home safe yet and that was my only goal and concern.

When I was still in Syria, I was getting e-mails from my agent about the "benefits" of a media frenzy to welcome me home at the airport in order to generate a buzz and revitalize the story. I made it clear that if there was any media frenzy at that airport, I would completely lose it. I left it in my family's hands to keep our date of arrival to themselves and I also told them that if this request was not respected, I was going to hold them responsible. Pretty strong words to be telling a family that had done nothing but support me and sacrifice with me throughout this whole nasty ordeal. I just did not know how otherwise to express the depth of my aversion to this scenario.

When we finally did hold a press conference a few weeks later, I was asked by a journalist to comment on reports that actress Angelina Jolie was interested in the movie rights to my story. By this point I was a little sick of having my life exposed, and I told him that even members of my family knew better than to begin discussing such matters, and that my agent would handle those sorts of things. I had not asked to be drawn into this spotlight, I said. I just wanted to be a mom to my girls.

I was sleeping in the girls' room at home when Patrick came in with the newspaper one morning. He said that he had something to show me (the Angelina Jolie mention) but he begged me to find it funny and to laugh. Everything in the media about my story seemed to anger me and he was trying to get me to lighten up a little.

* * *

When the plane touched down at the airport in Calgary, I breathed a small—but only a small—sigh of relief. Even here, on home ground, our cloak-and-dagger routine persisted. There would be no throng of family and friends with "Welcome Home" signs, no camera flashes popping. I had been told that the only visible greeters would be people from the roundtable—two Calgary police detectives quite familiar with my case, Theresa Garagan and John Hebert.

But even before then, the girls and I had to go through customs and immigration. And it was during that process, to my great surprise, that I felt the most emotion on this, my homecoming day. The uniformed immigration official, a young woman, stamped my passport and said, looking straight at me, "Welcome home, Melissa. Welcome home to Canada." That moved me a great deal.

Patrick, meanwhile, went through immigration with all the other passengers and he gathered our luggage at the carousel. A friend of his picked him up and brought him to our house in the foothills. The old Copperfield Gardens team were all at the airport—in a security room watching us on surveillance cameras as we disembarked. Theresa was apparently getting agitated at seeing Patrick film us from behind (she knew he would be in trouble for using his camera at a security-conscious place like customs and immigration). Sure enough, he was quickly asked to turn the video camera off.

There, too, at the airport was my old high school friend, Andy, who had helped design the web site that had helped us find the girls. Dressed incognito in baseball cap and sunglasses, he was skulking around the airport hoping to surprise us, but he never actually saw us and we never saw him. It was not until later in the week when we had breakfast with him that we discovered he had been there.

Caught up in the excitement surrounding our return, my father had called Andy's wife, Simone, and given her a very funny and cryptic message. We all laughed so hard when they told the story at that breakfast. His message was something like, "Our package is arriving from Germany tomorrow." And then he hung up.

Beyond the immigration desk waited John and Theresa, who whisked us to a corridor and a backdoor staircase where the welcoming committee grew to include Darryl Stark from Bison Security, Dave Chittick from the Missing Children Society of Canada and my brother Doug. We were all led to a back door and then outside where Darryl's van was waiting, along with John and Theresa's unmarked police car.

My brother and the girls sat in the van's back seat while Darryl and I occupied the front. Dave said goodbye at the back door of the airport but Theresa and John followed us in their car to make sure we were not being followed. We took a roundabout route home, just to be sure.

Snow blanketed the ground in the foothills, and I was reminded of that first time the girls and I had gone up into the mountains in Lebanon, my reconnection with my daughters still so recent and fresh. Once home, Hannah and Cedar ran out of the van to play in the snow as my family—Mom and Dad, the rest of my family and their partners—all spilled out of the house onto the front lawn. I had taken with me to Lebanon pictures of the new house to prepare the girls, and they were thrilled at seeing it. Patrick and my brothers had spent days before Patrick left for Syria hanging up Christmas lights. A good thing the neighbours could not see them through the trees hanging Christmas decorations at the beginning of February!

Everyone was crying, but not me. I had left my tears in Lebanon and Syria.

In one corner of the living room stood a fully decorated artificial Christmas tree, with presents for everyone—all, of course, unopened. (Mom had been dutifully dusting the tree for months.) Hannah and Cedar were beside themselves with excitement. Christmas 2006 had been delayed and now it would be properly celebrated—with turkey and dressing and two kinds of pie (apple and pumpkin). Among their presents were Fisher-Price kids' cameras, so the girls could film everything.

For Cedar, there was a bonus. Back in September, we had baked a chocolate birthday cake in her honour and decorated it with dragonflies. The cake, of course, was history, but all of Cedar's birthday presents were waiting as well.

Downstairs was their new bedroom, which had been decorated to match almost perfectly the one at Copperfield—with a patchwork of pastel colours on one wall, the same decorations and the same bedspreads and a pink lava lamp, the gold sparkles inside rising and dropping like gently falling snow. Outside, the girls tried out the swings and then explored the tree house that previous owners had built.

For so many months, I had dreamed of this moment. Of setting foot on Canadian soil, of us all being together as a family.

* * *

One day, not long after we were back in Canada from our "adventure" in the Middle East, the children of two friends I had played ball with—Damon, nine, and Chase, four—stopped by for a visit, along with their parents. We were all walking up the stone path to the house, and Damon, somewhat indiscreetly but in all innocence, asked Hannah a question.

"So, your dad finally let you go, eh?"

We all drew in our breath, worried about how she would respond.

"No," said Hannah very matter of factly, "my mom came and got us."

EPILOGUE

The Aftermath

Lovell Bowen, the now meek, now bold "Auntie Leslie" character from our encounters in Sydney with the Hawach family, has strawberry-blonde hair and the bluest blue eyes. A straight-talking spitfire of a woman with an athletic build and fingernails painted bright orange, she is as handy with a quilt as she is with a sidearm. Lovell is a grandmother who worked almost five years in the child abuse unit of the Calgary police force. One of the first things she did when Hannah and Cedar got back from what we still call "our adventure in Lebanon" was to bring her own grandchildren over to play with the girls. Lovell and her husband, Don, live in a small town not far from my house.

A few days later, Lovell, fifty-six as I write this, went for a mammogram. The results were at first reassuring, then devastating. She was told she had cancer of the breast, which had spread. Radiation and chemotherapy treatment commenced almost immediately, and there would follow good days and bad days, days when Lovell felt entirely herself, and other days when she could not lift herself off the couch.

In May 2007, the business community in Saskatoon, Saskatchewan, put on a fund-raising dinner meant to help us defray the enormous costs of the search and rescue. Lovell and Don drove eight hours to get there, and, though she could hardly walk due to complications from her treatment, she formally presented the girls and me with the hope quilts they have slept under every night since. As I and others spoke at the podium that night in front of some 400 people, the quilts behind us formed a striking backdrop. Our entire journey seemed to have been encapsulated on those breathtaking quilts. Full size and exquisite, those quilts are two of the most beautiful presents the girls have ever received.

I remember going to see Lovell with the girls in mid-June 2007. I did not know which Lovell I was going to see that day: the formidable woman I knew from our time in Sydney or the patient laid low by a relentless disease and the attempts to cure it. She sat on the couch in the TV room upstairs while we were there, as if this was, indeed, her base of operations. Pictures of her children and grandchildren adorned every shelf and wall, in the same way that pictures of Hannah and Cedar gaze out from almost every wall in my own house.

Lovell was perky that day, her old self. Almost. "How ya feelin', sweetie?" were the first words she uttered. My health (I was four months pregnant) not hers, was the first topic of discussion. (Lovell's own health would steadily improve, by the way, and she seems robust once more as I write this in late November 2007.)

That day we talked about quilts, of course. It was not long before she had her son (whose children were playing outside on the sidewalk with Hannah and Cedar as we chatted) hauling up quilts from downstairs. Like a game-show model, he smiled for us and dutifully held up each quilt so the careful stitching, the elaborate detail, the many motifs could be explained to me, and admired.

Lovell had started working on the hope quilts for Hannah and Cedar as soon as she got back from Sydney, and she vowed that she would not stop working on them and detailing them until we were home. Lovell and Don also collected funds from their church members to help with our costs. Like many professionals working on this case, she had gone far beyond the call of duty and become emotionally involved. Strangers, I have often thought to myself, championed our cause—except that many of them are no longer strangers at all but close friends.

"I've slept with you," Lovell would tell me that afternoon. "I held you when you were crying as if I was your mother. There were times when you were ready to give up and I had to be able to comfort you. I remember you asked me once, 'How will I know the right thing to do, if the courts don't give me back my children?' And I told you, 'Your mother's heart will know.'"

Lovell knew that working on the quilts would create hope for everyone involved in the search and that making the quilts was a physical manifestation of that hope. Lovell asked my mother and father for the girls' photos, and they had to be of the best quality and precisely the right size to fit the blocks on the quilt. The process is lengthy and complicated, and it took several tries and several printers before the images could be properly transferred onto muslin. Finally, Lovell stitched each cloth image into the quilt.

Lovell knew that the words "hope" and "love" had to be inscribed on each quilt, and that each quilt would be festooned with flowers, bunnies and dragonflies large and small. On trips into small-town Alberta, on holiday in Hawaii, she hunted in fabric shops for material. At a fabric show in Calgary, just when she was starting the quilts, she found dragonfly charms made of metal and beads, and she deftly sewed those onto the quilts. The pattern for Cedar's quilt came from Australia—where, Lovell says, some of the best quilt patterns in the world are made. In all, Lovell told me, the two quilts were a hundred hours in the making.

Hannah and Cedar are obsessed with the quilts. Hannah has taken hers proudly into her classroom and picked out the words love and hope, and explained to her classmates why the dragonfly figures so prominently. On cool mornings, I will drive Hannah to school in the mini-van and Cedar comes with us, of course, but only after she has wrapped herself in her hope quilt. Every morning the quilts are neatly folded at the foot of their beds. Every night, the quilts cover the girls and keep them warm and feeling safe.

"It's a security thing," says Lovell, who knows a thing or two about the subject.

* * *

I wish the quilts were magic quilts, that they could provide actual security for Hannah and Cedar and me. The flight of the dragonfly looks to be over, but maybe not. After our return, friends and family would say, "You must be so happy this is all over." It may not be.

Patrick and I still worry that another attempt may be made to grab the girls—either by their father or his emissaries. Finding the girls in Lebanon was a difficult task; far easier would be to find the girls in Alberta.

My father shares our fear of another abduction. "There's always the risk," he says. My mother, on the other hand, does not worry about another kidnapping, but the first one continues to haunt her. "I'm still scared," she says. "I think of how it could have gone, how it might have ended in a different way. I don't feel quite finished with it all."

My mother and father both feel guilt for not speaking up earlier and loudly. We have all learned that hard lesson—that instincts should sometimes be obeyed. Krista, the partner of my brother Brendan, told me that as she watched Joe leave "on vacation" with the girls, she had a powerful feeling that we would not be seeing Hannah and Cedar for a long time. Krista has a friend who knows of four abductions quite similar to our case. Maybe, had we all—including me—been a little less polite and quiet, this thing could have been avoided.

I look back on my decision to let Joe take the girls to Australia and I can see that my instincts were still clouded by my need to buy peace between him and me. Even then, separated from him, he had a way of making me doubt myself. He could be so persuasive and I was still vulnerable to him.

Ask Jim and Judy Engdahl if they have an ounce of sympathy left for their counterparts, Louie and Gladys Hawach, and my parents will at first say no. But press them, and they will soften their stand. Dad feels bad that the Hawaches have no contact with two granddaughters, while Mom tries to imagine what it must be like to have a son do what Joe did. What really astonishes my parents, though, is that Louie and Gladys have made no attempt to get in touch with Hannah and Cedar or to respond to any of the letters and photos the girls and I have sent them.

This part of the story, at least, has ended and ended reasonably well. The girls are back home, with their mother, and no one was physically hurt in the process. We feel relatively safe, and the civil court in Lebanon (like the family court in Canada) has recognized that I am the sole custodian of Hannah and Cedar. That breakthrough occurred on February 10, 2007, and was important for several reasons. With that document in hand, our Lebanese lawyers were able to prove in criminal court that I had proper custody of the girls, had therefore not committed any crime by taking them, and neither had Brian and David. The ruling meant that they, like me, were guilty of nothing more than a misdemeanour (obstruction of justice) and this eventually led to their release from jail.

Getting the Lebanese judicial system to recognize the custody rights of a woman (a non-Muslim woman living in a foreign country at that) may well be unprecedented in the Arab world, and may offer some encouragement to other women in similar circumstances. Before trying, I had been told there was a precedent—that a woman had won such a victory in Lebanese courts, but I never heard or saw anything to support this. And after I won, the Canadian embassy in Beirut, Foreign Affairs and many other Canadian government departments wanted copies of the civil judgement for their records. There exist so many stories of Western women losing their children into the Arab world and never seeing them again. My story goes against that grain. As for the Lebanese criminal court, the kidnapping charges against me were considered by the judge but never laid. I was, like Brian and David, charged with a misdemeanour—obstruction of justice. And the religious court ceased to matter once my lawyers successfully challenged the Maronite bishop's custody ruling.

Richard Bennett wonders if the Lebanese authorities simply got tired of dealing with us. Constant pressure was coming from the Canadian mission in Beirut (in no small part reflecting pressure from the Canadian government behind the scenes). This squeaky wheel got the grease.

As for the lawsuit I launched against the Hawach family, it quietly faded from view. My Australian lawyers had questioned Louie, Sid and Pierre Hawach on November 30, 2006, and we subpoenaed Suzie and Janet Hawach to appear next for questioning after Christmas. But once I got Hannah and Cedar back, the lawsuit—which had cost me more than $50,000—became a moot point.

When I dropped the suit, the media reported that fact. The families of Brian and David thought that I was releasing the pressure on the Hawach family because I had the girls back. The reality was this: Getting Hannah and Cedar back was the sole reason for the lawsuit. There was no reason to pursue it. Indeed, the financial risks of losing were huge. I agreed to drop the suit if Louie, Sid and Pierre agreed not to press me for their lost wages. To continue the process would have offered no help in getting

Brian and David released from prison. I had not considered, though, that their families would perceive all this as they did. But I did understand when I found out about their reaction. I'm just glad that we are all out.

What offers me a small measure of safety is that Joe still faces criminal charges in Canada of parental child abduction and fraud (charges that have yet to be tested in court), along with a civil case stemming from the unpaid HSBC Bank Canada loan and other unpaid Amcan debts. Canadian extradition orders remain in effect and his name has been flagged by Canadian immigration authorities. If Joe has remained in Lebanon, he is safe from these criminal and civil matters but vulnerable the minute he comes back to Canada. Still, I well know how borders can be crossed, police avoided, authorities bypassed.

Back in 2006, Joe borrowed $100,000 from HSBC Bank Canada for his paper plant, then deposited the money in his parents' account in Sydney. I'm speculating that perhaps in Joe's eyes he was simply repaying money loaned by his father. In the eyes of the bank, however, he had defaulted on a business loan. On July 24, 2006, the bank's lawyer sent a letter to our Mountain Park address in Calgary seeking precisely $101,239.61 or legal action would be taken. "Govern yourself accordingly," the letter ends. I wish he had.

Perhaps Joe believed that because I was also named in that loan and he was in hiding, the bank would chase me for the money and let him be. When that did not happen (it was easily determined that I had not benefited from the loan), Joe called the HSBC lawyers (the girls and I were back in Canada by then) and offered to settle for $50,000—but only if they added my name to the judgement (the classic "It wasn't me, it was her" defence)! The lawyer declined the offer and immediately reported the telephone call to my lawyers.

In the meantime, the question of some sort of contact between the girls and Joe has been discussed by lawyers on both sides. On hearing this, some friends have reacted with shock. How, they ask, could you be so naive as to trust Joe Hawach? Such a notion is not as warm and fuzzy as you might at first think. Self-interest guides my thinking, too. Some would argue that no connection is the safest and that Joe has brought such a fate upon himself.

There's the challenge, then. Give my daughters a full life without putting them and me at risk.

I am still angry, however, that this whole situation—the words *stupid* and *ridiculous* seem apt—ever had to happen to the Engdahls of Canada and the Hawaches of Australia. It was difficult reliving everything for this book and actually writing the book, and I have yet to fully come to terms with baring my life for all—but clearly that ship has sailed already. I am not happy about having to postpone my education because going back to school was so pleasurable and rewarding. And I still resent having to concoct some sort of working relationship between the girls and their kidnapper—who happens to be their father. That said, I never want to deny the girls anything, let alone such an important relationship.

* * *

For the first three weeks back in Canada, I was extremely unsettled. For almost eight months, I had been obsessed with two things: getting my girls back in my arms, and getting them back home. I had accomplished what I had set out to do, but all my engines were still revving. During the search for my daughters, I felt empowered, driven and terribly alive. The worst moments were when nothing happened.

How to rediscover those old routines, how to settle into this house that still felt unfamiliar, how to stop the dreams and nightmares: Those were the challenges in the early days. By the summer of 2007, I was feeling more normal. But the process of readjustment continues.

My parents, the Calgary police, the Missing Children Society: They all had access to my e-mail throughout the crisis, and they continue to monitor incoming messages. They are still trying to protect me.

* * *

When Dave Chittick speaks, I listen. So when he says that I am a changed woman, I take him seriously. "The fascinating aspect of this whole story," he said when we got back, "is that the experience with Joe [he meant the marriage and its trials] almost destroyed your confidence. But you got it back. The Melissa who walked into the al-Rimal Resort and picked up her kids was not the Melissa whom Joe knew when he left with them. You were transformed by this experience."

The old Melissa—the one my family knew and loved before Joe, before the marriage, before the kidnapping—has come back, but she is not the same woman. She is less trusting, less inclined to give the benefit of the doubt, less gullible. My brother, Doug, puts it bluntly: "That whole experience added ten years to your age. But it also brought a close family closer."

* * *

Through my time in the Middle East, I carried with me two books. One was a thick textbook called *Abnormal Psychology* (not a bad choice, given some of what we had to contend with). While the girls were creating things with my homemade Play-Doh in Lebanon, I was immersed in the workings of the aberrant mind. I had to write a year-end exam three weeks after I got home. I must know the subject: I got a mark of 94 per cent.

The other book I carried with me, and read to the girls every evening (in fact, I read it every night in the girls' bedroom in Calgary during the days and weeks and months they were gone) was one called *I Promise I'll Find You.* Written by Heather Patricia Ward and illustrated by Sheila McGraw (both Canadians), the book is aimed at missing children and assures them that they will be found by one who loves them—be it by plane or train, by horse or boat or submarine, whatever it takes and however long it takes. The illustrations depict a devoted mother and her rambunctious dog searching the world's cities and mountains and seas, and even outer space, for her lost child.

A high school friend of mine (the only one other than me to have children at that point) had given me the book upon hearing of the kidnapping. Jackie included inside the most heartfelt letter about how she could not possibly fathom the pain of my loss. The book was a beautiful gift.

Through rhyming verses and very playful illustrations, the book aims to comfort any young child who knows what it feels like to be lost or separated. It is dedicated "with love to all the missing children in the world and to the memory of Kelly Cook."

The last verse reads:

And if I had no other way,
I'd walk or crawl or run.
I'd search to the very ends of the earth,
For you, my precious one.

In the summer of 2007, I wrote a note to Heather Ward to tell her what impact her book had had, and how it managed to comfort both the girls and me through a long ordeal. I wanted to know, too, what had inspired the book, and I was curious to learn the story of Kelly Cook. From her home in Hanna, Alberta (some one hundred kilometres northeast of Calgary), she sent back this note almost immediately:

"Dear Melissa, I wrote *I Promise I'll Find You* in 1994, and it was the first manuscript I had ever sent to a publishing company. I wrote it as a song to my two young children and sent it in at the urging of my sister who said it should be in print for all parents. Within two weeks, the president of Firefly Books contacted me and said he had two thousand manuscripts on his desk but he wanted to publish mine. He then asked if I would mind if Sheila McGraw did the illustrations." Heather went on to explain that Sheila McGraw had done the illustrations for an enormously and internationally successful kids' book—by Canadian author Robert Munsch and published by Firefly—called *Love You Forever*, about the enduring love between a mother and her son. Heather, of course, knew all this, and it had been for that very reason that she had decided to try Firefly first.

Heather goes on:

"*I Promise I'll Find You* sold sixty-five thousand copies in the first six months after its release, and is still available across Canada, the U.S., and Korea, where it has been translated. Over the years I have received many telephone calls, letters and newspaper clippings, regarding the ways the book has touched people's lives. Many people have said I should do a book about the book.

"A child in Georgia was lost in the woods for over four hours and when search and rescue found him he was not upset at all. When questioned why he wasn't worried, the boy commented, 'I just knew I would be found—I knew because of the book!' His story made the headlines and I was sent a copy of the article.

"After the events of 9/11, I was contacted by Firefly Books and learned that a young girl—she had a cousin who was killed in the attack on the Pentagon—had started a campaign to provide a copy of my book to every child who had been affected by the terrorist attacks." Some eight hundred signed books were sent to those children.

"You asked about the dedication in *I Promise.* Kelly Cook resided in a tiny community I visited often as a young girl. She lived in Standard, which is approximately half an hour outside Calgary. Kelly was sixteen when she was abducted in 1981 from her home by a man pretending to need a babysitter. Kelly was found a few months later in the bottom of an Alberta lake. She had been murdered. I was fourteen at the time and while I never knew Kelly, because of her disappearance, my aunt introduced me to her younger sister and we became fast friends. I spent many hours with the family as they grieved for their daughter. Kelly's death remains unsolved to this day.

"The impact of her disappearance was powerful and when I had my own children I was determined to have them know—

I'd walk or crawl or run.
I'd search to the very ends of the earth,
For you, my precious one.

"I did not write this book to become well known. I am simply a mother who wanted to share a message. *I Promise* is the only book I have had published. I am hopeful that the book will continue to offer comfort to people for many years to come."

Heather ended the note by saying that she'd be happy to meet me and the girls some time. It hasn't happened yet, but it will.

In November 2007, I gave Hannah a picture to take to school. It was part of a project—each pupil was to create a "me box" and fill it with five things that made them special or unique. One of Hannah's defining traits is that she was born in Australia, so I dropped into the box several pictures of her and her parents outside the Sydney Opera House.

What I did not know, and only discovered later when I spoke with Hannah's teacher, was that Hannah had also taken to school our copy of *I Promise I'll Find You.* She used the book to tell the class of her long episode in the Middle East. I was stunned. The teacher reported that Hannah had told the tale simply and without assigning blame. "My dad took us. He wasn't supposed to. My mom came and got us" was it in a nutshell. "I didn't know you were a celebrity," one of her classmates later told her.

Hannah is at the top of her class, she helps other children learn to read, she constantly worries about everyone else, she's a natural leader. She's doing really, really well.

At the same time, though, she's been through a bruising experience. She knows that what her father did was wrong, but she loves her father very much. Everything I have read, all the advice I got from psychologists and the Missing Children Society of Canada, tells me that Hannah (not Cedar, whose youth and innocence spared her) will need counselling. There are many wounds to heal and lies to undo. Hannah's meetings with a psychologist may go on for years, and while their frequency may diminish, her cognition will increase. She may have new questions as time passes.

What I wanted, and what this treatment enables, is for Hannah to be able to talk about what she experienced without fear of hurting my feelings or displeasing me.

When Hannah and Cedar talk about their father, it's usually in the form of a question. "Why doesn't he come and see us?" is the most common one.

"It's complicated," I tell them. "He's made some mistakes and it's hard for him." I tell the girls that he loves them, that he's safe, and that he's thinking about them.

When I reconnected with the girls in Lebanon, I had with me arts and crafts (some of which I had brought, some of which the Canadian embassy had sent over at Christmas via the General's brother). I knew it was important that the girls express themselves through art if they felt the need. Cedar seemed not to have been wounded at all by her experience. It was Hannah who, every once in a while, would draw a picture of sad faces and it would break my heart to see that. It was hard for me to watch my eldest child struggling with the pain of what had happened. At the same time, it made me very angry: This just did not need to happen to them.

Hannah understood that her father had done something wrong, she understood that they did not belong in Lebanon (she hated all the war images of tanks on the corners and soldiers holding automatic weapons everywhere) but she was only just turning six—and quite simply she loved her dad.

Thankfully there was not a lot of turmoil at this point and the girls never got upset at not seeing their father, had no nightmares or episodes like that. I answered Hannah's questions as truthfully and as simply as possible without disrespecting her feelings for her father. I do not understand why any parent would want to insult the other parent in front of his or her children. The children are damaged by hearing this, not the former spouse. We keep pictures of Joe (and the four of us as a family) in the girls' room where they can look at them whenever they want.

We have sent to the Hawach family recent photographs of the girls, them in their gymnastics and ballet classes, a Father's Day card from Hannah and art by Cedar—all via my lawyer in Calgary, Kelly Stewart.

There is no doubt that the girls love their father, and no doubt that he loves them. (In his own weird way. He loved them so much he kidnapped them—perhaps after convincing himself that removing them from me was best for them.) The damage done stems mostly from the girls' being uprooted from their home, security and routines, and from the lie Joe told them: that their mother had abandoned them and no longer loved them.

From my conversations with the girls, though, I also know they often had a delightful time during their almost six months with their father—both in Sydney playing with their cousins (whose photos adorn their bedroom walls) and at the Lebanese resort on the Bay of Jounieh playing with their young relations (the daughters of Joe's Lebanese uncle), all of them terrifically happy children. The girls also played with two young girls named Lynn and Leah at the resort. In their time together, Joe taught Hannah how to ride a two-wheeler and they went fishing on the ocean (she insisted on catch-and-release). They spent a lot of time swimming. I may have been going through hell, but these were mostly happy days for Hannah and Cedar. (One thing they did not like was the school they briefly attended. Hannah remembers being told to "shut up" by her teacher and she also recalls Cedar crying for her sister.)

I did worry about their teeth when the girls were gone. Sometimes I would lie awake at night, wondering about my girls' dental hygiene on the other side of the world. If I sent toothbrushes to someone in the Hawach family, I thought, would they be passed on to the girls? (Such talk baffled my friends, who would ask, "Mel, your girls are in a battle zone and you're fretting about their teeth?") Still, I wanted to know: Was Joe ensuring that the girls brushed every morning and evening? Were they flossing regularly?

In Damascus, I went to a brilliant pediatric dentist—she had trained in California—who looked over the girls' teeth after one of Hannah's fillings came out and she complained of pain. A Lebanese dentist had installed the filling but had evidently done a poor job. Hannah would require several "baby root-canal operations," complicated procedures that were begun in Syria and continued in Canada. This all became increasingly trying for my daughter, so much so that for a time I had to put her dental surgery on hold.

We are now under the care of a very skilled and fantastic pediatric dentist who heard of our circumstances and reached out to us. He has helped to change the negative experience of the dentist for Hannah, and the girls actually look forward to going to his office, which—like the Syrian dentist—caters exclusively to children.

Before this transformation, however, Hannah was angry. "Why didn't Daddy," she asked me, "take care of my teeth?"

I told her that children's teeth are sometimes the mommy's job, and maybe he just forgot. Worse, she might have added, "Why did Daddy lie to me and say you had left us?" Some day, perhaps, Hannah as a young adult will put those same questions to her father.

* * *

Since the kidnapping, the dynamic between Hannah and Cedar has changed. Cedar had always gotten a lot of attention. She can be so endearing: Early in the morning, she'll come into our room, smiling sweetly and asking to be let into the bed. How can I say no?

Sisters know which buttons to push, and Cedar used to tease Hannah. I worried that Hannah's complaints about this were not always taken seriously. I know how magical Hannah is, and I know her needs—for structure and sleep. When those needs are denied her, it's easy to miss who she is. Cedar, either by default or by grabbing it, usually gets the spotlight.

All that has changed now. At Cedar's birthday party in September 2007, I watched Cedar stand on a chair and talk to the room of children and adults. She was, as usual, at the centre. And I looked over at Hannah to see how she was taking this. She was so elated by the joy Cedar brings, her imagination, her delight, her laugh.

That Cedar. I have a painting downstairs, an original, done by a friend in Australia. Someone had used black marker on it—a little three-inch squiggle. Hannah would never do that. I asked Cedar about it.

"No, it wasn't me."

"When you say what's untrue," I told her, "that makes me more upset than the fact the painting has been spoiled. I'll let you think about it." Then I told Patrick, and he decided to have a chat with Cedar.

Patrick: "Do you know who coloured the painting?"

Cedar: "You did it."

Cedar actually tried to convince Patrick that he had done the dirty deed. Then, finally, she fessed up.

Hannah recently did something similar. After an altercation between my daughters, I asked Hannah, "Did you smack Cedar?"

"No." She's the worst liar.

"We'll talk later," I said.

Five minutes later, she asked me downstairs to their bedroom. "I did smack Cedar," Hannah admitted. "I'm sorry I lied. I was just embarrassed to admit it in front of Patrick and Uncle Brendan" (who happened to be there).

I've been proud to watch the evolution of Hannah and Cedar, to watch Hannah mature and grow into herself. It's been really special.

* * *

In the summer of 2007, Hannah, Cedar and I went to Montana for a brief camping holiday. The customs and immigration official at the American border looked at our passports, saw all the stamps and visas from the Middle East and asked about them.

"Do you want the short story or the long story?" I asked her.

"The short story," she replied.

"The kids were on holiday," I said, "and I picked them up."

I was grateful that ours was an easy crossing, but disappointed that a lone parent was allowed to cross a border with so little questioning.

* * *

I had been back in Canada several months and was working on this book when Dave Chittick paid me a call. A father himself (he has two young children), he is another highly professional man who became a close friend through the experience of helping me retrieve my missing children. "I hope," he told me, "that you can use this process of telling your story to the benefit of your own mental and emotional health. That there will be some catharsis for you. That it will give you an opportunity to rebut some of your critics, but some things you'll just have to let go. My broad hope is that the book inspires other left-behind parents, and people generally, to realize the value of hard work and perseverance."

"I hope, too," he continued, "that you end up with a book you're happy to have your children read. There's no shame in anything that you've done. I know you carry a tremendous amount of guilt over what's transpired. We've talked about it on numerous occasions: 'How could a caring mother have allowed this to happen?' At times, you have really beaten yourself up over it—unnecessarily but understandably."

What set our case apart, Dave observed, was the extraordinary backing I received throughout my nearly eight-month-long quest to retrieve my daughters. "The hook for me," he said, "was the support of your whole family. That's what really touched me, was seeing everyone in your family and Patrick suffering through this whole thing with you. I think that's quite rare. Your family rallied."

Dave was once asked by a journalist to explain why the abduction of Hannah and Cedar became such a cause célèbre. "Melissa," replied Dave, "is typical in many ways, remarkable in others. The reason the story resonated with so many people is that it's about an average person thrust into an extraordinary circumstance and dealing with it."

Dave liked the fact that I had been forced to contemplate a radical solution to getting the girls (a dawn raid by commandos) and rejected it in favour of something entirely in keeping with my own character. A mother simply held out her arms to her daughters and they came running to her. As

Dave put it, "You were able, on your own strength, using your own courage, and in the right circumstances, to go and do what needed to be done."

The Missing Children Society of Canada had never sent an investigator beyond North America. They had never sent an investigator into a war zone. For whatever reason, they did this time.

Rhonda Morgan later explained her decision to me. "We felt we could best assist you," she said, "by guiding you through the legal and diplomatic systems in Lebanon. You were occasionally given advice that we thought would only harm your case in the end. Dave Chittick was the voice of reason and you listened to his advice. We wanted to be there for you 'til the end, so I approved Dave's request to go with you."

Dave hoped that the book would be truthful but not damaging, and that one day I would be happy to have my children read it. I'm not sure, though, that one book can serve all those masters. Others can decide. I have described the events as best I can recall them, only changing names when I worried that harm might come otherwise. The Aussies have an expression to describe something real and genuine. "Fair dinkum," they say, and I hope the book is that.

I now realize how blessed I was in so many ways as I searched for my daughters. I had my own intellect and abilities, exceptional family and friends, access to finances to make it all happen, superb expertise and more than a little luck. I would not wish my experience on anyone, but there have been some benefits: It made a tight family tighter, and it has made me stronger. I have learned much about international diplomacy, how debts and favours between countries are repaid behind the scenes, how opposing truths can coexist: Governments can do so little, governments can do so much.

I learned some difficult truths about relations in the Middle East, and between countries there and Canada. Those relations are fuzzy and often informal and below ground—and there are some who see wisdom in keeping things just as they are. If the Canadian government, in a very public way, had whisked me out of Syria or Lebanon, there would have to have been some sort of payback. The honour system would have insisted on it. Maybe a terrorist would have been released, or some other hard bargain would have been struck. No, quiet diplomacy is the way to go.

When the Israeli army inflicted billions of dollars in damage on Lebanon's infrastructure, Canada pledged $90 million to help that country rebuild. At the same time, I know that senior people in Canada's foreign affairs department were asking of their Lebanese counterparts: Can anything be done to help the case of Melissa Hawach? We had been made to jump through all three levels of the judicial system in Lebanon to get my custody orders recognized, with delays and roadblocks, and then suddenly the way was paved. Maybe the Canadian pledge coming through and our court orders doing likewise were not related at all. I will never know.

I know only that while high-profile politicians played a role in my getting home safely (especially after my case was raised in the House of Commons), it was consular officials—those working, often behind the scenes, in the diplomatic trenches—who helped me most. I will always, always, be grateful to them.

When I got back to Canada, I was asked repeatedly: "Were you helped enough by Canadian consular officials in Lebanon and Syria?" The question was a natural one, given all the criticism heaped on those same officials in the wake of the Maher Arar case. I told my questioners that I was more proud than ever to be Canadian and that embassy officials care. They are hardworking and they take care of Canadian citizens—as best they can and as much as they can. I always felt I was in good hands.

I also learned several hard truths about the media. Some journalists, such as Gwendolyn Richards at the *Calgary Herald*, Vanessa Lee at Global TV, and Sandra Lee and her photographer, Sarah Rhodes, of the *Sunday Telegraph* (in Australia) were very sensitive and caring as well. Staff at *Woman's Day* magazine in Australia were likewise very helpful—even before my story had achieved the prominence it later would. All of these people perfectly understood my circumstances and always reported my story fairly and responsibly.

Still, I often abhorred the headlines to stories. Editors would put in quotations things I would never say. "How I stole my kids back," etc., etc. "Tug-of-love Mom," as I was referred to repeatedly in headlines, assigned a frivolous, almost light-hearted shading to what was for me—and surely many readers—a heartbreaking story.

And I understand now what a double-edged sword newspapers and television and radio can be. Though I am an intensely private person, there were times when I did agree to be interviewed, times when I wanted aspects of my story told to the widest possible circulation—to apply pressure when that was called for, to increase the likelihood of witnesses seeing the girls. But what you tell a journalist and what goes in a newspaper or magazine or television news clip can be two different things. My experience with being interviewed means that I will never read or watch the news as I once did. Even speaking in generalities can come back to haunt you.

Rhonda Morgan, speaking for the Missing Children Society of Canada, was furious when her general comments about cases like mine were twisted to sound like she was talking specifically about my case. Some stories had it that my "mercenaries" had taken the girls at gunpoint! Nonsense masquerading as news. The Canadian media were generally good to me, but a national magazine, one I had long admired, mightily muddled my story.

And I'm still trying to figure out how private e-mails about my case, from Bison Security in Calgary to an Australian private investigator, ended up in the Australian press. One story was headlined, "Private eye tells of role in return of 'abducted' children." The P.I. had no role in all this. He suggested a Melbourne security firm, one we never used or much considered. The story made me look like I was ready to hire commandos.

I followed the reportage of the death of actress and model Anna Nicole Smith in February 2007 and the shooting rampage at Virginia Tech in April 2007 and was reminded how irresponsible some reporters and broadcasters are. Hiding behind "freedom of information" and "the world has a right to know," they sometimes ignore facts and just spin out what they believe is the most pleasing angle.

Not long after I returned to Canada, I gave a speech at a dinner meant to raise funds for the Missing Children Society, and I told my audience that the sensationalized treatment of my story in the media had done a real disservice to the battle that we had actually waged and to the battle that many left-behind parents must fight. It seemed like the media wanted to focus only on the five men I had hired—not on the root of my story. Seated close by as I spoke was an entire table of television executives, who cannot have missed my message: Shame on you, I said, and that needed to be said.

Rhonda Morgan has her own thoughts on why two missing children—Hannah and Cedar Hawach—achieved such a high profile. "I've been doing this for twenty-three years," she once said. "Different parents will do different things. But I can't think of any who would have done what Melissa did—gone into a war zone. She is absolutely the most courageous woman I have ever met."

In Rhonda's experience, only one other story compares—that of Betty Mahmoody, whose story was told in *Not Without My Daughter*, a book published in 1987 and made into a film in 1991. Mahmoody was an American married to a Persian doctor who convinced his wife to join him on a two-week vacation to see his family in Tehran along with their daughter, Mahtob. For Mahmoody (and her daughter), this marked her first visit to the Middle East and she was nervous at the prospect. She should have trusted her instincts telling her not to go. Only in Iran did she learn the truth: Her husband's family were intensely devout and conservative Muslims, he had been fired from his job in the United States, and there would be no going back home. Mahmoody escaped with her daughter via Turkey through a risky underground network but only after enduring eighteen months of virtual confinement and no small measure of violence—and even death threats—from her husband.

If you ask Rhonda what she learned from the Hawach case, she will say my circumstances simply reminded her of something she already knew: that teamwork is the key. She also believes that the statistics on missing children in Canada and elsewhere almost certainly understate the gravity of the problem. Countless cases unfold below the official radar and are not reported.

Before 1980, it was not a crime for one or the other parent to abduct his or her own child in Canada. That year, specific provisions in the Criminal Code of Canada came into effect making parental child abduction a criminal offence. Section 273.3(1) of the Criminal Code (revised in the summer of 2007) makes it a crime to remove from Canada "a person ordinarily resident in Canada who is under the age of sixteen years." Section 282 prohibits parental child abductions in situations where a custody order has been made by a Canadian court. Section 283 applies to situations where parents continue to have joint custody of their child by law, where there is a written agreement, where there is a foreign custody order or where the abducting parent did not believe or know there was a valid custody order in place.

* * *

In October 1998, new guidelines were introduced by the Canadian ministry of justice. They were aimed at police and Crown attorneys to help them decide when and how charges may be laid. Dr. Carl MacGuigan, minister of justice when the Criminal Code was amended in 1980, said at the time, "The new law puts the child first and recognizes that the children have rights; the right to security, stability and continuity in their lives." Still, these guidelines are just that. The ultimate decision as to whether or not to lay charges in a particular case rests with the appropriate local authorities.

In recent decades, says Rhonda Morgan, the courts in Canada have changed in other ways, and it is now as likely for fathers to gain child custody as mothers. The result: Today, as many mothers abduct their children as fathers do. Child kidnapping has become an equal opportunity crime.

And as the world becomes more and more integrated, with more marriages between people of different races and religions and cultures, understanding between those groups is likely enhanced. But so is the risk of marital upheaval either caused by, or aggravated by, cultural and religious differences. As Rhonda points out, in some Muslim cultures the mother has custody rights of the child until the age of eight (when religious training commences), but after that the father has the greater right. When custody battles are lost, sometimes the losing parent's first instinct is to flee. In 90 per cent of parental child abductions, says Rhonda, the abductor crosses a border—and countries in the Middle East, which typically are not signatories to the Hague Convention, are a favourite destination.

I met with Rhonda as I was writing this book, and she expressed hope that *Flight of the Dragonfly* would give people a better understanding of what parents go through when children are taken from them. There is this false understanding, she says, "that children taken by a parent are safe." In most cases (depending on how long the children are held and the lies told), there is far-reaching emotional trauma. "The children are lied to," says Rhonda. "They grow up not knowing who to trust. In many cases, the children are forced to go by different names. They are made to lie about who they are, where they come from, and they move constantly."

Some children are permanently damaged by their experience, some recover nicely. Some children, as adults, never forgive the abducting parent and refuse to speak to that parent ever again. In some cases, the child is so brainwashed against the left-behind parent that even years after reuniting the resentment lingers. There is even a term for it: "parental alienation syndrome." Some left-behind parents never see their children again, an experience that some of them describe as worse than actually losing a child to death.

A powerful documentary film called *Victims of Another War: The Aftermath of Parental Alienation* explores the lives of three adults who were uprooted when their parents' marriages soured. In each case, the left-behind parent was demonized, so much so that sometimes the child came to fear that other parent. Produced by PACT (Parents and Abducted Children Together), the film underscores the damage done when a child is used as a weapon by one adult against another.

The precursor to parental child abductions, almost always, is an acrimonious separation or divorce. In many cases, the scarring of the children starts with the father and mother fighting in the home and then in the courts during custody battles. Experts in the field will tell you that revenge against the other parent is the prime motive in many of these abductions. Child kidnapping is not only another form of child abuse, it's a means by which one adult can inflict torture on another.

* * *

I do not miss the sleepless nights, the phone calls in the dark, the rushes of adrenaline, the months in hiding, the speaking in code (on the telephone the General and his men always addressed me as "Juliana"), the fear that I was being listened to, watched and followed. I do not miss being judged by complete strangers (though I suspect this book will provoke a new round of judging). I worry about finances and will go on worrying until our debt—which peaked at $700,000—is fully paid. Legal bills in Lebanon alone came to $65,000 (U.S.). (Some $47,000 went to the criminal lawyer, $10,000 went to religious lawyers, and another $8,000 to the civil lawyer.)

By degrees, and thanks in part to fund-raisers in both Alberta and Saskatchewan, we have paid back a large chunk of this staggering debt. We still get the odd cheque in the mail from someone who has read our story and wants to help out. On the other hand, the bills, especially legal bills, keep coming and the debt collectors keep telephoning every day. That black rain of debt, sad to say, continues to fall on my shoulders. One day in June 2007 the sum of $1,000 was deducted from my bank account to satisfy a creditor (in this case the Canadian Imperial Bank of Commerce). A day later, Joe sent me an e-mail demanding to hear the kids' voices. For my own mental health, I must separate those two things—the financial fallout and the personal.

Though I do not want to, I have to at least consider declaring bankruptcy. In a way, I have parked the matter of the debt, set it aside in my mind. Put in perspective, set against everything I have endured in the past year, money woes seem inconsequential. The man who was kind enough to loan the money is also kind enough not to pressure me. All I can do is pay him back at my slow pace.

I regret very much the toll that this whole business took on my father (in June 2007 he had heart surgery, a quintuple bypass) and on Brian and David—who had to endure three horrific months in a Lebanese prison. At one point, I was told that Brian's wife, Alex, then the mother of a two-month-old baby, had received a death threat. The call was reportedly traced back to a police station in Beirut. Brian and David were so generous to me, and they and their families suffered greatly for that generosity.

Brian and David were sometimes portrayed in the media as hired mercenaries who simply got caught doing one more dirty job, and it was just not like that, at all. These men were even criticized by their peers for not going in brandishing weapons and for letting a "mini-van mom" (that would be me) dictate the terms of the rescue. The men no doubt took heat from their superior for going against his orders and for siding with me. All this was their reward for their kindness and their professionalism, for the huge risk they took to help me.

Woman's Day magazine in Australia interviewed Brian and his wife quite soon after his release from Lebanese prison. Alex described in that article how Brian had removed himself from a celebratory meal with family members. After searching through the house, she found her husband sitting on the edge of his young son's bed, watching him and his baby brother sleeping. For three months in that jail, Brian had tried to conjure that image. The sight of the boys asleep, the smell of them.

Brian's eldest boy (five or six years old I would guess, from pictures I have seen of him) would apparently walk around the house in his father's shoes when he learned his dad was in prison. He was very distressed and told his relations how he missed his father and wanted him home. The boy kept a scrapbook of newspaper clippings, intending to present them as a gift to his father.

For the first week of their incarceration, Brian and Dave were kept in a rank, five-by-six-metre, concrete underground cell, with a hole for a toilet. They were cheek-by-jowl with twenty-one other prisoners. It was twenty days before the two men were allowed to call home. Alex, who must be a very strong woman, moved in with her mother and sister for support, hired a lawyer and girded herself for a long and emotional legal battle. At one time, it was feared that the men could face fifteen years in prison. In the end, the charge of kidnapping minors was never laid, only the misdemeanour of obstructing justice, and the men were allowed to go. They face legal costs of several hundred thousand dollars.

Brian regrets the anguish he caused his family and their financial debt is a horrible cross to bear, but he told the Australian magazine journalist precisely what he had told me. That he and David and the other two men are all fathers, and they could not have lived with themselves if they had boarded that plane without helping me. Alex feared that her husband would come back a broken man, but she remarked on the great peace he feels. The photograph of him in the magazine shows a pale man with a tempered smile.

I would never judge any parent of a missing child, but if a parent ever asked my advice I would counsel him or her not to resort to commando-style reclamations. We did consider that option, especially after half a dozen "special units" called us to offer their services, and we even made a video to be used in case we followed through. This was a measure of my desperation. But the second I visualized strangers taking my daughters, I shook my head and said no.

When I had been back in Canada less than a day, I sat at home and thought back to all that had happened. Emotionally, I was numb. But then came a great gift—a feeling of peace with the realization that during the entire episode, there is not one thing I would have done differently. Dave Chittick had so often told me that I needed to remember who I was, that

I had to stay true to that self, and that the girls needed to come home to their mother and not a lost soul.

On that day I did not feel a bit lost. I was home, with my girls.

* * *

Our lives in the country are as normal as you might expect. We take our young Bernese mountain dog, Cena (a blend of Cedar's name and Hannah's), to puppy school. The kitten known as Treats attacks the window by the couch, my bare legs and the toy mouse dangling on a blue string from the closet doorknob—all with equal abandon.

I remember one night in mid-July 2007, taking Hannah and Cedar over to Andy and Simone's house in Calgary. They had set up a projector in their backyard and used the side of the garage as a screen so their two girls and mine could watch a movie outdoors under blankets while Patrick and I went out to dinner. I felt relaxed, knowing the kids were safe. We talked about the girls sleeping over, but I am not quite ready for this yet. That day will come.

Simone remembers how teary-eyed she was as she had to explain to her daughter, Lola, precisely one year earlier, why Hannah was going to be away for a while—"because her daddy had done a naughty thing." Both Andy and Simone marvel at how I managed. "I would have fallen to pieces," says Andy, "but you were a rock. You did not crack or crumble. You were so focused on your mission."

Have I changed? I asked them. "No," Andy reassures me. "You still have your sense of humour. You're still the smart-ass." Andy reminds me of the old days when I would get laughing so hard I would come perilously close to wetting myself and I would skedaddle to the washroom for relief. I can still laugh like that.

Back in July 2006, just days after I learned that Joe had the girls in Lebanon, Joe was telling me on the phone how we could handle this outside the courts.

"Handle this?" I asked. "Like a dance-off or something?" He was talking about a parenting plan and my response was pure me: funny, dripping with sarcasm. The call had been taped and when we replayed it, everyone in the room cracked up.

Simone likewise remembers how certain calls from Joe would set me off on loud and comic rants. One time he had said on the phone that he wasn't sure he could trust me. "You can't trust *me*!" I began my replay of the conversation while Andy and Simone howled. Sometimes, humour is the only possible response to life's absurdity.

But Simone is also more sanguine about the impact of what she sometimes calls "my situation." "You've been transformed," she tells me. "That experience aged you a bit. It took away some of your innocence." But she likes the fact that I am not on high alert all the time, that I do allow the girls their freedom, that life goes on much as before.

More and more, our place feels like home. By the fireplace upstairs are the two large photographs in green frames of Hannah and Cedar, ones that Joe left behind in his rented house. There must be three dozen photos of Hannah and Cedar in our house. But that was true in the house at Copperfield, too. Those girls were, and are, and always will be, paramount in my life. I never want to know again the panic of not being able to hold them.

* * *

The last word must be a word of thanks. So many people helped me on my way—in Canada, Australia and the Middle East. Lynda, the wife of my baseball coach, virtually did not sleep the whole time the girls were away. She wrote to everyone she could think of—including lesbian groups in Lebanon (!) in hopes they could help me find my girls. So I have a powerful connection now with my baseball team, even greater than it was.

I remember several snow-pitch baseball tournaments in fall 2006. One raised $37,000 to help defray our expenses. In another, umpires donated their wages and players their prize money, and those who received jackets as prizes had Hannah's and Cedar's initials embroidered on the sleeves. When we sold the house on Copperfield, the real estate agent—who was a member at the golf course where Patrick works—refused to take a commission, knowing our straits. In a hot real estate market, as Calgary has been for years, that is a sizeable sum of money.

Friends and colleagues of Patrick's would give him cards with several thousand dollars inside. Members at the golf course offered us the use of their vacation homes and formed a committee to help raise money to pay for our legal costs. Over and over, strangers offered help. It is a humbling and emotional experience to be in need of assistance and to have it come in waves, to see how generous people can be to each other. Patrick would call me in Lebanon, crying after receiving such gifts. Patrick left home when he was seventeen, his father died several years ago and he has never relied on anyone other than friends. Such generosity in Canada touched him deeply, just as it did me in the Middle East.

In Lebanon and Syria, strangers took the girls and me in, sheltered us, welcomed us in every way. Some were paid for their trouble, some were not. The compassion was the same.

* * *

Every night that Cedar and Hannah were gone, Andy's daughter, Lola, said a prayer for them. And when her mother, Simone, told her the good news that the girls were home, Lola was overjoyed. "I did it, Mommy," she said. "My prayers worked! I brought them home."

Indeed you did, Lola. When Hannah was home, she made a card for Lola that read, "Thanks for praying us home."

Lola's prayers and those of countless others. At so many times in my journey, I could feel all these great gifts of spirit sustaining me, willing me forward and the girls home. Consistently, all the myriad pieces of this grand puzzle that had to fall into place did just that.

I feel like I have been given a second chance, and I tell friends and family not to dwell on small and menial matters. Celebrate your life and that of those around you. You never know when, or if, it will be turned completely upside down.

People sometimes ask me what I learned from the whole experience. I tell them that I came to realize how good people are, that there's more reason to trust than not. I'm more trusting of people in general. There are days when I feel completely normal, others when I feel like I'm still back in Lebanon, deep down that rabbit hole, unsure of what the next moment will bring.

A friend of mine trains horses, and he says that "time and miles" cure a lot of horse–human relationships. My hope is that time and miles, and a new baby boy, will eventually do the trick. In November 2007, Tristan Lalande—a beautiful baby boy weighing seven pounds, fourteen ounces—entered the world and made it seem a little brighter.

I have also learned what I'm capable of. When you're in a crisis like this, you do not ask yourself, How can I do this? You just do it. It was a matter of survival. Remember the story of the man who cut off his own arm with a dull pocket-knife? In May 2003, Aron Ralston was a twenty-seven-year-old hiker exploring a remote desert canyon in eastern Utah. While he was moving through a narrow opening in the rocks, a thousand-pound boulder shifted and pinned him to the spot for five days. Out of water and with no other recourse, Ralston applied a tourniquet and amputated his right arm below the elbow. He did what he had to do.

Acknowledgements

There are so many people to thank for their help on my journey these past few years, and although there is no way that I could even begin to mention everyone, I am going to try.

First and foremost, I wish to thank my family: my father, Jim; my mother, Judy; and my three brothers, Doug, Adam and Brendan, and their wonderful wives, Celeste, Shauna and Krista. Special thanks to my mother for knowing intuitively when I needed to hear some words of inspiration, for keeping us strong and focused when we were in Lebanon, and for loving my daughters in the most special and touching way, as only a "Nanna" can. I want to thank my family for their sacrifices, for being there for my daughters and me, but also for helping me find my own voice again—and, more importantly, to help me believe in it. Thanks to my extended family, cousins, aunts and uncles, in particular my uncles David and James. I felt you in my corner and I needed that. To Gordon, Anne and Marjorie—my grandparents—for keeping the faith when things felt hopeless.

A very big thank you to the Missing Children Society of Canada—in particular, Dave, Rhonda, Conor, Liz and their families. Your work to help parents and children is difficult and emotional, and I am honoured to be assisting you to "light the way home" for so many others. It has been your torch and it is now mine because the search must continue.

My legal team in Canada at Edy Dalton: Richard Bennett and Kelly Stewart. My legal team in Australia at Slater & Gordon: Anthony Cheshire, Bill Madden and Mark Whelan. My legal team in Lebanon: Roger Abiaad and Antoine El Kozah. Thanks for believing in the heart of a distraught and frantic mother. You saw the humanity in a difficult situation, and your families are lucky to have such fathers in their lives.

Thanks to the Calgary Police Service (especially Theresa and John) for going above and beyond the call of duty. Thanks to Bison Security Group, especially Darryl, John and Lovell. Lovell, you are a woman with the biggest, bravest heart I know and a beautiful and loving family to show for it. A big thanks to Michael Rumore and Associates in Australia for all of their efforts. Thanks to the Canadian government for their tireless and thorough assistance, in particular Jean-Marc Lesage and Helen Harris. Thanks to Heather Ward for writing *I Promise I'll Find You.*

Thanks to the staff at the Canadian embassies throughout the Middle East and in Sydney. All Canadians should travel confidently knowing that their embassy staff is extremely competent, genuinely caring and willing to go to bat for them. Especially our new best friends, Steve and Carole, and their beautiful family and pets!

So many friends and businesses helped out in any way that they could. It was overwhelming and heartwarming.

Thanks to all my friends, especially Rayanne, Steph, Jay, Andy, Simone, Sydelle, Eamon, Bryanne, Jackie, Brent and Betty, The Calgary Hawks (particularly Roy and Lynda), the Calgary Women's Fastpitch Association, Perry Fleming, Brett Greenslade, Dillon, Fuzzy, Regan, Paul and the whole gang at The Monk, the Golf Depot (Rob and Cher), Big League Sports (Greg, Gloria, Dave), the NSA and their umpires, Jazz, Sysco Foods, Dakota Dunes (MacLaren), Priddis Greens Golf and Country Club and its members (especially the Board and Special Committee), Sherry and Sean in Australia, *Woman's Day* magazine in Australia for all of their help beyond the reporting of a sensitive story, Vanessa Lee and Gwendolyn Richards for reporting the story before it was a story, Judy Saba, Don Bowen, the two Bills and their lovely wives (our family's rock and Angel), Elizabeth (who was the voice of Hannah and kept me going), Wendy and Cody, the McMillans, Joanne, Beverly D. for her Mother's Day painting, the big-hearted and special board of fundraisers in Saskatoon, and our supporters in Yorkton, Kelvington, Melville and throughout Saskatchewan, as well as the strangers and friends who sent me thousands of emails of support and encouragement. (I read every one and they kept me strong—and busy!)

A huge and special thanks to the business community in Saskatoon. I am so proud of where my roots are. I'm thinking of all those who supported my family and me—through fundraisers and through their words. I want to particularly thank all the friends and colleagues who held my mother and father up during this time. You were all a part of our battle.

A very big thank you to my friends in Lebanon. You welcomed us into your homes and treated us like family. You are like angels, and I will never forget you. To the one Lebanese man from whom we asked so much and who delivered every time: thanks from my heart to you and your family for keeping us safe, for picking us up when we were down and for never giving up. Your ability to see the funny side of things in a very unfunny situation is truly a gift. We are forever in your debt. Thank you, thank you, thank you.

I am eternally grateful to the other men who assisted me in Lebanon. You are heroes. You sacrificed time with your own families to help unite me with mine. I am forever indebted to you.

I want to thank my astute editor at HarperCollins, Iris Tupholme, and her fantastic team, for their faith in the book, their care and their diligence. And a big monkey hug and banana for the man Hannah and Cedar call "Turkey Baby." You took the time to make me and my daughters laugh, and you will always be welcome in our home. You have a big heart and a great talent. Thank you for caring so much.

I wish to thank two very important and special men: Patrick, you have stood beside me and at many points carried me through the toughest time in my life. You are one of the most selfless, generous and loving people I have ever met, and I am a lucky woman to have you in my life. Secondly, my father. Most daughters would like to think that their father is a hero. I now know that you truly are. I am so blessed to have had such a brave and loving man as my role model. The support and generosity of the Saskatoon business community for our family is a direct testament to the kind of man you are and the depth of your friendships.

Lastly, I wish to thank, from the depth of my soul, my children. Hannah and Cedar, you continue to amaze me with your grace, intelligence and ability to find the sunshine in all areas of your lives. You have inspired me to be a better person, and you always will. I love you both, "infinity times." Tristan James, your birth has brought a great new joy to our family. I want you to know what a miraculous gift you were, and are, to all of us.

APPENDIX A:

The Missing Children

The number of children who go missing staggers the mind. In the United States, an organization called the National Center for Missing and Exploited Children cites American Department of Justice data. Here are the numbers: Some 800,000 children in the U.S. (under the age of eighteen) were reported missing over the course of the year studied (2002).

Of that number, some 204,000 were the victims of family abductions (although some estimates put that number as high as 350,000). In Canada in 2006, an estimated 60,461 children went missing—most of them runaways, though there were also 326 reported parental abductions (down from the average of 400 cases a year listed by the RCMP Missing Children Registry).

According to the Missing Children Society of Canada, when one parent abducts a child, that parent will cross a border 90 per cent of the time to try to avoid detection. The worldwide numbers are elusive, but I'd wager they're also numbing figures. And those numbers are on the rise, as messy divorces in many parts of the globe are followed by bitter litigation in the courts over child custody.

Given such numbers, needless to say, many cases end badly or simply have no ending. Dave Chittick tells of a case he is pursuing of a baby girl who was taken by her mother and who is now thirteen years old and likely living somewhere in South America. The father has not seen his daughter in all that time. Another case, this one being investigated by one of Dave's colleagues, involves a two-year-old boy abducted by his father. That boy is now a twenty-one-year-old man and he, likewise, has not seen his mother in all those years.

Another man's child was abducted and taken to Costa Rica, and, after taking out a second mortgage on his house, the man is now $25,000 in debt from legal costs. As Dave put it, "He's tapped out. We had to make a decision recently not to do something that might have proven useful"—because he simply could not afford to do it. His daughter has since been returned to Canada under the Hague Convention but authorities would not press charges against her mother. Dave spent numerous hours on the phone with the acting sergeant quoting the Criminal Code around parental abductions but this particular officer did not consider the girl missing. She was with her mother and it was known they were in Costa Rica, so the officer did not feel the mother should be charged! After the Hague process finally brought mother and daughter home, the woman began stalking the father and eventually broke into his house with a golf club and beat him with it in front of his little girl. Only now is she finally being charged.

I repeat: There are so many misconceptions about parental abductions. In my opinion, any parent who chooses abduction as a viable option is not mentally stable. Police officers need training so that abduction cases are handled according to a set standard—and not just the opinion of the handling officer.

Despite such gloomy examples, Dave's work is ultimately driven by hope. "Much can be done," he says. The Missing Children Society of Canada, the strategies of local police and foreign police, Interpol notices, all, he points out, "can create opportunities to catch people up as they're moving about. But at the end of the day, the efforts of the searching parent are considered to be one of the key factors in bringing about a happy ending."

Under "much can be done" is one of the most important strategies a left-behind parent can deploy: filing an application with the nearest office of the Hague Convention. The aim of the Convention is to see that a child wrongfully taken from one signatory country to another is promptly returned, and to ensure that rights of custody and access in the child's home country are respected in the other country. Some seventy-five countries, including Canada, have adopted the Convention since it was ratified in 1983. More than 400 Canadian children have been returned with its help.

My lawyers, Richard Bennett and Kelly Stewart, were and remain great admirers of the Hague Convention and they were likewise very impressed with the quick responses of Canadian Foreign Affairs, the RCMP and Calgary city police. My lawyers were less impressed with Interpol, Lebanese authorities and the federal police in Australia—where parental child abduction is not a crime.

After my own experience, I would urge any mother or father whose estranged, separated or divorced partner wants to take young children to another country to at least ask him- or herself some hard questions. Is there trust between you and your former partner? Does the partner have substantial ties in the other country to be visited? And what are that partner's ties in the adopted country (where the children reside)? If those connections are strong, it's less likely that he or she would abscond with the children.

The RCMP's Missing Children's Registry has examined the literature on parental abduction and offers the following information. Be aware, they say, that both mothers and fathers are equally likely to abduct their own child. Mothers tend to abduct their children after a court order, while fathers typically do so before a court order. Abducting parents are usually twenty-eight to forty years of age, while most abducted children are between three and seven. Children tend to be taken from the home, typically during weekends or holidays. Communication between the searching parent and the abductor is common, and most parental abductions are resolved within seven days. Fewer than half the cases involve accomplices, usually the abducting parent's family members or current partner.

* * *

Obviously, prevention is the key.

On its web site and in its literature, the Missing Children Society of Canada (MCSC) has some timely advice—which I will summarize. (You should know that the MCSC often gets what Rhonda Morgan calls "the cold cases"—parental abductions that have not been easily resolved and that may remain unresolved for months or even years.) The MCSC notes that since 90 percent of their cases involve a second country, any parent who meets certain conditions may attempt to abduct his or her child and take that child abroad. Was the parent raised in that other country? Does he or she have family there? A religious affiliation with that country or dual citizenship? These are not red flags necessarily, but they are cause for vigilance.

To guard against your child being taken to a foreign country, try to set in place stiff penalties for abduction, specific visitation terms and restrictions on travelling with the children.

Contact the passport agency in your country and ask about restrictions regarding the issuance of a passport to your child. Post a significant bond as a deterrent to a parent considering abduction. Request that the parent with connections to another country obtain an order or decree from a court in that country that recognizes the decisions of the court in the child's home country. This order could include a clause stating that a child must be returned to his or her home country after any visit overseas. Consider, too, asking the courts for restricted or supervised visitation unless guarantees can be made that the child will not be abducted.

While the other parent is with the children on vacation in another country, the parent at home should possess current information about the other parent: particulars relating to job, family, friends (here and abroad), passport numbers, immigration information, visas and permits, and current living arrangements.

If trips were made abroad, note the airlines used and other travel details. Be prepared in the event you have to travel to search for your children. Have a zero-balance credit card and update your own passport.

If your child has been abducted by the other parent, contact the police immediately. Report your child to the police "missing person" department, and provide the child's name and a description.

Ask the police to put the child on CPIC (Canadian Police Information Centre) computer system and also on the United States National Crime Information Center (NCIC) computer system. Register the abduction with the Missing Children Society of Canada (MCSC) but ensure your lawyer is involved in this process.

Contact a lawyer to secure sole custody with a prohibition that your child not be removed from the jurisdiction (if you have not already done so). Have the child's name entered in the Canadian Passport Control System with a prohibition on issuance of a Canadian passport to your child from anywhere. List the addresses and telephone numbers of relatives, friends and business associates of the abductor (both here and abroad).

Collect all information on the other parent regarding passport number, driver's licence number, social insurance number and bank accounts, etc.

Have a written record of your child's specifics such as height, weight, hair colour, eye colour, special physical characteristics.

Provide the police with a colour photo of your child taken within the past six months. In your court order, seek provision to enable the Canadian Passport Office to refuse to issue a passport to the child. If the child is a dual national, ask the foreign embassy not to issue the child a foreign passport by providing your sole custody order to them. Contact your child's school and provide them with your custody order (since the abductor may try to access school records for your child). Contact your child's doctor and ask that the doctor inform you if the abducting parent seeks the child's medical records.

Have your local law enforcement agency obtain a search warrant or subpoena to access credit card information on the abducting parent to determine where purchases are being made, any large withdrawals or cash advances made or plane tickets purchased. Do the same regarding the telephone records of mutual friends and relatives. File a Hague Application with the Central Authority (usually a department of the provincial attorney general).

You may consider contacting the media for assistance. However, the MCSC recommends that you consult the police or a reputable missing children agency (such as the MCSC) before doing so. Media can prove helpful or harmful to a case, depending on individual circumstances.

Check the abductor's employment records. If the abductor has a vehicle, check with police to confirm the make, model and licence plate number. Have police check immigration, customs and airport records and airline manifests. Try to contact the abductor's family and friends. Keep detailed records of all contacts, and events prior to, during and following the abduction. Work closely with law enforcement and keep them abreast of any changes or new information in the case.

Contact the Missing Children Society (or any reputable agency dealing with parental abductions in your area). Their investigative services are offered free of charge to searching families.

Finally, Foreign Affairs Canada, and specifically its Consular Affairs Bureau, has published a thirty-page document called *International Child Abductions: A Manual for Parents* (available online at www.voyage.gc.ca).

This is another useful resource—both for a parent hoping to avoid a child abduction and for a parent coping with one. "You must be directly involved in the search in the anticipated return of your child," the manual reads. "This is a bewildering and often prolonged experience." Indeed it is. I wish I had read this document before granting my husband permission to take my girls on "a holiday." Reading the document would have made me fearful, and I might well have obeyed the manual's warning: "Do not ignore your fears. Act upon them and seek assistance."

The cover of the manual, at least the one I read and reread, features a globe stamped with footprints, an aquamarine suitcase perched atop the globe and, atop the suitcase, a teddy bear. Inside my copy of the manual, I have highlighted countless lines of the document in marker pen (ironically, the same colour as that suitcase). I had taken a crash course in a most unsavoury subject, and I would learn just how complex child abduction is and how many organizations—in Canada alone—exist, at least in part, to fight it. The Canadian Police Information Centre. The Passport Control List. The Canadian Border Services Agency. The Missing Children's Registry. The RCMP's Travel Reunification Program. International Social Service Canada. An entire bureaucracy built in part around the grief of countless mothers and fathers and their children.

* * *

I will be eternally grateful to all the individuals and officials involved in bringing my children home. Ours was an incredible, collaborative effort and it was a constant comfort to feel that those involved cared and that I mattered. Not every left-behind parent feels that. In fact, few do.

Parental abduction was a term that I had never heard until it happened to me. Like any traumatic event, it focuses your attention, your energy and your motivation. My journey took me into three different countries, and I experienced the frustrations of different legal systems, languages, religions and cultural norms. Along the way, though, I believe I gained a few insights into the issue of child abduction.

First, and most importantly, the issue has to be taken more seriously. Perhaps if it were, reaction would be speedier, recovery quicker. These are the sorts of comments that a left-behind parent often hears:

"Well, at least they are with a parent and are not in danger."

"There must be a reason that the mother/father did that."

"This is not a kidnapping; it's just a custody issue."

Let me be really clear on this point: The kidnapped child is in danger, and great and lasting harm to that child often results. Any parent who chooses parental abduction as a viable option never has the children's best interests at heart—though that parent is delusional enough to believe that he or she does. If people could hear the stories that I have heard about the effects of being a parentally abducted child, they would never take the situation lightly again.

The Criminal Code of Canada regarding parental abduction is quite clear. I am proud and thankful that my country considers parental abduction a criminal offence. Canadian law and Canadian courts constitute vital leverage to get parents to return children to their country of residence. Yet why are some parents charged and some not? Why is there no standard procedure? My case—and this point should be underlined—was handled in the most professional and expedient manner by the officers and investigators involved. But less than a year later I was very disturbed to learn about a left-behind father in Calgary whose case is being handled with entirely different protocols and standards.

Until both the general public and responding police officers in Canada take the matter more seriously, the left-behind parent will feel alone and dismissed.

Another step in preventing parental abduction would be to enlist the help of the airlines, or, at the very least, Canadian airport authorities. What about a standardized form to be filled out by every parent or adult who is travelling alone with children? The form would have to be shown before boarding a plane or crossing a border to exit Canada. If we could take this one step further and have countries that are signatories to the

Hague Convention adopt this same procedure, then in theory it would be nearly impossible for a parent to remove a child from a Hague country into a non-Hague country.

In Australia, for example, I could not even file a missing persons report for my daughters. Parental child abduction is not a criminal offence Down Under. It is a civil matter for the family courts. While Australia is very proactive in the Hague amendments and stays up to date with all of the new policies, this does no good when any parent can easily fly out of Australia beyond the reach of Hague laws—with no criminal ramifications. Over 500 children go missing from Australia each year through parental abductions, leaving the left-behind parent with almost no options.

Lost to that parent is the leverage that the criminal justice system can bring to bear on a case, along with police expertise and tools in locating missing persons. Let my own case illustrate the point.

In November 2006, Dave Chittick met with a sergeant/team leader in charge of the Missing Persons Unit of the New South Wales Police. The latter was in Canada speaking with police officers and non-governmental organizations about the missing persons business. To file a missing person's report in Australia, the officer told Dave, two conditions must be met. First, the whereabouts of the person for whom the report is being filed must be unknown. Second, someone (that is, the person filing the report) must be concerned for the well-being of the person reported as missing. Naturally, Dave strongly advised me to go to the Australian police and file a missing persons report. Surely I met those two conditions: I had no idea where Hannah and Cedar were, other than that they were in an embattled country and I desperately feared for their safety. You would think, then, that the police in New South Wales would respond.

Wrong.

When I spoke with the officer from the Missing Persons Unit (shortly after Dave did), I was told that because I knew the girls were somewhere in Lebanon and thought to be with their father and grandmother, the girls were not technically missing. Dave Chittick had hoped that the police would put pressure on the Hawach family but as far as the Australian police were concerned, the girls were not missing nor were they in any danger.

The problem, as Dave sees it, is not attitudinal but more procedural and legislative. "You have to remember," says Dave, "that the Hague process and the criminal justice process are completely separate from one another and, in many cases, blind to each other's existence. The Hague Convention is purely a civil remedy designed to prevent abducting parents from accessing the courts (to obtain custody orders) in participating countries where they may arrive with abducted children. From what I am told by lawyers who work with Australia, they are an excellent performer on Hague cases, notwithstanding the fact that Australia has no criminal sanctions in place for parental abduction."

Desperate mothers or fathers searching for their children are financially taxed and emotionally drained. The child is being used, all at once, as weapon, pawn and hostage. Studies by psychologists—some of whom argue that "child stealing is child abuse"—have shown that the abducted child often suffers later from depression, loss of stability, security and trust, loneliness, anger, helplessness and fear of abandonment. The agenda of the abducting parent, meanwhile, is often to control, provoke or psychologically torture the other parent.

A final point. Parentally abducted children should be automatically included in the Amber Alert system, whereby Interpol flags certain passports to alert border authorities. Not doing so only furthers the impression that parentally abducted children are not in danger. The Amber Alert simply cuts down the opportunities of an abductor to travel further.

I understand that there exist many logistical issues surrounding my suggestions and it is never as simple as it seems. Single parents whose partners were never in the picture and never will be may feel harassed by some of the precautions I'm suggesting. I would argue that these stipulations are for their protection too.

I hope that this book sheds some light on a subject that needs all the light it can get. If I can do anything to help stop any parent from getting to that point, I will do it. The turmoil inflicted by parental kidnapping on a wide swath of people—family, friends and people in their circles—is indescribable. I would not wish my experience on anyone, but it has taught me a great deal. I hope and I pray that others will learn from it.

APPENDIX B

Light the Way Home

Few words can express the emotions I felt when Hannah and Cedar ran into my arms after we had been separated for six months. I can honestly say that my children are back at home because the Missing Children Society of Canada (MCSC) was directly involved in our case. To help the MCSC continue the search for other children, visit www.mcsc.ca or call 1-800-661-6160 to make a donation. With your help, the search will continue.

The Missing Children Society of Canada—operating apart from any government funding and relying on donations from individuals and the private sector—provides invaluable support to parents and guardians of missing children. Since being established in 1986, the society has helped more than three hundred families each year and has assisted police in closing more than 5,300 cases.

Each year on May 25, the MCSC runs its "Light the Way Home" for missing children campaign, and Hannah, Cedar and I hope to be part of it for years to come. This campaign aims to heighten public awareness of the plight of missing children and to raise funds so that the society can continue its good work. Hannah, Cedar and I have agreed to be the face and voice of this campaign, one that asks Canadians to get involved in the search for missing children by doing two things: turning on their porch lights on the evening of May 25 and making a donation to the society.